trotman

Guide to
STUDENT MONEY 2010

15th Edition

GWENDA THOMAS

This 15th edition published in 2009 by Trotman Publishing an imprint of Crimson Publishing Westminster House, Kew Road, Richmond TW9 2ND

© Gwenda Thomas & Trotman Publishing 2009

© Gwenda Thomas and Trotman & Co 1992, 1994, 1996, 1998, 1999, 2000, 2001, 2002, 2003, 2004, 2005, 2006, 2007, 2008

Previously published as *Students' Money Matters*

Author Gwenda Thomas

The *Guide to Student Money* is developed from a survey conducted among students throughout the UK by Trotman Publishing.

Developed from an original idea by Andrew Fiennes Trotman

British Library Cataloguing in Publication Data
A catalogue record for this book is available from the British Library

ISBN 978-1-84455-186-6

Typeset by RefineCatch Ltd, Bungay, Suffolk

Printed and bound in the UK by MPG Books Ltd, Bodmin

Contents

CONTENTS

9 Postgraduate study: where to find funding   217

10 Making the money go round   261

Index   283

Berlin Mathematical School

The Berlin Mathematical School (BMS) is a joint graduate school of the three mathematics departments at the universities in Berlin: Freie Universität (FU), Humboldt-Universität (HU) and Technische Universität (TU). It combines the broad expertise in mathematics at the three Berlin universities into an excellent environment for postgraduate studies. Chosen for its innovative concept, its strong cross-disciplinary focus and outstanding teaching schedule tailored to the needs of international students, the BMS obtains major funding as a Graduate School in the framework of the German "Initiative for Excellence" since October 2006.

The BMS PhD programme consists of two phases:

In three to four semesters Phase I leads from a Bachelor's degree level to an oral qualifying exam. The study programme for Phase I covers a broad mathematical background and the specialization required for high-level research.

Phase II (four to six semesters) is dedicated to thesis research, preferably within one of the focused training programs provided by Research Training Groups (RTGs) and International Max Planck Research Schools (IMPRSs), or in research projects such as the DFG Research Center MATHEON, the Collaborative Research Center "Space, Time, Matter", or one of the interdisciplinary projects. The BMS integrates mathematics RTGs and IMPRSs as certified units that provide the research environment and supervision for Phase II students. For entering straight into Phase II, applicants are expected to have a Master's degree or equivalent, or must pass the BMS qualifying exam and meet the regular admission requirements of the Berlin universities' Ph.D. programmes.

The BMS offers a wide range of

support for its students. At least half of the Phase I and all Phase II students at BMS receive financial support -- either from one of the projects or from the BMS itself. In addition the BMS offers mentoring programmes, conference funds, summer schools, additional financial and organizational support for students with children, guidance and encouragement for female students, transferable skill trainings as well as German language courses for international students, and a "Buddy" programme for new students. Moreover students have access to all facilities at each of the three universities. Lounges at FU, HU, and TU serve as social meeting places.

The One-Stop Office provides support on matters ranging from the application process to visa, housing, and child-care, all the way to applying for post-doc positions.

For further details please visit the Berlin Mathematical School website at www.math-berlin.de or call us on +49 30 314 78651.

ESMT European School of Management and Technology is an international business school based in the heart of Europe in Berlin. The School was founded by 25 internationally operating companies and institutions to develop entrepreneurial leaders, who think globally, act responsibly and respect the individual.

ESMT offers Full-time MBA and Executive MBA programs, as well as executive education in the form of open enrollment and customized programs. The School also features in-house research-oriented consulting services. ESMT strives to generate relevant and ground-breaking knowledge for managers, business and policy makers through the integration of world-class research with a practice-oriented approach. Members of ESMT's faculty come from a wide variety of international, academic, and professional backgrounds. ESMT's campus is located in the historical center of Berlin, with an additional location in Schloss Gracht near Cologne.

Founders and sponsors of ESMT

Allianz SE; Axel Springer; Bayer; Bayerische Hypo- und Vereinsbank; BDA; BDI; BMW; Daimler; Deutsche Bank; Deutsche Lufthansa; Deutsche Post; Deutsche Telekom; EADS N.V.; E.ON; GAZPROM Germania GmbH; KPMG; MAN; McKinsey & Company; Munich Re Group; Robert Bosch; RWE; SAP; Siemens; The Boston Consulting Group; ThyssenKrupp

ESMT Full-time MBA – Empowering Future Professionals

Our Full-time MBA program is composed of two main phases: Mastering Management and Taking the Lead.

During phase one, you gain a solid foundation in the fundamentals of management such as organizational behavior, corporate finance and marketing. At the end of the first six months you get the chance to discover new business environments during an international field project.

Past field projects took our MBA participants to China, India and Mexico.

The second phase stresses the areas where future leaders must excel: innovation, entrepreneurship, governance and leadership.

An integrative part of "Taking the Lead" is the practice project, in which you work in a team on an assignment submitted by one of ESMT's partner organizations. The nature of the seven-week assignment is similar to that of a consulting project with the aim of proposing applicable recommendations to the company's management. The practice project also serves as the background for your master's thesis. This master's thesis aims to test your ability to review an area of management studies, to synthesize the main theories and models, and to discuss their applicability.

Entry Dates: January 2010

Program Duration: 12 months

Financing

Tuition and Fees: The MBA has a value-based price of €50,000.

Corporate rate: € 50,000

The tuition and fees for the MBA program in 2010 for students sponsored by a company are €50,000. This includes all learning materials, office supplies, food and drinks on campus on weekdays while the program is running, and the field project. Not included are meals during vacation periods, accommodation in Berlin, private insurance or personal expenses for the duration of the MBA program.

Self-sponsored rate: € 38,000

Tuition: € 29,000

Fees: € 9,000

The compulsory fees of € 9,000 are for learning materials, office supplies, food and drinks on campus on weekdays while the program is running, and the field project. Not included are meals during vacation periods, accommodation in Berlin, private insurance or personal expenses for the duration of the MBA program. In accordance with the educational vision and mission of the School, ESMT awards every individual applicant that is accepted to the MBA program a base scholarship of € 12,000. The outcome is the self-sponsored rate of €38,000.

Substantial Scholarships for Full-time MBA
ESMT's founding companies offer scholarships

Student Testimonial:
"The learning experience at ESMT is simply overwhelming: ESMT offers an outstanding learning environment with international and highly experienced professors and classmates from all over the world that bring in a vast amount of experience and opinions. The small class sizes, the support of corporate and faculty mentors and the great amount of group work ensure a high learning experience and self-reflection. I don't think that any established business school can match this high amount of dedication to every single student."

(Mirko Wagner, MBA Class of 2008)

that support Full-time student study. It is anticipated that most candidates will receive a scholarship. The scholarship can cover full tuition and fees in exceptional cases, depending on the assessment by the MBA Scholarship Committee of the applicant's merits.
ESMT has decided to offer two special full-scholarships for female candidates covering tuition and fees for its MBA class of 2010. We invite all interested candidates to apply for the ESMT Full-time MBA program and for one of our prestigious scholarships.

You will find more information about the ESMT Full-time MBA program at:
www.esmt.org/eng/mba-emba/full-time-mba/

Contact:
ESMT European School of Management and Technology, MBA Admissions Team
Tel: +49 (0)30 21231 1400
Fax: +49 (0)30 21231 1409
E-Mail: mba@esmt.org

Accredited by
Association
of MBAs

Mannheim Business School: Management Education on the Highest International Level

The Mannheim Business School is one of Europe's leading institutions for business education. Through its close ties with the University of Mannheim and its faculty for business administration, it offers a strategic concept for lifelong business education and is a leader in undergraduate, graduate, postgraduate and executive education.

At Mannheim Business School, students receive a comprehensive business education from an internationally recognized faculty. Its professors are all leaders in their respective fields of research and have a strong network into industry.

In addition, Mannheim Business School regularly invites experienced executives from leading companies as well as faculty from its partner institutions to teach. Program participants also benefit from projects realized with partner companies, which give the students hands-on experience and insight into current business issues.
Mannheim is considered to be the leading

German business school in nearly all national and international rankings. In addition, it is the only German institution to be accredited by AACSB International, AMBA and EQUIS, the three leading international accreditation organizations (so called 'Triple Crown').

The Mannheim Business School has a range of programs that interested students can apply for. Its full-time course, the Mannheim MBA is offered as 12-month intensive course for young professionals with at least three years work experience. Students also have the opportunity to spend time abroad at partner institutions throughout the world. All in all, four tracks are available (German, Eurasian, Transatlantic, European).

The stays abroad are not the only parts of the program allowing for an individual setting of preferences. Next to the obligatory "core courses", which convey the fundamental business know-how in the first two terms, the students can choose from among the "electives" according to their interests. Some examples among the many options are courses in Innovation Management, HR Management and Logistics. In addition, the curriculum includes as integral part training in "soft skills", qualities essential to people in positions of leadership. Examples of this aspect of the program are courses and workshops in topics such as "Intercultural Competence", "Negotiation" and "Presentation Techniques". Rounding off the program is a three-month team project at an international company: Small teams of students work on a complex challenge from the real business world and get the opportunity to apply the skills they acquired in their studies.

An indicator of this quality is Mannheim Business School's career service. Individual coaching and support in the search for the right job after the MBA are an integral part of the program. This has proven successful in the past, as the numbers of the last class to  graduate show that all students got at least one job offer and 70 percent signed a contract before they even graduated. The school has business relations to more than 300 international corporations in all industries. More than 50% of Germany's top 500 companies are based within 250 km of Mannheim. The international headquarters of companies like BASF or SAP are located just a stone's throw away from the campus.

"The Mannheim MBA brings highly qualified up and coming managers from the whole world to our school. The program gives them the opportunity to complete a management education at the highest international level in the heart of the world's third largest economy," says Mannheim Business School President Professor Dr. Dr. h.c. mult. Christian Homburg.

Visit:www.mannheim-business-school.com

Introduction

When I first compiled *Students' Money Matters* (now the *Guide to Student Money*) back in 1992 (this is its 15th edition), student loans were being introduced for the first time, and I felt there was a need for such a publication. I opened the book then by saying: 'When it comes to money, there is no doubt that for most UK students going on to higher education things are tough and are likely to get tougher.' I was right. But I had no idea then just how tough the going was to get and how sweeping the changes would be over the next 17 years. If this book was needed then (and it certainly was popular), it is even more essential today with the introduction of top-up fees. Unless your family has a bottomless purse, or you have a private income, getting through university financially is going to tax your ingenuity to the full.

But don't let this put you off university. It is still the great experience it always was. Students will have fun. The social scene is as active as ever. Students are resourceful by nature, and most are managing to get by financially. Certainly, they are leaving university with massive debts to pay off, but remember, as a graduate with a good degree you are likely to earn considerably more during your lifetime than you otherwise would. Currently there is a blip in this happy story. It's estimated that starting salaries for graduates are not increasing in 2009 as they have done in previous years (they are stuck at last year's median figure of around £25,000), and graduate vacancies are falling, which, according to the Association of Graduate Recruiters (AGR) Graduate Recruitment Survey 2009, Winter Review, hasn't happened in a long time. With luck, the credit crunch will be a distant memory by the time you graduate and the picture will have changed totally. But it's the financial hurdle of the next three to four years that you have to get over first, and this is where the *Guide to Student Money* can help.

How this guide can help you

In this new edition of the *Guide to Student Money*, we investigate the means and methods by which students can support themselves while studying for a degree, HND or other HE qualification. The book is aimed primarily at students starting their HE studies this year (2009–2010) and beyond.

The book does not set out to argue the rights and wrongs of the financial situation students find themselves in; neither does it tell you what to do. Our aim is to give helpful information and advice, and to point out the pros and cons to be considered when seeking loans, overdrafts, work experience, a job, a roof over your head, etc. It is for you to weigh up the evidence and information and make your own decision – because what's right for you could be totally wrong for somebody else.

However, it does include comments from employers, university tutors, careers advisers and, above all, students. As you might expect, the undergraduates with whom we discussed students' financial situation were very forthright in their views. These comments have been included, uncensored. There is nothing more valuable or illuminating than a report from the battlefield.

Here's how the book is organised.

- ► Chapter 1, 'That's the way the money goes', looks in detail at how students spend their money. An important section gives information on how much it is likely to cost you to live as a student in different parts of the country, plus detailed budgets from several students so you can get a picture of your likely expenses. There is information on the cost of university accommodation and a number of actual students' budgets showing exactly how the money goes.

- ► Chapter 2: now you know how much you are going to need, the second chapter, 'Fees and funding' takes a good look at where the money is likely to come from. Topics covered include top-up fees, loans to cover fees, maintenance loans, grants and bursaries.

- ► Chapter 3: so the funding is out there, but how are you going to get hold of it? This chapter looks at applying for loans and grants, means-testing, paying back your debts, additional hardship funds and why some parents have never had it so good.

- ► Chapter 4 provides advice for students who fall into special categories (such as Scottish and Welsh students, mature students, students from abroad); and the financial and social implications of studying for part or all of your degree abroad are discussed.

- ► Chapter 5 deals with working and earning money during your course. A high proportion of students work during vacations, and a growing number work during term time. What do they do? How much do they earn?

► Chapter 6 takes time out with a gap year and provides full information on organisations to contact. There is a special section on the student travel scene.

► Chapter 7 highlights one possible source of additional finance – sponsorship – and looks into how to apply and what you should look out for.

► Chapter 8 focuses on other sources of funding such as scholarships, trusts, charities and professional institutions and has tips on how to approach different funding bodies.

► Chapter 9 examines funding for postgraduates.

► Chapter 10: 'Budget like a bastard' was the advice given by a first-year student at Northumbria University in our student research. With that in mind, the final chapter of the *Guide to Student Money* gives you all the information you need to budget without it becoming a burden. It also includes useful information on how the banks can help you with overdrafts, loans and freebies and explains why the bank is the students' friend.

How to use this book

To produce the *Guide to Student Money* we drew up a list of all the questions we thought you, as a student, would want to ask about financing your studies. We then set about finding the answers. As a result, the book is written largely in the form of a dialogue.

The answers given have been kept as short, simple and direct as possible. We've cut through all the red tape and official jargon. Where we felt that you might want to dig deeper into a topic, alternative reference material has been suggested, along with appropriate organisations you can contact.

Occasionally you will find that information has been repeated. This is to help you, the reader, find the information you need quickly, rather than having to flick from one section to another.

The book is written in a logical order. You will probably find the next question is the one you would want to ask. However, it is a reference book, and readers need to be able to dip into it, seeking answers to questions as they arise. To help you find the section you require quickly there is a contents list, which covers the main points addressed, and an index. Each chapter opens with a list of the main topics covered. If your exact question is not there, turn to the section covering that topic and you will probably find the answer. In the unlikely event you don't find the answer, do contact us – we are always interested in hearing of any omissions. Throughout the book you will also find useful nuggets of information such as thrift tips from current students.

Money, and more particularly the lack of it, can be a depressing subject. We hope you'll find the *Guide to Student Money* an illuminating, helpful and amusing read, and that the information in the book will make your time at university or college less worrying and a lot more fun.

In the last edition we asked for your comments, criticisms and suggestions for the next edition. These are included here along with updated facts and figures taken from new surveys of the student scene, in particular the *NatWest Student Living Index* and our own *Guide to Student Money* research undertaken among 140 student contacts. But nothing is static, least of all the pecuniary plight of students, so please keep those comments coming. It is only by being vigilant and keeping in touch with 'campus correspondents' that we can pass on the right information to those who follow.

Our thanks for helping to prepare this book must go to all those students who were an invaluable source of so much of the information – and also to the employers and financial and higher education institutions who have given vital assistance in the research of the material.

Gwenda Thomas

CHAPTER 1

That's the way the money goes

How much is it going to cost you to be a student? This chapter answers questions on:

- ► So how much will it cost you? (page 2)
- ► What makes so many of you do it? (page 3)
- ► What will university cost? (page 4)
- ► Your living expenses (page 4)
- ► Student budgets around the country (page 26)
- ► Typical student budgets (page 32)

So how much will it cost you?

Take a deep breath. How does £13,626 a year – and a staggering £15,769 a year if you are studying in London – sound? Horrifying? Well, that is how much the National Union of Students (NUS) estimated students needed last year, and that was just for a 39-week academic year. Multiply those figures by three or four, depending on the length of your course, and you'll have some idea of what your university degree could cost – £40,000–£50,000 and more.

You might be able to do it for less. As you'll see from the budgets at the end of this chapter, the students we interviewed were having to manage on what they could get through grants, loans, bursaries, sponsorships, parents, and their own hard work and endeavour and it wasn't as much as this. Making ends meet while also enjoying yourself is possible: there are over a million students in our universities to prove it. So don't let the headline figures scare you off university. It won't be easy, but it can be done and it will be fun.

Where does the money go? Around a quarter goes on fees, books, course equipment and travel (see this and the next chapter); the rest on your living expenses – accommodation, food, socialising, clothes, general expenses and having a good time.

Many factors can affect your financial situation. Some students are luckier – or perhaps more determined – than others in:

▶ raising additional finance
▶ managing to work as well as study
▶ choosing to study in cheaper parts of the country
▶ finding/receiving additional bursary funding
▶ living at home
▶ choosing a generous university
▶ being excellent money managers.

While others:

▶ find that money slips through their fingers like water
▶ are great socialisers and imbibers
▶ take courses for which they have to buy expensive equipment or books, or to travel
▶ have expensive tastes and hanker after all the good things in life
▶ have a wide range of hobbies and interests
▶ study in expensive areas such as London.

Obviously you should not pick your course on the basis of where the living is cheapest, but it is as well to know what costs you are likely to face. This chapter looks at what it is likely to cost you to gain higher qualifications. But first . . .

What makes so many of you do it?

Last year around 588,000 people applied for higher education courses in the UK. What is the great attraction? Why did they want to forfeit the chance of having money in their pockets to become near-penniless students and pile on the debt?

These students taking part in the *Guide to Student Money* research had no doubts:

'I want to get a job I enjoy.'

'To improve my job prospects with the hope of getting a varied career. I'm not a 9 to 5 person.'

'I wanted to continue learning; university was the obvious path.'

If we asked everyone now studying in universities and colleges across Britain, we'd get thousands of different answers. Most would be positive, but not all:

'I don't rate uni at all. I wish the government would encourage people to do something they are good at and not waste money and time pushing people into a place they don't want.'
        Law and Japanese student, Oxford Brookes

Many, however, would say 'money' – or the potential for earning it. And there is no doubt a degree can help increase your earning power. Graduates can expect to earn on average 20–25% more than A level students over a lifetime, and much more if they study medicine or engineering, according to a report published by Universities UK. But whatever your reason for studying,

Facts and Figures

What makes a student decide on a university? Key factors:

▶ quality of teaching – 54%

▶ reputation of course – 44%

▶ reputation of the institution – 43%

▶ teaching methods – 35%.

Less important factors:

▶ how seriously the institution takes global development issues – 6%

▶ environmental issues – 5%.

(Future Leads Survey based on research carried out with 25,000 university applicants by Forum for the Future and UCAS and sponsored by Friends Provident)

Can't get a
university
place? Increase
in demand for
university places, especially
at the new universities, is up
by nearly 40,000 this year,
according to UCAS. Only
10,000 extra places have been
allocated for the 2009 intake,
so it looks as if there could
be thousands of disappointed
students. If you are one of
them, think gap year – and
try again next year.

it's going to be hard going financially for
the next few years. How are you going to
manage?

What will university cost?

Fees: will I have to pay them?

Yes, unless you're a Scottish student or EU
student studying in Scotland (more of that
in Chapter 4).

Most students who started their course in
or after 1998 have had to pay something
towards the cost of it. But in 2006 the maximum tuition fee per annum was
hiked up to £3,000. With year on year 'inflationary' rises, this year it will be
£3,225. If you are a non-EU student, your fees are going to cost you a great
deal more than this, wherever you study (see also Chapter 4).

3290 ~ 2010

Will the government take the cap off fees, as many universities want? There
is talk of fees of £7,000 p.a. or worse. But it is still just talk. As we publish, no
decisions on top-up fee changes have been announced. If you have already
started your course, any change won't affect you. It will be those who come
after you who will suffer.

Your living expenses

These have to be paid for largely by you. More maintenance grants and
bursaries are being given by the government and universities than ever
before, so there is more help available, especially for low-income families (see
Chapter 2 for full details). Managing is not going to be easy, but it shouldn't be
impossible. However, wherever your money comes from, it's you who will have
to eke it out and make ends meet. So here are the facts.

Accommodation: the major demand on your finances

Accommodation will probably soak up half your income. If it's full board in
university accommodation you are looking at over three-quarters of your total
income.

Finding the right place to live is important, especially in your first year. It can affect your whole attitude to your college, your course, your study, the town or city where you are staying, making the right friends, and whether you actually do well. If it's half an hour's walk or a bus ride across town, to get to the library, you may think twice about going there. If you're stuck in a bedsit with a grumpy landlord and no other students around you, the weekends could be very long and lonely. Halls are generally thought to be the best for first years, but they aren't right for everyone:

'It is impossible to get a decent night's sleep because of noisy students returning after a night out.'

1st year Arts student, Robert Gordon University

'Occasionally you'll hear people running along the corridor at two in the morning. But mostly people are considerate.'

Modern Languages student, Cambridge

Most institutions give first-year students first claim on halls of residence and most students jump at the chance. It gives you a circle of ready-made friends and a great social life. But for some students, living with a hundred or so other people, sharing bathrooms, meal times, TV programmes, problems, passions – even bedrooms – can mean unbearable strain. Others thrive on the camaraderie. Criticising mixed halls, one student told us:

'Coping with an ex-boyfriend over cornflakes and coffee at 8a.m. is something not to be endured.'

Where can I get information and help?

College prospectuses will generally give you details about halls of residence, though these may not be altogether bias-free. Students' unions may also have a view – ask if there's an alternative prospectus or students' union handbook. If it has to be accommodation in the private sector, ask for the university approved accommodation list.

Above all, check out the accommodation for yourself if you can when you make your first visit. Look at:

► cost
► whether rooms are shared
► eating arrangements – full board, half board, kitchen/do-it-yourself?

- facilities provided
- distance from college
- transport availability – and frequency and cost
- shops.

Students in the South East, but studying outside the London area, are thought to be suffering particularly badly, as they are being asked to pay London-equivalent rents while not qualifying for larger student loans given to students who study in the capital.

The college accommodation office is responsible for placing students in halls of residence, and will send you details once you've accepted a place. It will also help you to find rented accommodation.

Accommodation in halls of residence

Costs vary significantly between different types of accommodation and different universities, with much higher costs in the London colleges in particular. Be aware that the number of meals per day, the number of days per week that meals are served and the number of weeks in the academic year can vary between institutions. Some establishments offer accommodation other than the norm, such as en-suite, up-to-the minute facilities or out-of-town accommodation.

When comparing university self-catering accommodation in halls of residence with the rented sector, remember that in college accommodation gas and electricity are probably (but not always) included. This is unlikely to be the case in the rented sector.

Will I have to share a room?

Possibly. In some colleges, especially the older establishments, you may have to share a room for one or two terms. If you do have to share, you will probably be sent a questionnaire designed to find out what sort of person you are and the kind of person you could live with. Typical questions are:

Would you want to share with a smoker (where it's still allowed)? Are you an early riser? Do you like to go to bed late and get up late? Are you a party person? What kind of music do you like – is there any kind you can't stand? Honesty is the only way to harmony. Even if you are easy-going about smoking, do you really want to sleep in a smoky atmosphere? And, although your intentions may be very laudable at the moment, how are you going to feel about your room mate stomping around at eight in the morning when you've been out partying until two?

'Halls are great except you don't get to pick who you live with; sharing a flat with six other people can be a nightmare, especially when food goes missing and the kitchen becomes a garbage site.'

1st year Management
Studies student, Middlesex

'I'd never shared a room with anyone before and didn't really like the idea. At first it was strange, but after a couple of weeks you got used to it. Having someone around most of the time is fun.'

1st year Economics student, St Andrews

'I thought I wouldn't like sharing a room, but actually it's nice to have someone to come home to.'

1st year Modern Languages student, Durham

'I don't get on with my hall mates, I want to move.'

1st year, Ancient and Medieval History, Lampeter

'I strongly believe the London weighting should be further increased. My loan has never done more than barely covered my accommodation and that has made everything really, really stressful. If I hadn't found a job I don't know what I would have done.'

3rd year Mathematics student, UCL
(job: football statistician; pay: £15 p.h.)

it's a Fact

Have you found yougo yet? It's a student-only social network site developed by UCAS (http://yougo.co.uk). Dedicated to helping young people thinking about a move into higher education, it has recruited some 250,000 members.

The idea behind the site is to connect, online, current Year 12, S5 or equivalent students with those considering similar courses or universities, so they can 'meet' each other before they arrive on campus. As a member you'd have the opportunity to 'make friends' with current students so you'd know what to expect when you arrive.

What's it going to cost?

Most of the figures given in this section on what students are likely to have to pay are based on the *NatWest Student Living Index Survey*, August 2008, which was carried out among students in 26 major university towns throughout the UK; and research undertaken by the *Guide to Student Money*, which homed in on a smaller number of students, most in five universities. Both revealed some interesting facts. Here are the results.

cash crisis

If you are renting in the private sector, remember that a deposit may have to be paid up front – the average is around £232.

(NUS/Unipol Accommodation Costs Survey)

How Much is Accommodation Going to Cost?

Average outside London: £73 per week; average in London: £90.24 per week.

While on average students throughout the country, excluding London, are paying £73 per week, the average rents among students in London were predictably higher than anywhere else, at around £90.24 per week, except for Oxford, which came in at £91.80 per week. You could pay less if you're living outside the centre, but you would then have travel costs. Among the cheapest places to rent were Belfast at £58.27 and Lancaster at £57.74 per week. These are of course average figures; there were pockets of the country where rents varied considerably.

Don't forget that on top of rent you may have utilities (gas, electricity, water) to pay for. The *Student Living Index Survey* estimates these costs will be around £13.53 a week, which is something you probably won't have to pay in university accommodation. Full details of rents in different parts of the country are shown on page 129.

Action

Check out the length and terms of your contract. A recent survey of university students found that more and more landlords were asking students to sign 52-week contracts for accommodation. This means they are paying rent during the Christmas, Easter and three-month summer vacations, when they are likely to be at home – something you don't have to do in university accommodation.

Another problem we encountered was that students, such as medical students, who have to undertake a placement away from their university may find they are paying for accommodation away for a couple of months while still paying for the accommodation in their university town.

From one who knows:

'If your landlord won't fix something, take a photograph of the problem so you have evidence that it's not your fault. With this in hand, the landlord will find it difficult to play the trick of docking your deposit when you leave. Our curtain railing has come down and the landlord won't fix it. But he won't pull a fast one over us.'

Law student, Northampton

Possible problems when renting accommodation

'Exploding shower, broken-down washing machine, dangerous housemates.'
3rd year Entertainment Crafts student, Cleveland

'Entertaining unwanted visitors – cockroaches from the café downstairs.'
1st year Modern European Studies student, Thames Valley

'Lodgings miles from anywhere. Buses stopped at 7p.m. so late study and going out meant paying for a taxi home.'
2nd year Engineering student, Brunel

'I'm living with my landlord and a horde of mice – they eat everything – the mice, that is!'
3rd year Mental Philosophy student, Edinburgh

'Ex-prisoner broke into the flat – he was living there, unbeknown to us, for four days.'
4th year Archaeology student, Lampeter

'A mouse chewed through the kitchen wiring and we lost the use of our oven and boiler. Agent said: "mice don't eat wires, they eat cheese".'
4th year Medical student, St George's

'Landlords hate spending money. Learn some basic DIY and plumbing and you'll be fine.'
2nd year, DPhil in Education student, Oxford

'Typing in fingerless gloves and arctic wear was a good solution. At least the rent was cheap.'
1st year Classics master's student, Oxford

'Bullying landlord and agent.'
4th year Biochemistry student, Exeter

'Heating non-existent! We all wear gloves and thick socks around the house and jumpers in bed. But the mice are quite content.'
3rd year Creative Imaging student, Huddersfield

'I'm living with thieves. My mail has been opened and "things" taken out.'
2nd year Music Technology and Digital Media student, Huddersfield

advice note

Landlords who don't give deposits back should be a thing of the past in England and Wales. A new tenancy scheme has been introduced. Check www.direct.gov.uk/en/TenancyDeposit/index.htm for full details before handing over your deposit, and check that your landlord is adhering to the new law. Of course, if you trash the place, you can't expect to see your money back – it works both ways.

'Only one small common room for 600 students, and only nine washing machines.
1st year History student, Manchester

'Two dogs and the landlord, not the best of housemates.'
3rd year Biochemistry student, St Andrews

'Hall is competing in an energy efficiency scheme: consequently my room is 14 degrees.'
1st year Modern Languages student, St Andrews

'The gas man called the house a "death-trap".'
3rd year English and Social Anthropology student, St Andrews

But it's not all complaints:

'Our landlord is very sweet; he bought us a huge packet of biscuits for Christmas.'
2nd year Psychology student, Queen's University, Belfast

'Our landlord is ace. When the security system started beeping at 1a.m., he came out to fix it.'
2nd year Law student, Reading

Alice's story

Problem: my bedspring broke. Sleep was impossible. Exams were looming. I needed rest but my landlady was very slow to get things done. Strategy was called for. I invited the landlady over and got her to sit on the bed while we talked. I asked her if she was comfortable, and she had to agree she was not. I then asked her if she would like to sleep on the bed – every night. A new bed arrived within four days.

Should I take out insurance?

That's something only you can really decide.

A recent survey completed by Endsleigh shows that, on average, students now take £4,200-worth of belongings to university, and this is not going unnoticed by thieves. These possessions are often highly valuable and portable, for example laptops, iPods and mobiles. If you lost them, how would you replace them?

Insurance is another drain on your resources, but it could be money well spent and save a lot of heartache. Endsleigh receives some £350,000-worth of claims from students during their first month at uni, which is fairly substantial.

If you are living in halls you may find there is a comprehensive policy covering all students and that this is included in your rent bill. If you are living in rented accommodation, the landlord of the house or flat you rent should have the premises covered by insurance for fire and structural damage, but this is unlikely to cover your personal possessions. Students tend to keep open house, and because people are coming and going all the time security is often lax. If you do have a lot of expensive possessions it might be worthwhile considering taking out your own insurance, especially if you carry expensive belongings around. Ask yourself: what would it cost me to replace my iPod, stereo, TV, DVD player, camera, gold watch, PC, course books, whatever? Compare that with an outlay of, say, £30 a year. Rates for personal insurance depend on where you live. It costs more if you live in a big city than a sleepy rural town. In a crime hot spot, rates can be prohibitive.

'Everybody round here hires a TV so if it walks it's covered by the TV rental company. The same goes for washing machines and all other appliances.'

1st year student, Liverpool University

'We had a microwave and sofa cushions stolen! But mainly it's computers, TVs, stereos.'

3rd year Genetics student, Birmingham

Are you covered by your parents' insurance?

If you are, that is obviously the cheapest form of cover, but don't assume that your possessions are covered by your parents' home insurance once you go to uni. Some standard home insurance polices specifically exclude students – I wonder why? Get your parents to check the small print.

You can also take out insurance to cover the fees you have paid, just in case you are ill – or worse – and can't complete your year.

NatWest's Essential Contents Insurance seems ideal for the student living in rented accommodation because it offers a 'pick and mix' cover for the things that are valuable to you, such as laptops, iPods, mobile phones, which means that you don't pay cover you don't need. It can include cover for walk-in theft (not money). The cost varies according to what you choose to insure, and there is a lot of detail you should look into before deciding, but it sounds like a good deal.

Endsleigh, who specialise in helping students, offer student possessions insurance starting at £16 for £2,500 worth of cover for halls of residence, and £25 for £2,500 worth of cover off-campus in a 'good' area. They also offer the option of cover for just your laptop, with all risks cover starting at just £6 per £100 (prices correct at November 2008).

Do you make music? Whether you play in an orchestra or drum for a rock band, or whether it's part of your course, whether you do it for pleasure or to make extra money, if you lost that valuable guitar, violin, double bass or cello you'd be stuck. Insurance rates vary depending on whether you are in the UK or travelling in Europe, and what kind of instrument you have. Endsleigh offer flexible cover against theft and accidental damage for any musical instrument, subject to a minimum premium of £20. Cover is available for orchestral instruments (such as violins or double basses) and non-orchestral instruments. There is a choice of where cover can operate: UK only; UK and up to 30 days in the EU; and anywhere in the world. Shop around to get the best cover before making a decision.

Where to live?

Halls, rented accommodation with friends, at home? We asked some students what they thought.

Living in halls – Luke's story

Luke is a first-year student studying sports science at the University of Exeter.

'Bring a doorstop if you are coming to Exeter,' is Luke's advice. He decided to live in halls for the first year, to give him time to find friends – he has certainly done that. He lives in one of two blocks on campus, on a corridor with 10 other students. They each have their own room – 'Not spacious, but large enough to accommodate my guitars and sports gear' – and share two bathrooms, a shower, and a minute kitchen with just a microwave.

'It seems to work okay,' he says, 'we are never fighting over the bathrooms.' In fact, life on his floor works so well, they all leave their room doors open and live as a community – hence the need for a doorstop. 'People are always dropping in. It's open house. You're never alone or short of someone to talk to.'

The annual cost is £3,536 including food, heating, internet connection and insurance. 'We get two meals a day – breakfast and dinner – seven days a week. The food isn't too bad, but rather short of protein,' he says. 'As a sports student, actively playing three major sports, and spending free time on the ski slope, swimming and the golf range I need to supplement my diet, which costs another £8 a week.

'It can be noisy on our landing late into the night when people come back from an evening out, but then what do you expect? My friends and I make our fair share of noise when we return, enough to bring out the "resident-shooter" – a fierce female employed to keep the noise down after 11.30p.m.

'We go out twice during the week and every other Saturday – more if someone has a birthday. Sometimes we're a group of 30. We tend to gather in someone's room and have a drink or two before we go, to keep the cost down. There's a union bar on site and Exeter has a good range of night clubs.'

Sharing a flat – Matt's story

Matt is a third-year forensic science student at Nottingham Trent.

This is a story of contrasts. Last year Matt had a bad experience. He moved into a newly converted flat in what had been a telephone exchange.

'You could say there were eight of us living in that flat – three boys, four girls and a ghost. The building had a chequered history. Extraordinary things went on there – including a suicide. I can't say I actually saw an apparition, but I certainly heard a lot of creaks, bangs and strange laughter.'

13

The flat had a kitchen with a large dining area plus a TV and seven large bedrooms with en-suite bathrooms. There were no bills to worry about: all the utilities were included in the rent which, at £84.99 a week, wasn't exorbitant for Nottingham. Sounds perfect!

But it wasn't a happy household. 'Things went missing,' says Matt, 'including my champagne. There was no togetherness. We each catered for ourselves, which is an expensive way to live. My food bill alone was £25 a week. If only people could have been bothered to put their dirty dishes in the dishwasher it would have helped.'

Matt's advice: 'Get the whole sharing thing sorted before you move in and don't air your grievances on Facebook: it just makes things worse.'

This year things are different. He has moved into another new block of student flats built on top of TX Maxx in the centre of Nottingham. He is eight floors up and has a fantastic view right across the city. He shares with four other students. It has similar accommodation to his last flat and they all have en-suite bedrooms.

'This is the best accommodation I have had,' says Matt. Why? 'We are five blokes sharing. The flat is tidy, we all get on, there are no arguments, nothing goes missing, and there's a good atmosphere. If we are all in, then we will cook together – Tesco's is just round the corner. Weekly food bill: £15–£20. Rent is £89 a week: £4 more than last year, but worth every penny. What's more, the rent includes a travel card for the buses.'

Sharing a house – Emma's story

Emma is now a third-year modern languages student at Durham University.

Last year she moved into a house. 'There were five of us living in the house – three girls and two boys. We all met in halls so we were already good friends. We had three bedrooms upstairs for the girls, plus a bathroom, and two bedrooms and a shower downstairs for the boys. There was also a large kitchen/living-room.

'One of the girls had a boyfriend so she generally ate with him; the rest of us catered together – which is the cheapest way. We girls made a list and went out and did the weekly shop which was then delivered. Cost £10–£15 a week each. On top of that we had "The Kitchen Mug", a kind of kitty into which we all put £5 every two weeks to buy general stuff for the house.

'I am not sure how it worked, but it did. It was not arranged; there was no cooks' rota; it just happened. One person cooked and we all ate. Once I cooked for everyone for a week, and then did nothing for weeks.

'I can't say I'm a good cook, but when you're hungry (and students always are), people will eat anything. We ate a lot of pasta, rice and frozen vegetables. Sausage and mash was a great favourite. Not a madly healthy diet, but cheap. One memorable occasion I cooked a roast dinner.

'All utility bills were divided by five and we had a special utilities bank account into which we paid the money. Getting the housework done was more of a struggle to organise. But we were all good friends so eventually it happened.

'The great joy of our house was that you had your own space. But you were never lonely. Go down into the kitchen and there was always someone there. Maybe it was the atmosphere, maybe it was because we had the space, but people were always dropping in. We didn't arrange parties – we didn't have to, they happened. My bill for socialising crashed from around £500 in my first term, when I lived in halls, to a mere £170.'

Summing up the year, Emma thought it had been a good year and a great experience, but by the end cracks in relationships were beginning to surface and it was time to move on. This year is providing Emma with another great experience: as a language student she is spending half in France and half in Sicily, but that's another story.

Thrift Tips

'Book travel in advance. I travelled from Durham to London for £10.'
2nd year Modern History student, Durham

'Work as a TV extra or catalogue model.'
3rd year Psychology student, Wolverhampton

'Sell your work.'
3rd year Visual Studies student, Norwich School of Art and Design

'Use your hobby – I photographed a family on holiday and pocketed €100.'
Wolverhampton student

Living at home – Aysha's story

If Aysha Tezgel manages her future clients' finances as well as she is managing her own while at university she will go far. Aysha is 21, and in her second year at City University's Cass Business School, where she is studying banking and international finance with German.

She was determined to have a good time while at university, but without getting into debt

'I chose a university so I could live at home,' she says. 'This was not really a problem. City's Cass Business School has an excellent reputation.

'I then have generous parents who said I could live there rent free. So I have no worries about bills and shopping. Even my laundry is done, so I can concentrate on my studies.' With end-of-year results in the 70s and 80s in her first year, that has certainly paid off.

Her major expense is her monthly travel card which, even with her student discount, is £120. 'Again, my parents often pay for it.'

She receives a partial maintenance grant and a university bursary of £1,000. But it was only when the Worshipful Company of Needlemakers came up trumps with a £1,000 scholarship (given through the university) that Aysha knew that she was going to make ends meet, at least for her first year. The scholarship was for only one year – 'I didn't get the chance to apply again this year,' she says.

During two gap years Aysha had saved more than enough to cover her fees, but decided to take out a fee loan and leave her own money happily earning interest. 'My rainy day fund,' she says. 'I have also taken out a £1,000 student loan, which was a great help during the long summer vacation. I need £4,000–£5,000 for living expenses over the year, which covers travel, books, food, drink, clothing, and other day-to-day expenses. If I were to live by myself, even in halls, I would need at least £12,000–£13,000.'

Aysha doesn't feel she misses out on the social life by living at home. When something good is going on – a party, clubbing, whatever – she just beds down with one of her many friends.

'I feel I have more stability than some friends who are living away from home. Around February every year, they must start thinking about where they will live the following year: I do not have any of these worries.'

Asked about the major drawbacks to living at home, Aysha was in no doubt. 'The commuting, especially when you have a 9a.m. lecture.'

More and more students are choosing universities where they can continue to live at home because it is cheaper. In fact, 65% of our student contacts said they knew of someone who had decided to study in their own home town for financial reasons. As you will see in the next chapter, the amount of loan you can borrow if you live at home is smaller, but then that means less debt. For some students, this idea would be unthinkable. Going to university is all about gaining independence. But if that results in you having to abandon your course because of debt, then you could be back where you started – at home! It's worth thinking about.

Do I have to pay Council Tax?

Students are largely exempt from paying Council Tax. Certainly, if you live in a hall of residence, college accommodation, student house or somewhere in which all the residents are students, you will be exempt. If you live in a house where there are already two adults, your presence does not add to the bill. If you live in a house with one adult, that person will not lose their 25% single occupancy discount, providing they can supply proof that you are a student.

However, things are never quite that simple, as Paul Hubert, the welfare officer at Leeds Metropolitan University pointed out to us. 'Frequently,' he said, 'students in external accommodation do not spot the problems coming and these can prove intractable.'

Some examples:

▶ A full-time student moves into a house shared with non-students, and housemates expect them to contribute to the Council Tax bill.

▶ The flatmate who drops out of their course during the summer and fails to claim benefit.

▶ The part-time student who thought they would be exempt.

▶ The student/postgrad who is writing up work and is refused student status by local authorities.

Thrift Tips for Drinkers

'Make your own beer – it's fun, cheap and tasty.'
3rd year Digital Media student, Wolverhampton

'Organise parties at home and get others to bring the drink.'
2nd year Journalism, Film and Media student, Cardiff

'Drink cider rather than beer – it's cheaper and takes less to get you drunk.'
4th year Biochemistry student, Oxford

'Become teetotal. Impossible? Try the next tip.'
3rd year Design student, Wolverhampton

'Learn to drink slowly.'
3rd year English student, Wolverhampton

If in doubt, go to your university welfare officer – they are usually on the ball.

Other living expenses

While your accommodation will probably take at least half of your available resources, how are you going to spend the rest?

Food

Average per week: £21.48 eating in, £15.22 eating out.

Once you have a roof over your head, the next major expense is food, and here the *NatWest Student Living Index Survey* showed that costs were fairly similar throughout the country, with an average weekly food bill of £36.70. However, when we started to look at individual areas within the UK the picture changed. The hungriest students, with an average weekly spend of £46.19, were in London, followed by Aberdeen, where students had an average weekly spend of £42.13 and Belfast, with an average weekly spend of £42.20. For frugal living go to Durham, where students' average spend is £24.41 (£11.85 in the supermarket and another £12.56 on eating out).

But statistics don't tell the whole story: take St Andrews, where our own student contacts collectively had a termly food bill of £502 (£45.63 a week approx.), just slightly above the average. But we found individual students who were spending much more, including a second-year management student with a termly food bill of £1,000, topped by a third-year International Relations and Management student spending £1,000 a term on eating in and a further £700 on eating out.

It's a Fact

Big social spenders:

Going out 1 alcohol	Weekly spend
Lancaster	£56.69
Newcastle	£55.67
Aberdeen	£51.61
Cardiff	£50.63
Brighton	£48.55
London	£48.38
Leeds	£47.37
Exeter	£47.36
Liverpool	£46.71
Bristol	£46.66

Source: NatWest Student Living Index Survey 2008

Socialising/entertainment

Going out – average: £15.97 per week.
Alcohol – average £28.06 per week.

The *NatWest Student Living Index Survey* didn't assess how good a 'good time' students were having, or how often they went out, but on average students spend £44.03 per week on clubbing, pubbing, gigs, cinema and drinking. The biggest spenders, with bills of around £56.69 per week, were to be found in Lancaster, followed by students in Newcastle, with a weekly bill of £55.67.

Thrift Tips for Hungry Students

'Give dinner parties and charge.'
2nd year Industrial Relations and Modern History student, St Andrews

'Make your own sandwiches for lunch and sell them to friends.'
1st year Medicine student, Cambridge

'Get to like pasta!'
4th year Psychology student, Paisley

'If each of your friends brings a potato, carrot, leek you've got a great stew for next to nothing.'
1st year Music student, Huddersfield

However, if you look at alcohol consumption alone, the top prize goes to Newcastle, with an average weekly spend of £39.10.

The most abstemious students can be found in Dundee, with an average weekly alcohol bill of £17.49, while the stay-at-homes are to be found in Durham, with an average weekly spend of only £7.60 a week on going out. And they don't make up for it on the alcohol, with an average weekly spend of a very reasonable £19.79.

Our own research showed that when it comes to socialising, it is a very individual cost. St George's students averaged a very modest £132 a term for socialising. One second-year female medical student told us she spent just £5 a term: 'I don't drink,' was her reason; while a third-year student, also at St George's, and also female, owned up to spending a massive £375 a term just on socialising.

What are students drinking?

Students told us:

University	Drink
Oxbridge	beer
St George's	lager
Lampeter	Coca-Cola
St Andrews	vodka and mixer

Books and course materials

Average: £9.04 a week.

All students said they spent more on books in the autumn term and in their first year than at any other time. Some reported that they'd then taken to using libraries instead of buying, as books were so expensive. It is difficult to give an average figure for books, because what you need to buy depends on your course and how well stocked your college library is in your subject. It's worth checking this out before starting your course if you can. As a very general guide, the average figure was £9.04 a week (*NatWest Student Living Index*).

While our student contacts at St Andrews estimated a termly bill of £89, at Lampeter they spent on average just £50 a term.

Book check

Your university or college may have a second-hand bookshop. Find out before you start purchasing: books are very expensive. Check out your college library. Is it well stocked in books on your subject? Is it close to where you study and where you live? Try the net, there are many sites for buying and selling textbooks.

> *'I'm currently on the most expensive course – 3D design. The financial strain of coping with the cost of materials is hindering my design capabilities and interfering with my studies; the annual cost of course equipment is £200.'*

Photocopying, library costs and fines, etc.
Average: £3.88 per week.

Many universities provide a photocopying card, which eases the cost. For those on courses where study covers topics in a wide range of books the cost can be considerable. On average £3.88 a week was spent on photocopying and library costs. Many of our student contacts said most of their photocopying costs went on ink and paper for their own printers.

Field trips

Up to £700.

Geography, biology, astrophysics, computer science, music, sustainable development, medicine, education, ancient and medieval history – the list goes on. All these courses included field trips Costs ranged from £2–£3 to £700. Of the 140 students the *Guide to Student Money* contacted, 16 mentioned field trips as an expense. Interestingly, they were all studying different subjects. The actual cost will depend on the course you are taking, so an average would be meaningless. We found one student at Oxford who gave a range of £4 to £700. Keep field trips in mind when checking out your degree.

'Geology is becoming very expensive. I have two compulsory field trips a year costing £150 each.'

3rd year student, Durham

Mobile phones

Average: £9.82 per week.

Most students today have a mobile. New deals have brought mobile phone bills down, as our research shows. Last year's figure was £12.90 a week, compared with £9.82 this year. More and more students rely on their mobiles rather than pay for a landline. Highest spenders, according to the *NatWest Student Living Index*, were students in London, with average weekly bills of £11.76 followed closely by students from Leicester, with bills of £11.68.

Internet

It would seem this is no longer a major expense for students. Many find it is included in their rent fees. For the 140 students who took part in the *Guide to*

Want to Cut the Cost of Your Phone Bill?

Certain 08 numbers (0844, 0845, 0870 and 0871, for example) masquerade as costing the same as local calls when in fact they may not be as cheap as you think, and may not be covered by any cost-saving phone deal you might have in place. Many mobile phone packages exclude free phone numbers such as 0800 and 0808, so you pay the going rate for calling these numbers. To find the cheapest way to phone an 08 number, log on to www. saynoto0870.com. They might give you an alternative local number, or show how your call can be routed in a different way.

Student Money research, buying computer equipment was more of a problem, and it could cost anything from £5 to £500 or more. A broadband connection can mean a monthly bill of around £20, but in most houses this would be shared between perhaps four or five students. Look for the special offers, and if you are hoping to hop from one special offer to another make sure there are no tie-in clauses in the contract.

Clothing

Average: £16.62 a week.

On average students spend £16.62 a week on clothes, which is down on last year's £18.50. Had the credit crunch already started to hit students? The change is very apparent when we look at the best-dressed universities in the *NatWest Student Living Index Survey*. Last year London came out top of the league, with a weekly average of £26.90. This year Nottingham is top, but with an average of £23.86. The university least bothered sartorially this year was Durham, with a weekly bill of £8.45, followed by York, with a bill of £12.13.

Turning to the *Guide to Student Money* research, remember the second-year student at St George's who spent £5 a term on socialising? At £400 a term her clothing bill was not nearly so modest; and it was way above the St George's termly average of £116. When it comes to clothes, how much people spend is as individual as style.

Best-dressed regions

Northern Ireland was streets ahead of the rest of the UK, with weekly bills of £20.11, according to the NatWest survey, with England coming a very poor second at £16.74. The least smart region seemed to be Scotland, with weekly bills of £14.96.

Best-dressed universities (of 26 looked at)

University	Average spend per week
Nottingham	£23.86
Lancaster	£22.92
Liverpool	£21.08
Belfast	£20.11
Oxford	£18.83
Brighton	£18.68

Source: NatWest Student Living Index

So Where is the Cheapest Place to Study?

The NatWest research this year gives a very confusing picture. For money management York, with a weekly bill of £145.75, comes out top, followed closely by Plymouth at £147.75 a week. Even when weekly rent is factored in, York still comes in as the cheapest place to study, with a weekly spend of £212.45, followed by Plymouth at £216.80. However, the lowest average rents were found in Lancaster. The most expensive place to study is, of course, London, with a weekly bill, including rent, of £311.55.

Travel during term time

Average: £10.58 per week

To survive, it seems you need to be fit. Students said that walking was their main way of getting about. For many, however, travel was a significant cost, with students in London experiencing the most severe problems in terms of expense (average £16.35 a week) and time taken to get to lectures. At the other end of the scale, Durham students had the lowest weekly bills at £4.78. Our average figure of £10.58 includes taxis. Students studying medicine and based in London can be the hardest hit, as their training often involves attachments to other hospitals, which may be as far as 40 miles away. Check with your local authority to see if you are entitled to financial help with transport. Scottish students can claim extra for travel as a grant if costs exceed £159 a year.

About a fifth of students are thought to own a car or motorcycle. This estimate includes many mature students, who tend to drive longer distances than younger students during term. While petrol is an obvious cost, with the current volatility of petrol prices we felt an average was not helpful. Cycling seems to be much less popular than it was a few years ago. Students complained that cycling was dangerous, and another gripe was having their bicycles stolen – even being mugged for a mountain bike. Students cited pollution and traffic congestion as problems.

Travel check

▶ The frequency of university and local bus services: a huge number of students complained about the infrequency and unreliability of bus services and the fact that they didn't run at night.

'. . . and when the buses do come they are often so full they don't stop. It's quite common to be late for lectures.'

2nd year International Tourism and Management
student, Robert Gordon University

▶ The last bus: a number of students complained that in many cities bus services finish early, with no regular service after 10.30p.m. – a major problem for sociable students in outlying districts. Check on this when choosing accommodation; you don't want to find ...

'The last bus was at 7p.m. Even a modest social life was impossible.'

Law student, Bristol

▶ The area at night: an increasing number of both male and female students in many more universities said it was dangerous to walk alone at night. They included students from Huddersfield, Staffordshire, London, and many more. Many also said taxis were expensive.

'Late night in London is often dangerous. Many confrontations!'

1st year Music student, City University

'Walking home in the dark'

4th year Social Anthropology student, St Andrews

'Walking at night. Irregular buses. Someone destroyed my bike.'

2nd year Pharmacology student, Oxford

'Walking through estate at night'

1st year Medical student, St George's, London

'Taxis can cost £4 for a three-minute journey after midnight.'

3rd year English student, St Andrews

'You need a car in Bradford; walking even in the early evening is dangerous. Somebody just up my road had a gun pulled on them. Fortunately most students don't have much money.'

2nd year Technology and Management student, Bradford

But there were more positive comments:

'Taxis are in good supply in Bangor and a journey across town is cheap.'
2nd year Psychology student, Bangor

Travel between home and college

How much will it cost to get to your college from your family home and back again during the year? Average: £11.75 per week spent on longer trips.

If you live in Exeter and decide to study in Glasgow, getting there is going to be a major expense and you won't be popping home very often. But if home is Birmingham and you study somewhere close at hand, like Manchester, it's relatively cheap and you might go home weekly, which over time would tot up. So an average isn't really meaningful.

Plan your trips home and book early – there are some fantastic bargains on trains and coaches (see page 28). Coaches are generally cheaper than trains, but they take longer and the amount of luggage you can take with you is usually limited. The most popular means of transport for students is the train. However, many students told *Guide to Student Money* that their parents might give them a lift at the beginning and end of the year when they have a lot of luggage. If you do have to stagger home with your luggage using public transport, remember your costs may have to include taxi fares.

Student budgets around the country

The budgets on the next page are based on research carried out in August 2008 for the *NatWest Student Living Index*. For students living in university accommodation, utilities (gas/electricity/water) are generally included.

Thrift Tips

Don't shop on an empty stomach – it's disastrous.

Shop just before closing and get the bargains.

Watch out for special coach company offers.

Check that water rates are included in your rent.

Look for special student nights at clubs, theatres, cinemas.

Students' union shops buy in bulk so they can give good discounts. Beer, stationery, dry cleaning, even holidays, could be part of their cost-cutting service.

Average budget according to 2008 *NatWest Student Living Index*

	England	Northern Ireland	Scotland	Wales	London	Oxbridge
Alcohol (all consumed at home and while out)	£28.29	£28.89	£25.47	£30.58	£27.93	£23.65
Supermarket food shopping	£20.79	£22.12	£24.29	£22.31	£25.16	£22.32
Buying clothes	£16.75	£20.11	£14.96	£16.46	£16.63	£16.42
Going out (cinema/clubs/gigs)	£15.96	£17.24	£15.29	£16.70	£20.45	£14.18
Eating out (café, restaurant, canteen, etc.)	£15.18	£20.08	£15.34	£12.96	£21.03	£19.13
Cigarettes	£14.33	£17.00	£12.64	£17.54	£16.29	£14.32
Utility bills	£13.77	£10.44	£13.41	£12.63	£18.95	£13.68
Transport costs for longer trips	£11.37	£14.54	£12.05	£13.70	£12.11	£10.52
Day-to-day travel (inc. taxis)	£10.86	£12.99	£9.00	£9.20	£16.35	£8.70
Telephone/mobile phone bill	£9.65	£10.94	£9.56	£11.42	£11.76	£8.40
Books and course materials	£8.70	£10.05	£10.68	£8.79	£10.32	£8.10
Buying CDs, DVDs and videos	£8.71	£11.93	£7.70	£8.27	£12.12	£9.81
Laundry/dry cleaning	£3.96	£4.05	£3.99	£4.49	£6.84	£3.28
Photocopying/library costs, fines, etc.	£3.80	£4.17	£3.86	£4.62	£5.37	£3.65
Rent	£71.12* £67.67†	£58.27	£72.0	£64.29	£90.24	£89.17

*If London and Oxbridge included.
†If London and Oxbridge excluded.

1   THAT'S THE WAY THE MONEY GOES

Student Rail and Coach Cards

Both train and coach services offer student reductions, provided you buy their special student cards. These last for a year. One longish journey will more than cover the initial outlay, which is:

16–25 railcard: £24 p.a. (February 2009)
Reduction: one-third off all rail fares.

Travel restrictions: check with station for full details.

16–26 coachcard: £10 p.a. (February 2009)
Reduction: up to 30%.
Travel restrictions: some journeys cost slightly more at certain times.

See the table below for some comparative travel costs from London. Prices are based on return fare prices in February 2009 using a 16–25 railcard or coachcard discount.

Typical Fares	Train	Train	Coach
	Advanced single. Two single tickets must be purchased. Limited number of tickets	Off-peak Return	Mostly off-peak, booked in advance. £1 booking fee charged
London to:			
Edinburgh	From £7.90 × 2	£71.80	£36.00
Newcastle	From £9.20 × 2	£69.30	£25.50
Manchester	From £5.30 × 2	£42.75	£27.30
Nottingham	From £5.95 × 2	£30.70	£23.50
Birmingham	From £3.30 × 2	£9.90	£20.00
Cardiff	From £7.60 × 2	£28.80	£28.75
Bristol	From £6.60 × 2	£24.40	£22.95
Exeter	From £7.90	£38.20	£25.50

Many tickets have special conditions, and advance booking conditions vary. With some rail tickets it is cheaper to buy singles. Train companies operating on the same route have different fares. Check with National Rail Enquiries on 0845 748 4950 and ask for a full list of options for the journey you are making. See also www.moneysavingexpert.com, and don't get taken for a ride.

Coach prices: travel on Friday is generally more expensive; reductions are available if you book in advance.

Can I afford to run a car?

If your only income is the standard funding for students, most rational people would say no. But since so many students do seem to have cars they must be managing it somehow. A recent survey by Reaction UK claimed that nearly half of all students own or use a car. Travel from your home to your university will probably be cheaper by car, but you may also find yourself going home many more times during term, acting as chauffeur to the party, and taking trips at weekends. And don't underestimate the maintenance bills: they can be astronomical, especially for an old car. Then there's the road tax, currently £120p.a. (£66 half-yearly) for cars under 1549cc and £185 p.a. (£101.75 half-yearly) for the rest. If your car was manufactured after March 2001 you'll be charged according to its CO_2 emissions. There are seven different bands, and costs range from zero for cars with very low CO_2 emissions to £400 a year (£220 half-yearly) for a mighty 4×4 gas-guzzler. Add to that your MOT and AA/RAC membership (which makes sense if your car has a tendency to break down) and your biggest outlay of all – insurance, which for third party, fire and theft (the cover favoured by most young people), is said to be averaging close to £1,000.

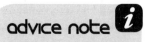

advice note

▶ Restrictions on cards can change, so always check what is being offered and when you can travel.

▶ Look for special reductions: occasionally the rail or coach companies will have special promotions such as half-price student cards, or half-price fares. They may also give discounts on things like CDs or subscriptions to magazines. Check out www.gobycoach.com.

How much to insure my wheels?

Two wheels or four, it's not going to be cheap or easy.

Four wheels

Students lucky enough to have a car may find they don't have much luck getting insurance, especially if they are first-time drivers and aged under 21. Try Endsleigh Insurance: in 1997 the NUS, worried that many students who ran cars couldn't afford the cost of insurance cover, asked Endsleigh (an insurance company that they part own) to try to find a way to reduce motor insurance premiums for students – which they did, by up to 30%.

A word of caution: think twice about 'fronting'; that's the old trick of mum taking out the insurance and naming the student as second driver. If there's a claim and it's discovered that the student is really the main driver, you could find the insurance company won't pay up.

Facts and Figures

▶ Students spend around half their money on accommodation.

▶ The number of students taking up university places in autumn 2008 was up by a staggering 10.4% on the previous year, making a grand total of 456,627 (UCAS figures).

▶ 22% of full-time students at UK universities fail to obtain a degree (*Staying the Course*, House of Commons Committee on Public Accounts Report 2007–2008).

▶ 14% of students drop out of their course (HESA).

▶ The NUS believes a major cause of dropping out is financial hardship (*NUS Student Hardship Survey*). Other reasons include exam failure, ill health and switching courses.

▶ Even at 14%, Britain has one of the lowest university drop-out rates for degrees on the global completion table.

Insurance costs vary, depending not just on who you are, but on where you live. Big-city drivers pay a higher premium than, say, those in the country. In London the costs are prohibitive. Endsleigh warns: 'Insurance premiums are based on the address where the car resides for the majority of the year. Therefore, if you are living away from home while studying, you must provide the address where you live for the majority of the year.' So even if it would be cheaper to take out insurance from, say, your parents' home address, think before you do it. Giving false information could lead to claims not being paid.

Two wheels

You might think a bicycle is much easier to insure. But any student intending to take a bicycle to university must think in terms of having it pinched, or at least borrowed without permission. Insurance companies certainly do.

Insurance advice: a good padlock and detachable wheel or saddle should be your first form of insurance. Consider exchanging that expensive mountain bike for something that looks as if it's come off the tip.

Who to try: Endsleigh offers bicycle cover for bikes and fixed accessories up to £1,500 against accidental damage and theft anywhere in the UK and up to 30 days' cover in Europe. Premiums depend on the value of your bike and where in the country you live, ranging from £27 for bikes worth up to £149 in a fairly theft-free area. Also try the banks – some offer fairly good deals.

Approximately half of all UK-registered bikes are scooters (about 0.5 million) and they have enjoyed an upturn in popularity because of TV stars such as Jamie Oliver. They are often regarded as a cheaper alternative to cars, but remember – they are easily stolen. Some insurers exclude theft cover unless the bike is garaged at night. Immobilisers don't always stop thieves either, as a bike/scooter can be bundled into even a small car.

Endsleigh provides insurance for scooters and small motorbikes. A lot of their enquiries in this area come from students with bikes under 250cc. They offer comprehensive; third party, fire and theft; and third party only.

Thrift Tips

'Rent out any extra room space.'
1st year Contemporary Photographic Practice student, Northumbria

'Visit car boot sales to sell, buy and sell again.'
4th year Environmental Science student, Stirling

'Offer to walk the neighbours' dogs for a couple of quid an hour.'
1st year American Studies and Computing student, Wolverhampton

'Never be afraid to ask if there is a discount for students. I found my NUS card reduced my swimming sessions from £1.95 to 75p.'
Computer student, London University

'A lot of websites pay you to fill out questionnaires to receive text message advertising – you can also sign up for offers on sites such as www. britishfreebies.com and find yourself with enough free samples of shampoo for the year.'
Sheffield Hallam University student

'Try www.moneysavingexpert.com for all kinds of savings.'
3rd year Media and Print Journalism student, Huddersfield

(Students from a number of universities suggested www.studentbeans. co.uk for great discounts.)

'Teach piano.'
English student, Oxford

'Coach A level and GCSE students.'
3rd year Medicine student, Oxford

A level students thinking of giving university a miss because of debt should remember that, on average, graduates can expect to earn 20–25% more than people who finish their education with A levels, which is £160,000 over a lifetime, and much more if you are taking medicine – a cool £340,315 more. (Universities UK report 2007). However government research put the figure much higher, at around 45%.

How much will you need to survive each year as a student?

£6,000 a year? £7,000? £8,000? £9,000? £10,000?

The NUS estimated that for the last academic year (2008–2009) students would need £15,769 if living in London and £13,626 in other parts of the country for the 39-week academic year. You'd be lucky if you had that. In fact, based on what you are likely to receive in funding, the NUS suggested an average shortfall in funds of £7,768 for a student in London and £6,614 for a student elsewhere. And that was last year. So in reality you're going to have to survive on what you can get and what you can earn. How much is that likely to be? See the next chapter!

Typical student budgets

Four students show how their money goes, and where it comes from.

Emma's budget

Second-year medical student at St George's, London

Emma shares a house with three other students – two girls and one boy – plus, as she says, 'a large contingent of uninvited residents who don't pay rent'. There are four bedrooms, one bathroom, a sitting room, kitchen with table and chairs but not enough room to sit and eat, and a washing machine, which she says seems to make their clothes dirtier. It's shabby. It hasn't been refurbished . But 'it's warm, only 10 minutes' walk from uni, and the rent is reasonable'.

Emma says: 'My course is likely to be six years and I expect to graduate to a debt of at least £40,000. It sounds horrendous, but once I'm qualified I

Outgoings	Per term	Comments
Rent	£1,460	52-week contract. Rent £365 each per month (£4,380 p.a. each), and that's good for Tooting (London)
Utilities	£70 approx.	Still waiting for our bills. Male student copes with bills and we just pay up. How stereotypical
Fees	£1,048	£3,145 a year
Food in	£180	Just-in-time catering – we girls tend to cook together – makes it cheaper. Sainsburys only 5-minute walk. Shop together when we need food – rice and pasta – usual student diet
Housekeeping	£45	House needs – take it in turns to buy. £15 a month each
Food out	£195	£15 p.w. food at uni. Lots of little restaurants around £8–£9 a meal, also pizzas/curries
Socialising	£5	Don't drink. Just hot chocolate
Entertainment	£40	Cinema, ice skating, uni disco
Hobbies	£30	Theatre/art exhibitions
Phone	£77.75	£2.75 land line. We have it for the internet. £25 a month mobile
Internet	£6	
Vices	£66	I'm a chocoholic
Travel term-time	£13	
Return fare home	£10	Petrol for car
Books	£140	Textbooks mostly. Reading for pleasure – £25
Car	£160	I pay the road tax and petrol, Dad pays the insurance and maintenance
Clothes	£400	You have to look smart when doing hospital rounds – well, that's my story!
Toiletries	£40	Shampoo
Printing	£4	
Total	**£3,989.75**	

don't think it will be too difficult to pay off. My advice to students: know your rights, especially when dealing with landlords and house agents. For example, a deposit should be returned within 10 days, not 40. And check for safety features before you move in – we had a bad carbon monoxide scare.'

Income	Per term	Comments
Fee loan	£1,048	£3,145 over the year
Student loan	£1,666	£5,000 over the full year
Parents	£200 approx.	They don't have to, but help out at the end of term
Grant	£900	Full grant £2,700 p.a.
Uni bursary	£400	£1,200 p.a.
Overdraft	Not using any at the moment	£1,250 facility available from bank. Not using any of it
Total	**£4,214**	

Matt's budget

Third-year forensic science student at Nottingham Trent

It was the murder of a local girl in his home town of Croydon that made Matt decide on this subject. 'Forensics played an important part in solving the case.'

He lives in a large flat with four other students – all males. It is on the eighth floor of a brand new student block built over TK Maxx and has a fantastic view over Nottingham. He has an en-suite bedroom with sofa, and shares a large kitchen, which includes an eating area, TV and dishwasher. This is how his money goes.

Outgoings	Per week	Per year	Comments
Rent	£89	£3,738	Contract 42 weeks. All utilities are included. Not exorbitant for Nottingham
Mobile	£11	£572	Covers whole year
Internet connection		£50	Upgrade. Double last year's cost but worth it
Food in	£17.50	£630	Occasionally we all cook together, but mostly I cater for myself. More expensive than sharing, but with Tesco just round the corner I buy to eat. It's much cheaper than last year and always fresh
Food out	£18.75 approx.	£675	

Outgoings	Per week	Per year	Comments
Laundry	£1.50	£100	Wash and dry £3 on premises every other week
Toiletries	£2.50	£90	
Socialising, entertainment & music	varies	£900	I've really cut back on the drinking and we we don't go out so much – tend to drink before we go. Last year's bill £2,556
Gym membership		£75	Two terms – I'm a cox for the uni team
Travel (in town)	£0	£0	Annual travel card, go anywhere in Nottingham – given free as part of rent
Travel (home)		£120	£20 return on coach to Croydon in Surrey. Twice a term
Books		£30	Mostly use library
Vices	£0	£0	Quit smoking, saved £416 p.a.
Clothes		£100	
Gifts		£40	Mostly over Christmas
Holidays	£0	£0	Can't afford them
Fees		£3,145	
Total		**£10,265**	

Income	Per year	Comments
Fee loan	£3,145	
Student loan	£2,808	Student loan
Parents	£1,000	They are not expected to contribute but they do
Grant	£2,700	From government
Bursary	£400 (anticipated)	This is what I received last year from university: £200 in second and then third term
Jobs		None around
Overdraft	£1,250	Interest-free from bank. Could get another £500 but haven't had to ask yet
Total	**£11,303**	

Matt says: 'My advice to all new students is to watch the first two weeks. Freshers' week is the killer; many students spend over a grand. By the end of my first term here I was down to having just £7 a week for food. I did better last year, but it looks as if I'm going to end the year in funds. People seem to be cutting back. We do go out, but there is more drinking at home. Not sure if it's the effect of the credit crunch, or just because I'm happier.'

Your First Term

The first term at university is expensive – and it can be the undoing of some students, condemning them to three years of anxiety and debt. Stories abound of students spending £3,000 just on socialising, though funnily enough, you never seem to meet anyone who has actually done the spending. But overspending there certainly is, especially during freshers' week, and once you get badly into debt it's very difficult to get out of it.

Beth's budget

First-year geography student at St Andrews

Beth is 18. She lives in a university house at Fife Park, a student accommodation estate of some 42 houses built in the 1970s. Next door is one of the most exclusive university halls of residence, so there is a large student community there and many facilities such as bars, restaurants, a tea room and a laundry. Beth shares the house with five other girls (some houses are mixed). Each has her own bedroom and there are two bathrooms plus a shower and a kitchen/diner. It is self-catering. Asked what it is like, Beth said: 'Adequate'. Major drawback: it is one and a half miles (half an hour's walk) from the centre of St Andrews and the university.

The figures given on the next page are for Beth's first term.

Beth says: 'It's a relief to find I can manage my finances. At first it was difficult moving into a house with five people you didn't know. We were such different personalities. People would eat and just leave the dirty dishes for someone else to wash up. And cleaning the house was a tussle. But we got it all sorted in the end, and now four of us have applied to share another house next year. This time it's only 20 minutes from the

Outgoings	Per term	Comments
Rent	£667	The actual rent is £2,000 p.a., which is good value
Food in	£100	I'm a vegetarian. I cook in bulk and freeze it. We each cater for ourselves. We tried eating together because it's cheaper, but it didn't work out, we were never all around at the same time. And some of us had a lot to learn about cooking
Food out	£30	Mainly 'bring a dish and bottle' parties and ceilidhs. You should taste my blue cheese canapés and cranberry sauce. Yum
Toiletries	£20	Shampoo, etc.
Laundry	£20	£1.80 for a wash, £1 for a dry once a week
Phone	£20	Top-up. I do have a landline in my room which my parents pay for and use
Computer	£14	Extra leads
Entertainment	£10	Mostly DVDs and the cinema – special late night showings. New Bond film champagne premier £15
Socialising	£40	No night clubs in St Andrews
Club membership	£70	I joined five clubs: trampoline £12, canoeing £15, Christian Union £3, hiking £5, Amnesty International £2. Gym membership £30
Travel term-time	£60	Visiting my sister at Edinburgh Uni
Fare home	£50	Return to Greater London – train
Vices	£0	Don't have any
Books	£60	Wait and buy from last year's students at half price
Field trips	£10	Edinburgh/Dundee
Clothes	£20	Biggest outlay – hiking sack University Hoody Hot pink Toastie Bar hoody – bright red – I work there for charity and fun Friday nights
Gown	£135	Essential for formal dinners
Bike	£150	Best buy! How else would I get to lectures on time?
Gifts	£120	Well, it's Christmas!
Away weekend	£55	Christian Union weekend away
Fees	£592 approx	£1,775p.a. – low because it's Scotland
Total	**£2,243**	

1 THAT'S THE WAY THE MONEY GOES

Income	Per term	Comments
Fee loan	£592 approx.	To pay for fees, £1,775p.a. – less than in England
Maintenance loan	£1,240 approx.	Full maintenance loan less grant (£3,720p.a.)
Maintenance grant	£905	
Bursary	£0	Not given in Scotland
Parents	£188 approx.	£75 a month
Grandparents	£800	£2,500p.a. while at uni
Overdraft	£0	Free overdraft facility of £1,200 from the bank but haven't used it yet
Savings	£800	I'm a great babysitter
Job	£0	Thinking of it. Only have 12 hours lectures, so every afternoon free
Total	**£4,525**	

centre of town and has a sitting room, but a rent of £2,400. The best advice I received when I arrived was don't take any money to the freshers' fairs, otherwise you'll join every club. As it was, I joined five – those third years are very persuasive.'

Luke's budget

First-year sports science student at the University of Exeter

Luke, who is 19, lives in halls, in one of two accommodation blocks situated on campus. There are 10 students living on his corridor and they share two bathrooms, a shower and a microwave. His room has a desk, fridge, lamp, shelves, a chest of drawers and cupboard space large enough to accommodate his guitars and sports gear.

The figures given on the next page are for Luke's first term.

Luke says: 'Save as much as you can before you come. The first term is very expensive, you go out more than at any other time and spend more than you think. I learned the hard way. Try and get a job and get it organised

Outgoings	Per term	Comments
Rent	£1,300	£3,536 for the whole year. Includes food – 2 meals a day – heating and lighting, internet, insurance
Additional food	£88	A sportsman needs protein – £16 every two weeks
Food out	£100	Nando's, takeaways – Indian/Chinese
Toiletries	£10	Hair gel. Mum stocked me up before I came
Laundry	£25	Sports kit. Cost just for soap – washing and drying is free
Phone	£120	Mum generally pays the bill
Entertainment/ socialising	£500	Mostly alcohol and clubs, the driving range £6p.w., ski slope £15, cinema
Club membership	£220	Cricket £75, football £70, squash £50, rifle shooting £30
Gym membership	£235	
Travel term-time	£30	Taxis to other campus – sports bags can be heavy
Fare home	£0	Would be £50 return but Dad collects me by car – too much sports gear
Vices	£35	DVDs and play station games
Books	£100	Can always sell them to new students next year
Photocopying	£20	Ink for my printer
Clothes	£40	Stuff for themed nights – vampire teeth and other essentials
Equipment	£10	Mostly stationery
Gifts	£15	Birthdays mainly
Away weekend	£20	Four days in Wales with friends
Fees	£1,048	£3,145 for the year
Total	**£3,916**	

before you come to uni because when you get there you'll find all the jobs have gone. I was already working for the Ernest Jones group at home in Surrey, so just transferred to the local shop here in Exeter. I am the only one in my group with a job – it doesn't quite cover my socialising, but it certainly helps.

it's a Fact

Great news, guys, it looks as if you are going to be outnumbered yet again. Of the students starting courses in 2008, 251,932 are females and just 204,695 males. Have a good year!

(UCAS figures)

Income	Per term	Comments
Fee loan	£1,048	£3,145 for the year
Maintenance loan	£1,233	
Maintenance grant	£780	
Bursary	£0	Nothing yet!
Parents	£275	£25 a week from Mum. Had been saving for my uni years
Phone bill	£120	Mum pays
Overdraft	£200	Free overdraft facility from the bank of £1,000 approx. Did borrow £200 but have paid it off
Job	£412.50	£37.50p.w. Work in Ernest Jones – 7.5 hours at £5p.h. every Saturday
Total	**£4,068.50**	

Fees and funding

This chapter answers questions on the main sources of finance for students embarking on higher education in 2009–2010.

- ▶ Top-up fees: the lowdown (page 42)

- ▶ Fees: what you pay (page 44)

- ▶ Maintenance: grants, bursaries and loans (page 48)

- ▶ Further information (page 59)

Note: the information in this chapter is based on the funding package for students starting university in the UK in 2009–2010. Any variations in Scotland, Wales and Northern Ireland and additional help for special case students are covered in Chapter 4.

Top-up fees: the lowdown

The arguments are over – top-up fees or, as they are officially called, variable fees are here to stay for most students and already inflation is hiking them up still further. And now there is talk of taking the cap off how much universities can charge UK students for fees. The government is likely to make a decision some time soon. However, that is not for this year, and whatever they decide on fees will not be retrospective, so students who are already at university will stick with the current fee arrangement – around a 2.5% increase each year.

While student debt is rising at an unprecedented rate, and will continue to do so, some ingenious ways have been introduced to help alleviate some of the financial anxieties while you are actually studying. So it's not all doom and gloom.

Student funding: the main points

Fees

▶ Universities can charge different (variable) fees for courses, but most do charge the maximum.

▶ The maximum a UK student starting study for a first degree in 2009–2010 can be expected to pay in fees is £3,225 p.a.

▶ Welsh-domiciled students studying in Wales will effectively pay fees of £1,285 (see page 91).

▶ Scottish students studying in Scotland do not pay fees at all (see page 88).

▶ Students can take out a loan to cover their fees, which they will pay back gradually once they have graduated.

▶ Payback for loans will begin in the April after you graduate if you are earning over £15,000.

▶ There will be no help with fees for low-income families.

Maintenance

▶ Maintenance grants of up to £2,906 are available for students, depending on family income on a sliding scale up to around £50,000 (this is not as high as last year).

▶ Bursaries are available from universities, especially for students from low-income families.

▶ Main source of maintenance income is the student loan, available to all students, max. £4,950 (£6,6,928 in London).

- Part of the loan is means-tested on family income and on the amount of maintenance grant students receive.
- Non-repayable Special Support Grants of up to £2,906 are available for students receiving government support – largely lone parents/disabled students.

Remember, not every student gets everything. How much support you can receive will depend on three factors:

- where you live
- family income
- where you choose to study.

Looking at the detail

Am I a special case?

If you fall into any of the categories listed below, check out Chapter 4.

- Scottish students and those studying in Scotland (see page 88).
- Welsh students and those studying in Wales (see page 91).
- Northern Irish students and those studying in Northern Ireland (see page 93).
- Students from another country in the EU or outside the EU (see page 94).
- Refugees/asylum seekers (see page 98).
- Sandwich/industrial placement students (see page 101).
- Part-time students (see page 101).
- Foundation students (see page 103).
- Second undergraduate degrees at Oxbridge (see page 104).

- Full-time distance learning courses (see page 104).
- Attending a private higher education institution (see page 105).
- Nursing/midwifery students (see page 105).
- Healthcare students (see page 105).
- Medical/dental students (see page 106).
- Trainee teachers, Wales (see page 108).
- Social work students (see page 108).
- Dance and drama students (see page 109).
- Married/independent students (see page 110).
- Single parents/students with a family to support (see page 110).
- Students with disabilities (see page 111).
- Students studying abroad (see page 114).

Fees: what you pay

How much will I have to pay towards my fees?

Your university will set a price for each course up to a maximum of £3,225 p.a. Fees are flexible, but most universities charge the full amount.

However, we did find a few universities that were charging lower fees to 2009–2010 entrants. These included:

Institution	Fee
Greenwich	£2,900
Leeds Met	£2,000
Writtle College	£2,906

Who will pay my fees?

You. There will be no help from the your local authority (LA) for fees and your parents will not be asked to contribute. What's more, family income will have no bearing on what you pay. Universities can charge what they like for a course up to the maximum of £3,225 p.a., and what they ask is what you must pay, but you may take out a loan to cover these fees.

Will every student pay the same fees?

Unless you come from outside the EU, students on the same course at the same university will pay the same fees – they are not means tested – but course fees can vary even in a university. Your university will decide what fees it is going to charge.

Remember: Scottish students studying in Scotland do not pay fees at all, while non-Scottish students who study in Scotland do, but at a different rate to students in England. Wales also takes an independent line. For full details and reasons why the rates are different, see Chapter 4.

Do fees ever go up?

Yes, every year. When the top-up fee programme was first mentioned, the government said that fees would not go up before 2010, but the original top-

Note: LA stands for local authority in England and Wales. When the term LA is used in this book, please read SAAS for Scotland (Student Awards Agency for Scotland) and ELB (Education and Library Board) for Northern Ireland.

up fee of £3,000 has been given an annual inflationary lift, so it is now £3,225. What will happen next year nobody knows, but there is plenty of speculation in the media. A report commissioned by the government published at the end of December 2008 recommended that universities should be free to charge whatever tuition fees they choose. There was also a suggestion that cheaper degrees should cost less, around £6,000 to £7,000 p.a., and more expensive degrees, such as medicine, up to £20,000 p.a. While this is only speculation at the moment, there will certainly be changes in 2011; and they won't be for the better, or cheaper. However, if you are starting your degree this year, you will be saved from even greater debt.

How am I going to pay my fees?

Where is a student going to find £9,675 or, at worst, £12,900 for fees?

They won't, at least not while they are studying. One of the better aspects of the current funding system is the fee loan, which all students can take out. And you don't have to start paying it back until you have graduated and are earning at least £15,000 (see page 75 for full details). So nobody has to pay fees up front; there will be no getting slung out of uni for not having the money to pay fees, and no juggling your finances between eating and studying – as in the past. You just keep piling on the debt.

Where will the loan come from?

From the Student Loans Company.

How do I get my loan for fees?

You apply to Student Finance England (www.direct.gov.uk/studentfinance), at the same time as applying for your maintenance loan and a grant. It is all done on the same form and processed together. Student Finance will then process your application and pass it on to the Student Loans Company, who will pay out the money. The form is available from www.direct.gov.uk/studentfinance to fill in or download, or by calling 0845 300 5090. For more information on applying for finance see Chapter 3, page 62.

How much can I borrow?

Whatever your course costs, up to £3,225 p.a.

Is it means tested?

No.

What will happen to the money I borrow for fees?

It will be paid direct to your university.

Who can get a fee loan?

UK first-degree students, EU students and those taking a PGCE (Postgraduate Certificate in Education).

Is taking out a loan for fees a good idea?

Yes. The big plus of the 'top-up fee' funding system is that, because students can take out a loan to cover their fees, they (or their parents) will not have to pay fees before they start university or while they are studying. So all your maintenance loan, any bursary and maintenance grant you receive, anything your parents give you and everything you earn will all go towards living. You should have fewer money worries than your predecessors during your time at university, but your debt will undoubtedly be greater.

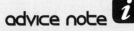 **advice note**

If your parents want to pay your fees but will have to borrow to pay them, it's worth remembering that the loan offered by the Student Loans Company is probably the cheapest money you can borrow, so it might be an idea to come to a family arrangement – you take out the loan for your fees and they pay it off for you.

If my parents want to pay my fees, can they do so?

There is nothing to stop parents paying your fees. Fees have to be paid at the start of each year. Most universities allow fees to be paid in tranches, but you will need to talk to your university. Some universities will give a discount if fees are paid in full up front.

Who gets help with fees?

Nobody, unless you:

▶ started your course in 2005 or before

▶ are a 2005–2006 gap-year student who had an exemption

- are a Welsh student studying in Wales (see page 91)
- are a Scottish student studying in Scotland (see page 88).

What happens if I drop out of my course? Will I have to pay fees?

Probably, but there are no hard and fast rules. If you drop out before 1 December you may be all right as your fees won't have been paid out before that date. But generally, it will be a matter of discussing it with your university – after all, they have all the expense of providing a place for you.

I want to change my course: what happens about my fees?

Again, it will be a matter of discussion with your university. If you are changing to another course in the same university, fees may not be a problem, but if you are moving to another university it might be more difficult.

Will I be able to get a loan for fees for any course I take at college?

No. Courses for which loans for fees will be given include: full-time (including sandwich) degree, HNC, HND, Postgraduate Certificate of Education, school-centred initial teacher training, or equivalent courses undertaken at a UK university, publicly funded college or comparable institution.

Courses for which loans are not available include: school-level courses such as A levels or Scottish Highers, BTEC and SCOTVEC National Awards and City & Guilds courses for those over 19, postgraduate courses (except teacher training), all part-time courses★ (except initial teacher training courses), some correspondence and Open University courses.

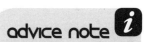

advice note

If a fee debt of £9,675+ (£12,900+ for a four-year course) fills you with horror, and well it might, don't abandon your degree aspirations – yet. There are some excellent bursary deals on offer and many students, especially those from low-income families, may find that while studying they are better off than their non-top-up-fee predecessors.

★See page 101 for details of grants for part-time courses.

What can I do to raise funds to pay my fees if I am unable to get a loan?

1. Talk to your local authority.

2. Talk to the college where you want to take the course.

3. Apply for a career development loan – see page 58.

4. Apply to professional bodies, trusts, foundations, benevolent funds – see Chapter 8.

Fast facts on finance

For students starting their course 2009–2010	
Fees	Max. £3,225 p.a.
Fee loan	Up to £3,225 p.a.
Student loans	£6,928 in London, £4,950 elsewhere, £3,838 living at home (less in your final year); 28% is means tested on parents' income and maintenance grant received if you have been assessed for a maintenance grant
Maintenance grant	£2,906 for low-income families (less in Scotland). Means tested on family income
University bursaries	At least £319 p.a. for those on full maintenance grant (most give more)
Access to Learning Fund (Contingency Fund – Wales; Hardship Funds – Scotland; Support Funds – Northern Ireland)	Random distribution; given largely to help with rent and other financial hardships
Part-time students	Increased levels of fee grants to max. of £1,210 plus course grant of £260 – slightly more for fees in Wales
Salary payback threshold for fee and maintenance loans	£15,000

Maintenance: grants, bursaries and loans

There are three elements to students' maintenance:

► maintenance grants

► university bursaries

► student loans.

Maintenance grants

What are they and will I get one?

Maintenance grants are not new: they have been creeping into the funding system since the year 2000. What is new, though, is the amount – up to £2,960 – and the number of students who will receive them. This is not government generosity, however, but because students no longer receive help with fees. Maintenance grants are means tested on your or your family's income up to £50,000, but note: this is only in England. In the rest of the UK the family income cut-off point is much lower – see Chapter 4.

Maintenance grants for new students in England: who receives what in 2009–2010

Family income	Grant
£25,000 or less	£2,906
£30,000	£2,240
£35,450	£1,574
£40,000	£908
£45,000	£242
£50,000	£50
More than £50,000	£0

How many students will receive a maintenance grant?

This year, in England, around a third of students are expected to receive a full grant, and around a third a partial grant, even though the grant eligibility has been cut back from a family income of £61,000 last year to a family income of £50,000.

When will I get my grant?

It will be paid in three instalments, one at the start of each term.

Who calculates how much I will get?

Student Finance England, based on the information you supply on your application form.

University bursaries

Universities have always offered bursaries to good students, but never on the scale that they are doing now. The government stipulated that to charge the maximum fee – currently £3,225 p.a. – universities must sign up to an

Access Agreement, which stipulates that students receiving the full £2,906 maintenance grant (i.e. those from low-income families) must be given a further non-repayable bursary of at least £319, making a grand total of £3,225 combined maintenance grant and bursary (the same amount as the full fees) – but your university bursary could be more.

Some universities stick to the guidelines. Others are far more generous; some use bursaries as an incentive to attract students. Many offer bursaries on a sliding scale to all those receiving a proportion of the maintenance grant. The average bursary given by universities in 2008–2009 was £1,000 p.a. for those receiving the maximum maintenance grant. This could be given in kind – e.g. reduced accommodation costs. Even students who don't actually fall into the low-income category are cashing in. Examples are given on page 51. For up-to-date information check out the bursary map website: http://bursarymap. direct.gov.uk.

Shop around. There are some fantastic bursary deals about, and every university has a different approach. Finding a university giving generous bursaries could be more cost-effective than trying to find a low-cost course, and probably better educational value too.

Where will the money for bursaries come from?

Universities have set aside over £350 million from the increased fee money to support students from low-income families, and it is estimated that some 400,000 students will benefit from this. But many universities are already heavily endowed by generous benefactors and have always awarded scholarships, awards and bursaries to selected students.

Where can I find out about university bursaries and scholarships, and what's being offered?

cash crisis

Many students are missing out on bursaries just because they didn't ask. Check with your university if you are entitled to a bursary even if you are not from a low-income family. They are not necessarily given out automatically. See the bursary map at http://bursarymap.direct.gov.uk.

University prospectuses and websites are a good starting point and should provide plenty of information. Also try:

- www.studentsupportdirect.co.uk
- www.ucas.com
- http//bursarymap.direct.gov.uk.

There is also more information on university awards and scholarships, including sports bursaries, music scholarships, location scholarships and awards for students from abroad, in Chapter 8 of this book.

Some examples of bursaries being offered by universities to students in 2009–2010:

University of Westminster, London	Bursary of £319 given to all students receiving a maintenance grant	
University of York	**Family income**	**Bursary**
	Under £17,910	£1,434
	£17,911–£26,500	£1,024
	£26,501–£38,330	£614
University of Manchester	All home students from households with income of less than £25,000 eligible for a bursary of £1,250 p.a. Advantage scholarships of £3,000. Success scholarships of £1,250 regardless of family income	
University of Oxford	**Family income**	**Bursary**
	Up to £17,999	£3,225 + £875 (1st yr only)
	£18,000–£25,000	£3,225
	£25,001–£49,999	£200–£3,255
Warwick University	£1,800 given to all students if household income under £36,000. Limited numnber of Alumni Scholarships of £1,000–£2,000	
Newcastle University	**Household income**	**Bursary**
	Under £25,000	£1,280
	£25,001–£32,284	£640
	Achievement bursaries also given	
University of Chichester	**Family income**	**Award**
	Under £25,000	£1,077
	£25,001–£29,999	£821–£1,026
	£30,000–£34,999	£564–£820
	£35,000–£39,999	£308–£563
	£40,000–£49,999	£256

To compare and contrast what universities are offering, take a look at *University Scholarships, Awards and Bursaries*, published by Trotman. As well as giving full information about the bursaries now offered by universities to students from low-income families, it lists over 100 institutions offering scholarships, awards and bursaries. Many are for people studying specific subjects, or are travel awards. Subjects vary from the more usual Engineering, History, Geography, Languages, Law and the sciences to the more specialised, such as Cultural Criticism Studies, Paper Science, Rural Studies, Retail and Textiles.

The NUS is calling for a nationals bursary scheme after a government survey showed a third of students based their HE decisions on the amount of financial support available.

cash crisis

Getting a bursary – Sam's story

Sam, 21, is now in his second year at Trinity Hall, Cambridge, where he is studying Archaeology and Anthropology. As an independent student with no family home, funding was extremely important to him.

'I knew Cambridge was very supportive to students in my situation, which was very reassuring,' says Sam, 'and they were very clear about what they would offer. I was given their maximum bursary of £3,100 for my first year, and this year it has gone up to £3,150.

'I was determined to go to university, bursary or no bursary,' he says, 'but the bursary does mean that I don't have to work during term time and have the time and resources to attend conferences and field trips relevant to my degree. I also use the extra time to volunteer with our students' union's access schemes. And I haven't fallen into debt.'

Sam also receives a full government maintenance grant, currently £2,835, and a student loan of £3,365, and he took out the full fee loan of £3,145.

'My grant and bursary cover my living expenses during term time and my loan goes towards the vacations. To top this up, I have been working during the vacations, mostly on website design and maintenance, earning around £10 an hour. Last year, I even managed to swing a week's work in Sri Lanka with fares paid plus a fantastic £14 an hour rate.'

Sam pays £69 a week for accommodation – food not included – and he has a weekly food bill of around £45.

Before university Sam took a gap year and worked in the university's Materials Science Department. 'I managed to save around £2,000, which is my safety net. Like most students, the bank gives me an interest-free overdraft which occasionally I dip into when funding doesn't arrive on time, but I don't see it as part of my income.'

Student maintenance loans

The student loan is quite different from the fee loan. The student loan is cash in the bank: the fee loan is paid direct to your university and you never see the cash.

How much can I borrow?

Not enough – at least that is what most students think. The maintenance loan is reviewed annually and usually increased. What you receive is dependent on where you are studying. (Note: the student maintenance loan, usually called the student loan, is quite different from the maintenance grant. The loan you have to pay back – the grant you don't.) The rates for a full maintenance loan for a full-time student in England in 2009–2010 are shown in the table below. Rates for Wales and Northern Ireland vary slightly.

		Full year max. available	Final year max. available
Students living away from their parents' home and studying:	in London	£6,928	£6,307
	elsewhere	£4,950	£4,583
Students living in their parents' home		£3,838	£3,483
Studying overseas		£5,653	£5,215

'When I started uni I didn't think I'd need a student loan. I'd taken a gap year and saved and was getting £500 a year bursary, but I spent about £800 in the first term – well, actually most in the first month – it was outrageous, it really was. Well, let's face it, the first year isn't exactly quiet. Most went on booze, pizzas and more booze. But that first month was probably the best few weeks of my life. I had worked continuously during my gap year, so when I got to uni I hit it hard.'

Jono, 3rd year student, Loughborough

Is the loan means tested?

Yes. Not everybody can take out the full maintenance loan. It is means tested on your maintenance grant and on family income. For low-income families part of the grant is paid in lieu of part of the maintenance loan, so those receiving the full maintenance grant, or a large proportion of the full grant, may find they are not entitled to the full loan. If you are from a higher-income family (earning over the £50,000 income threshold) a quarter of the loan allocation is means tested against your income or that of your family. It is hoped that any part of the means tested loan you do not receive will be paid by your parents or spouse.

This is the maintenance students can expect in England who are starting their course in 2009–2010:

Family income (£)	Assessed contribution (£)	Maintenance grant (£)	Maintenance loan (£)	Total grant plus loan (£)
Student living at home				
			Max. £3,838	
25,000	0	2,906	2,385	5,291
30,000	0	1,906	2,885	4,791
40,000	0	711	3,483	4,194
50,000	0	50	3,813	3,881
50,778	0	0	3,838	3,838
53,000	444	0	3,394	3,394
56,153	1,075	0	2,763*	2,763
Student studying in London				
			Max. £6,928	
25,000	0	2,906	5,475	8,381
30,000	0	1,906	5,975	7,881
40,000	0	771	6,573	7,344
50,000	0	50	6,903	6,953
50,778	0	0	6,928	6,928
55,000	844	0	6,084	6,084
60,478	1,940	0	4,988*	4,988
Student studying outside London				
			Max. £4950	
25,000	0	2,906	3,497	6,403
30,000	0	1906	3,997	5,903
40,000	0	711	4,595	5,306
50,000	0	50	4,925	4,975
50,778	0	0	4,950	4,950
55,000	844	0	4,106	4,106
57,708	1,386	0	3,564*	3,564

*The point at which the non-means-tested part of loan is reached.
Note: figures are not exact and should be taken as a guideline only.

How the calculations are made

Where students receive a maintenance grant, the amount of loan for which they are eligible will be reduced, pound for pound, by the amount of grant they receive. University bursaries are not included in this calculation. This means that if you come from a lower-income household you will have a smaller loan to repay. All students will be able to get 72% of the maximum student loan for maintenance.

Where the student is not receiving a grant, the other 28% will be assessed on family income over £50,778 at a rate of £1 for every £5 earned. As you can see, students from better-off families are very dependent on parents making their contribution. If you had started your course last year, the point at which parents had to start contributing was increased to a salary threshold of around £61,000.

Sixth-formers who started university in 2008 expected to pay on average £34,740 for a three-year degree course. This was up from £33,512 on the previous year, according to the *NatWest Student Money Matters Survey*. However, Vickie, a fourth-year medical student at Liverpool, reckoned she will have debts of around £45,000 when she graduates, and that's without top-up fees.

cash crisis

My academic year is longer than at most colleges: can I get extra money?

Yes. If your course is longer than 30 weeks you can claim for an extra loan, which will be means tested, for each week you have to attend your course. Weekly rates for 2009–2010 are:

London	£106
Elsewhere	£83
Living at home	£54
Studying abroad	£115

Where does the student loan come from?

The Student Loans Company, which is a special company set up by the government to provide loans for students.

Student loans: a few facts

When the student loan was first introduced in 1992 there was uproar. Many thought that higher education in this country should be completely free; others said that students should contribute to the cost of their education. At the time, the loan was around £580. People predicted student numbers would plummet. They were wrong. In fact, while the loan increased year on year, so did student numbers.

Facts and Figures

How do students feel about debt?

► 77% were worried about the amount of debt they would have on graduating

► 54% were concerned about debt

► 23% had considered packing in university

► 73% were concerned about the increasing fees.

Among A level sixth-formers considering university:

► 66% said their biggest concern was money

► 54% said they were concerned about workload, keeping up, failing exams.

(*NatWest Student Money Matters Survey* August 2007)

But 2006, the first year of the top-up fees, saw a drop in student numbers. Applicants for courses were down by 3% to 506,304. And the number of students actually starting courses was down by 3.6% to 390,809 (UCAS figures).

Fast forward to 2008 and, according to UCAS, application figures increased by a massive 10% to 588,689. And it now looks as if 2009 may well be another bumper year, with applications by March up by 8.8%.on the same time last year.

But the cost is still a deterrent for some. Our research amongst students in December 2008 showed that around 40% of students knew of somebody who didn't go to university because of financial reasons, and 65% said they knew someone who had decided to study in their home town to save money.

Whatever your views about funding yourself through university, if you are a student just starting in higher education in the UK, you will probably end up with a hefty loan and graduating with a sizeable debt. Most students do. Eighty-six per cent of the *Guide to Student Money* student contacts expected to be seriously in debt.

What students say about debt

'When my bank offered an interest-free overdraft I thought the £1,500 was mine to spend. Now I have to think about paying it back. Very distressing!'

'It is unfair to judge the financial status of a student on the parents' income, since it's the student who will be paying off the debt.'

'It's the middle-class students that are suffering, with no grants, and parents who can't afford to sub them.'

'In my first year I spent all my loan in two weeks, so I had to live on noodles for three months. Ugh!'

'I don't like living at home, but I have to because I'm skint!!!'

'Student debt is bad enough, but the "invisible" debt is worse – overdrafts, credit cards, borrowing from family – all of which has to be paid back.'

'Depression is a problem that hits everyone who lives on a tight budget.'

There are students who take a different view:

'Generally, studying is an indulgent luxury which improves prospects and so people should take as much responsibility as possible.'

'Most students don't mind the thought of paying back money once they are earning.'

Who can get a maintenance loan?

UK students who undertake full-time first degree or Diploma of Higher Education courses at universities or colleges of higher education. While there is no age limit on students taking out a fee loan, maintenance loans are available to students aged under 60.

I'm an overseas student: can I get a maintenance loan?

No. Even students from the EU who are classified as 'home' students for fees are not entitled to apply for a maintenance loan. For further details see Chapter 4, page 94.

Are there loans for part-time students?

No. But there is help (see Chapter 4, page 101).

I want to do a second degree: can I get a loan for maintenance and fees?

It depends on how long your first course was and the length of your second course. In general, support will be available for students for the length of a course plus one extra year. Say your new course is three years. Add to that one year. Subtract the length of your first course, say three years, and you would receive funding for one year. But if, for example, your previous course was three years and your new course is four years, add another year to that and you would receive funding for two years. Of course it could work the other way: if your previous course was four years and your new course is only three, you would end up receiving no funding at all. However, if you are thinking of taking a second undergraduate degree at Oxford or Cambridge you could be in fee loan luck – see Chapter 4, page 104.

I want to change my course: what happens to my loan?

If you change to another course in the same college, your entitlement to a maintenance loan may well stay the same, but your fees could be different. Equally, if you transfer to another college the fees may be different. The major problem arises if you change to a college/course that does not attract student support or if there is a break in your studies before you join the new course. If you transfer from one course to another or withdraw from your current course it is very important that you not only discuss this with your college, but also talk to Student Finance England as soon as possible.

I am doing a further education course: can I get a loan?

If you are doing a course that leads to a first degree, HND, HNC, PGCE or NVQ at Level 4 you can get a student loan. The information in this book is aimed mainly at higher education students. Students in the 16–19 age group attending further education colleges may be eligible for financial help through their college.

What are Career Development Loans?

They are designed for people on vocational courses (full-time, part-time or distance learning) of up to two years where fees aren't paid, and you can't get support from your local authority. They cover course fees (only 80% given if you are in full employment, 100% if you have been out of work for three months or more) plus other costs such as materials, books, childcare and living expenses. You can apply for £300–£8,000.

The scheme is funded by a number of high street banks (Barclay's, the Co-operative, the Royal Bank of Scotland) and administered by the Learning and Skills Council (LSC), who will pay the interest on your loan during training and for up to one month afterwards. If the course you take lasts more than two years (three years if it includes work experience) you may still be able to use a CDL to fund part of your course. Shop around the different providers and compare the terms offered before making a choice.

For a free booklet on career development loans phone 0800 585505. More information can also be found on www.lifelonglearning.co.uk and www.direct.gov.uk/en/EducationAndLearning/AdultLearning. See also Chapter 8 for Other Sources of finance to tap.

> 'Get a job – the student loan seems like a lot of money, but it doesn't cover even the essentials.'
>
> Psychology student, Hull
> (See Chapter 5)

Why are the student loan rates lower for the final year?

Because they do not cover the summer vacation. You are expected to be working by then, or can draw social security. However, if your final year is longer than 30 weeks you can apply for more loan for each week. If it lasts 40 weeks or more you can get a loan at the full rate. This is often the case for students on 'accelerated' degree courses. Rates for 2009–20010 are:

	Full year	Final year
Home	£3,838	£3,483
Elsewhere	£4,950	£4,583
London	£6,928	£6,307

Further information

Who to contact/what to read

- ▶ Student helpline: 0845 607 7577 between 8a.m. and 8p.m. Mon to Fri. 9a.m. – 5.30p.m. weekends for financial information, including information on your loans.
- ▶ Student Finance England – online: www.direct.gov.uk/studentfinance. Tel: 0845 300 5090.

Full information about fees, maintenance grants and loans is given in the following free booklets, which you would be well advised to get and study:

- ▶ For students in England: *Student Finance England – A Guide to Financial Support for Higher Education 2009/10* (which is the source for the loan statistics in this chapter). Tel: 0800 731 9133. Website: www.studentfinancedirect.co.uk. Braille and cassette editions also available.
- ▶ For students in Scotland: *Student Support in Scotland: A Guide for Undergraduate Students 2009/10*, available from any Scottish university or the Student Awards Agency for Scotland (SAAS), 3 Redheughs Rigg, South Gyle, Edinburgh EH12 9YT. Tel: 0131 476 8212. Email: saas.geu@scotland.gsi.gov.uk. Website: www.student-support-saas.gov.uk.

▶ For students in Northern Ireland: *Financial Support for Students in Higher Education 2009/10*, Student Support Branch, Department for Employment and Learning (Northern Ireland), Rathgael House, Balloo Road, Bangor, Co. Down BT19 7PR. Tel: 028 9025 7710; (for booklet) 0800 731 9133. Website: www.delni.gov.uk.

▶ For students in Wales: *A Guide to Financial Support for Higher Education*, National Assembly for Wales, Higher Education Division 2, 3rd floor, Cathays Park, Cardiff CF10 3NQ. Tel: 0845 602 8845. Websites: www.studentfinancewales.co.uk; www.learning.wales.co.uk.

Thrift Tips

'Reduce your "cuppa" expenditure – buy a kettle and a cafetière.'
3rd year Geography student, Oxford

'Move to eco-friendly products – e.g. homemade vinegar/bicarb cleaning sprays.'
4th year Classics student, St Andrews

'For the price of a sandwich you can buy a whole loaf, packet of meat and even the mustard.'
PhD English Literature student, St Andrews

'Market your talents. If you play an instrument, teach – £15 p.h. If you play tennis, coach – £10 p.h.'
1st year Music student, City

CHAPTER 3

Applying for funding and paying it back

In this chapter you will find information covering:

Applying for grants and loans

You should start thinking about applying for financial support as soon as you have applied for a place on a course. Do not wait until you have a confirmed place on a course: just quote the course you are most likely to attend. Apply even if you don't think you will be entitled to a maintenance grant, as you will also be assessed for how much loan you are entitled to and how much (if anything) your family is expected to contribute. From this year onwards, new students will apply to Student Finance England and not to their local authority. For existing students there is no change.

Important steps to follow:

1. You can apply online at www.direct.gov.uk/studentfinance (Student Finance England) from 9 February. You can download a paper application form from the website or phone 0845 300 5090 to get a form sent to you. Students from the rest of the UK, see Chapter 4: Scotland page 88; Wales page 91, Northern Ireland page 93.

2. Fill in your application form and return it on the web or by post to Student Finance England. The address is on the website and on the form. Give all the details you are asked for and say whether you intend to apply for a loan. Remember to include your National Insurance number if you want a loan. You might also be asked to send your UK passport or birth certificate as identification. Your parents/partner may also be asked to supply information.

3. Once Student Finance England has received your application you will be assessed to see what finance you are entitled to. You will then be notified by letter of what your entitlements are – that should be within six weeks of your application being received. You will then be able to track the progress of your application and to manage your own student finance account online. If you get in a muddle or need some advice, just log into their helpful webchat service or secure messaging.

4. Before you start your course you will be sent a payment schedule showing when you can expect to receive money.

Timing is important.

► You can apply to Student Finance England from 9 February.

► New students – try to return your form no later than 22 May 2009.

► Students not providing financial information should apply by 24 April 2009.

► Late applications may result in late payments.

If you want to discover what help you are entitled to, check out the online calculator at www.direct.gov.uk/studentfinance.

There is no change to the application process for students based in Wales, Scotland and Northern Ireland – turn to Chapter 4 for details.

When and how will I get the money?

Your student loan and grant: once you have registered your arrival at university and have started to attend the course your university will notify Student Finance England and your student loan and grant (if applicable) will be paid into your bank account. However, it could take three working days after your college has confirmed that you have arrived for the money actually to reach your bank account, so you may need funds to tide you over. Payments will be in three tranches, made at the beginning of each term.

Your fees: will be paid direct to your university.

Your university bursary: likely to be paid into your bank account by your university. It will generally be paid out in two tranches, one in the second and one in the third term. You may need to inform your university that you think you are eligible for a bursary. Make sure you have filled in the right section on your application form to ensure financial information is passed to your university so they can assess you for a bursary.

it's a fact

Student Finance England, the new online service for students applying to go on to higher education in 2009–2010, makes the process faster and more straightforward than ever before. You can now apply for student finance at the same time as making your UCAS application, so you only have to fill in your details once. See for yourself: visit www.direct.gov.uk/studentfinance.

advice note

You will need to have some cash in hand when you arrive at university, since your loan/grant payment will not hit your bank account on the first day and it could in fact be several days before you receive any money.

'I was living on £5 a week since an error had been made in processing my application form and I didn't receive my bursary until the last week of term.'

2nd year Biochemistry student, Oxford

'Major problem in student loan coming in late in the term.'

3rd year Classical Civilisation student, Warwick

Panic! My loan and grant haven't arrived!

It happens – not that often, but it can be dramatic when it does. In an ideal world your cheque should be waiting for you when you arrive at your university or college, but things can go wrong. Some typical reasons we discovered were:

▶ you applied late, so the amount of the loan has not been assessed

▶ loans company has been inundated

▶ wrong information on your bank account

▶ you didn't give all the information required, e.g. NI number.

Whatever the reason, it doesn't help the destitute student to eat, so …

What can I do?

▶ Try the bank. If you already have a bank account, the bank may help you out with a loan – most banks offer free overdrafts to students. Talk to the student adviser at the campus or local branch. This, of course, is no help to the first-year student who needs that cheque to open a bank account, so make sure you have an account before you start your course.

▶ Try your college. Ask your college for temporary help. Most institutions have what's called a hardship fund set up to cover just this kind of eventuality.

▶ Try the Access to Learning Fund, which has been set up to help students. Full details are given on page 71.

▶ Friends? They may well take pity on you when it comes to socialising, buying you the odd drink, but it is rarely a good idea to borrow from friends.

How late can I apply for funding support?

Up to nine months after you have started your course.

Applications can be made at any time during the academic year. The cut-off date for a maintenance loan application is one month before the end of your academic year.

Parents: what to expect

What are parents expected to contribute?

Last year the family income threshold for eligibility for a grant was raised (in England) to a generous £60,005 and it is still that figure for the lucky students who started their course in 2008. This year it has been cut back to £50,000, but that is still better than in the rest of the UK, where the norm is around £40,000. So parents earning over £50,000 should expect to contribute something.

The maximum amount parents/spouses in England are expected to contribute for one student in the year 2009–2010 is approximately:

▶ students studying in London: £1,940
▶ student studying elsewhere: loan top-up £1,386
▶ student living in parents' home: £1,075.

(See the table in Chapter 2, page 54.)

Note: Scotland has a different system of funding for students, and parents are expected to contribute substantially more than parents in the rest of the UK. The figures are also different for Wales and Northern Ireland. See Chapter 4.

Note to parents

No parent is expected to contribute more than the maximum means-tested portion of the loan for each student, however high their income – but many do. (See the paragraphs below for details of what you might have to pay.)

How do they calculate how much loan I can have?

The actual calculation of whether and how much your family is expected to contribute towards maintenance, and how much grant you are entitled to, is very complex. It is based on 'residual income': that means what's left after essential expenses have been deducted. The assessment will be on family income, so if both parents are earning, both incomes will be assessed.

So what are essential expenses? It works like this. They take your parents' or parent plus partner's gross income before tax and National Insurance and then subtract allowances for

Facts and Figures

Parents are contributing more than ever before.

▶ Almost two-thirds of students receive financial support from their parents.

▶ 26% give a regular amount.

▶ 23% give money as and when needed.

▶ 8% of students receive a lump sum at the beginning of each term.

▶ 4% received a one-off payment at the start of their studies.

NatWest Student Survey, August 2007

things like pension schemes, dependants and superannuation payments that qualify for tax relief, and whether you will be receiving any maintenance grant. Having done this they then assess what your household contribution should be. It is not until the family income is over £50,000 that parents are expected to contribute. See table on page 54.

My parents are divorced: whose income will they assess?

Your local authority will decide which parent they consider you are living with, and assess their income, while ignoring the income of the other parent.

I have a step-parent: will their income be included?

Yes: the income of a step-parent, if that's the parent you live with, or a cohabiting partner, whether of the same or opposite sex, will be taken into account. However, maintenance received from an absent parent will not be considered as part of the household income when assessing income.

What happens if my parents are not prepared to divulge their income?

You will not be assessed for a maintenance grant and will only be eligible for three-quarters (the non-means-tested portion) of the maintenance loan.

What if I have a brother or sister claiming for a maintenance grant and a loan?

If there are several children in higher education in the family, the grant and loan entitlements are calculated on the same scale as for one student; those parents whose residual income is below £50,000 would not have to contribute for either student and you would both be eligible for a full loan. If the family income is over £50,000 but below £57,708 (£60,478 in London), parents would have to contribute no more than for one student, and any additional loan received would be divided proportionately between the students. Any parental contribution should be divided in the same way. It must also be remembered that any other dependent children they have will come into the calculation. Parents with a higher residual income will have to contribute more if they have more than one child at university. The maximum parents can be asked to pay, regardless of how many children they have at university, is £6,210 if students are under the new top-up fee system.

Does the parental contribution ever change?

It certainly does. Last year in England the income threshold for receiving a grant was raised to £60,005. This year it has dropped to £50,000. A fall is unusual: it would seem the massive hike last year was a bad calculation by the government – there were too many takers, so they had to do a smart about-turn for new students this year. But in general, the threshold at which parents begin to contribute towards maintenance is likely to be raised each year as the loan is increased, since only 28% of the loan is liable for assessment. But if parental earnings are static they could find they contribute less the following year. Remember, parents are only expected to contribute – nobody can force them.

What if my mum or dad is made redundant?

If your parents' income suddenly drops, you should contact Student Finance England immediately, as you could be entitled to a maintenance grant and more maintenance loan. You should also tell your university, since many bursaries are linked to the amount of maintenance grant received.

If my parents can't afford to or won't pay the shortfall in my maintenance loan, is there anything I can do?

No. There is no way that parents can be made to pay their contribution towards your maintenance, and your local authority or Student Finance England will not make up the difference. Equally, your parents can choose how they give their contribution: cash in hand or paying for something like rent, utility bills, books.

Are there any circumstances in which my parents would not be expected to contribute towards my maintenance?

Yes – if you:

▶ are 25 or over
▶ are married
▶ are in care
▶ have been supporting yourself for three years.

Is the debt worth the struggle?

Judge for yourself!

Graduates earn on average 20–25% more over their lifetimes than people leaving school with A levels. On average, this amounts to £160,000, according to the research in 2006, but how much the difference is depends on what you study:

Medicine	£340,315 more
Humanities	£52,549 more
Arts	£34,494 more

(Report published by Universities UK 2006.)

Some important questions and answers

I want to go to a university in my home town, but don't want to live with my parents: can I get the full financial package?

Students living at home are eligible for the lower 'living at home' maintenance loan only. There is no regulation preventing you from living away from home, but funding is at the discretion of your local authority.

Our research for the *Guide to Student Money* showed that 65% of students knew someone who had decided to study in their home town to save money.

I'm thinking of getting married: will it affect my maintenance grant and loan entitlements?

Yes. Students who get married before the academic year are considered as independent and their support is no longer assessed on their parents' income but on that of their partner, provided he or she is earning enough. This is calculated in a similar way as for parental income.

I'm not married but living with a partner: will this affect my support?

Yes – you will be considered independent in the same way as a married student would be and income will be based on your partner's income.

What is the maintenance loan meant to cover?

Lodgings, food, books, pocket money, travel, socialising – but not fees.

My academic year is longer than at most colleges: can I get extra money?

Yes. If your course is longer than 30 weeks you can claim for an extra loan, which will be means tested, for each week you have to attend your course. Rates for 2009–2010 are:

► London: £106 per week
► elsewhere: £83 per week
► living at home: £55 per week
► studying abroad: £115 per week.

If your course year is 45 weeks or longer, you will receive a loan based on 52 weeks.

Which subjects are up and which are down among students applying for uni in 2008?*

Subject up	Percentage change	Subject down	Percentage change
Business & Administration	+21.9%	Media Studies	−0.5%
Economics	+19.8%	Philosophy	−1.2%
Dance	+17.9%	Business Studies	−2.5%
Civil Engineering	+15.4%	Electronic & Electrical Engineering	−2.7%
Architecture	+15%	Production & Manufacture	−2.9%
Software Engineering	+14.6%	Forensic & Archaeological Science	−3.1%
Finance	+13.6%	Crafts	−3.3%
Nursing	+13.3%	Planning	−3.6%
Management Studies	+13%	Anatomy, Physiology & Pathology	−6.6.%
Chemical Processing & Engineering	+12.7%	Pre-clinical Veterinary Medicine	−7%

*UCAS application figures for 2008.
Note: large combination subjects not included.

Avoid being a university drop-out. At the last count, around 14% of students, or one in seven, dropped out or failed to get a degree. Freshers who think they've taken the wrong course should beat a hasty path to their course director or careers service for advice as soon as possible. Nothing is set in stone. The critical date is 1 December: the Student Loans Company doesn't actually pay your fees before then.

If I work part time, will it affect my student financial package?

No. Students can work during their course – i.e. undertake vacation work – and the money earned will not be considered when their loan/grant is calculated.

What will happen if I drop out of my course?

You will have to pay off any loans taken out for fees and maintenance. Your local authority might also ask you to repay some of the fees they have paid.

When is the best time to take out a maintenance loan?

There are three options:

1. When you need it.
2. As late as possible – because it's index-linked to inflation (see page 75).
3. As soon as possible. Some financially astute students take out their student loan, even if they don't need it, and invest it in a good interest-paying account with a bank or building society. Not so easy to find in these credit crunch times. But these accounts generally pay more than the inflation rate and more than the interest on a student loan. Make sure you know what you are doing. Check out interest rates first, and ensure you can get at your money quickly and easily if you are likely to need it – some high-interest rate accounts give limited access.

'Because I had sponsorship, had worked for a year before uni and had a Saturday job, I didn't need a student loan, but I took it out anyway, and put it in a good building society account, just in case I wanted to go on to do further study. As it is, my sponsor has offered me a job that's too good to turn down, so I won't need it, but it was nice to have that security cushion there. I haven't checked it out yet, but I think the loan has actually made me money; at least it hasn't cost me anything, which has to be good.'

3rd year student

Do I have to take out the whole maintenance loan amount?

No. You can take out however much you want, up to the maximum for which you are eligible that year. If you do not apply for the full amount at the start of the academic year you can apply for the rest later.

Will the loan be paid all at once in a lump sum?

No. The loan will be paid termly, in two or three instalments depending on when you apply for it.

Is there any help with travelling expenses?

The first £303 of any travelling expenses is disregarded. Above that you can claim a grant for certain expenses if you are attending another establishment as part of a medical or dental course or attending an institution abroad for eight weeks or more as part of your course. The grant is means tested. (Scottish students see page 88.)

Additional help

Access to Learning Fund

What is it?

This is a special fund available through your college, which provides help to students who may need extra financial support to stay in higher education.

cash crisis

▶ As your loan cheque will not be banked until you have arrived at your university or college, you will need to have some money of your own to get yourself there, and possibly to maintain yourself until the cheque is cleared. Check out the cost of train fares.

▶ If you are living in halls of residence, your college will probably be sympathetic if your cheque hasn't arrived and will wait until it does. But don't be too sure about this – check it out. Some colleges will add a penalty to the bills of students who don't pay up on time. And if you run out of money and can't pay your bill at all, you will not be allowed to re-register for the next academic year. If it's your final year, you will not get your degree until the bill is paid.

▶ If you are living in rented accommodation, you can expect no leniency. Landlords expect to be paid on the dot, usually ask for rent in advance and may request an additional deposit. You will need funds to cover this.

advice note

Postgraduates are not entitled to a student loan unless they are taking a PGCE course. So if, as an undergraduate, you do not need the loan or all of the loan now, but are thinking of going on to do a postgraduate course, it might be worth your while taking out the student loan and investing it, so the money is there to help you through your postgraduate studies later on. If you are not a financial whiz kid, take advice. The student loan is a really cheap way of borrowing money, but you don't want to build up debt unnecessarily.

Who gets Access help?

If you are in real financial difficulty this is the source to tap. The fund is open to both full- and part-time students studying 50% of their time on a full-time course. It is there to help those facing particular financial hardship, those in need of emergency help for an unexpected financial crisis and those who are considering giving up their studies because of financial problems. Priority is given to students with children, mature students, those from low-income families, disabled students, students who have been in care, and students in their final year.

'Ask for help as soon as you realise you have a financial problem as it takes at least four weeks to assess an Access to Learning Fund application. But in the end I got £200 – a lifesaver when you can't pay your rent.'

4th year Astrophysics student, UCL

'I was having trouble meeting my mortgage repayments: the university was very helpful with an emergency loan and very understanding. Talk to them. At the end of the day, they don't want you to drop out.'

4th year Pure Mathematics student, St Andrews

How much can you get?

That depends on your college. It could be just a few hundred pounds to tide you over a sticky patch, it could be £3,000 plus. Your college will use its discretion. The amount given will depend on a number of factors – your circumstances, how many other students are applying and how much they have in the kitty. You can apply for help more than once in a year.

Wales: similar payments are made through the Financial Contingency Funds (FCFs) scheme.

Scotland: provides help through Hardship Funds.

Northern Ireland: provides help through Support Funds.

'Because I have no family and have to spend the whole year in halls, my college asked the Access Fund to help out with my rent.'

1st year student, Cambridge

Will I have to pay the money back?

Access payments are usually given as a grant, but they could be given as a short-term loan.

'I tried to get funds from Access but felt I was on trial.'

Mature student, Physics and Engineering, Heriot-Watt

'The college hardship fund is a wonderful scheme to help you survive.'

Mature Midwifery student with four children, Canterbury Christ Church

How do I set about getting money from the Access to Learning Fund?

Apply to your college. Every institution will have a different procedure and different criteria for measuring your needs. You will probably have to fill in a form giving details of your financial situation. Most institutions will have somebody to help and advise you. They may even have a printed leaflet giving you details.

When should I apply for Access funding?

As soon as trouble starts to loom. The fund is limited to the amount that is allocated, so it is largely first come first served. We have heard of institutions that have allocated most of their funds by the end of November of the academic year.

I'm a student from abroad: can I apply for Access money?

Sorry, but no. The Access to Learning Fund is restricted to 'home' students only, so overseas students are not eligible.

Are there any other hardship funds?

Some institutions, and also some students' unions, have resources to help students in real financial difficulty. They all vary depending on the institution, and they will pay out money for a variety of reasons. Funds are generally given when all official avenues are exhausted. Priority is often given to students who are suffering financially because of unforeseen circumstances such as a death in the family or illness. Sometimes small amounts are given to tide you over or to pay a pressing bill. Increasingly, hardship payments take the form of an interest-free loan, which can be especially useful if your grant/loan cheque doesn't arrive on time. They may also offer help to students from abroad.

Leeds University Union, for example, offers a range of financial assistance to students who find themselves in difficulty. There is a Fundraising Group, which considers all applications. As most of the money comes from external charitable trusts, their hands are tied to some extent because they are governed by each individual trust's guidelines and criteria. But they do offer much-needed support.

Are there any other allowances, grants and bursaries I could apply for?

Yes. Check the next chapter: you might fall into a special category. Otherwise try Chapter 8, 'Other sources to tap'.

Gordon's story

Gordon is a Latin American studies student at Glasgow.

'When I came to university I had an electric guitar, an amp, a bass guitar, a stereo and a camera. In times of financial need these have all had temporary lodging in the pawnshop. Gradually this became less and less temporary so that now I no longer have a bass guitar, a camera or a stereo.

The loss of the latter is no great hardship as I have already sold my CDs/DVDs one by one to the second-hand record shop.'

Thrift Tips

'Try the Access to Learning Fund: it isn't widely advertised. I got £200.'
3rd year Sociology student, Aberdeen

'Try to get your booklist early and be first in line for second-hand books – then sell them back to your uni library later.'
3rd year Physics student, UCL

'Take a gap year and save.'
3rd year Geography Management student, York

'Find food nearing its sell-by date and being sold off cheaply, then freeze it.'
1st year Social and Political Science student, Cambridge

Loans: paying them back

Will I be able to afford to pay back my loans?

It may take a long time, but a system has been worked out that allows you to pay back what you borrowed in line with what you earn.

When do I have to pay back my loans?

You repay nothing until the April after you have graduated, and then only when your income is over £15,000 p.a. will you begin to pay off the loans. The amount you pay is related to your salary, so whether you have borrowed £1,000 or £35,000, have had a maintenance or fee loan, or both, your monthly repayments will be the same if you stay on the same salary. You will go on paying until the debt is paid off. However, if after 25 years you still haven't paid it all off, the government will write off anything left outstanding (except arrears). Rates are currently worked out at 9% of income over £15,000. So the current scale looks something like this:

Annual income up to:	Monthly repayments	Repayment as % of income
£15,000	£0	0
£16,000	£7	0.6
£17,000	£15	1.1
£18,000	£22	1.5
£19,000	£30	1.9
£20,000	£37	2.3
£21,000	£45	2.6
£22,000	£52	2.9
£23,000	£60	3.1
£24,000	£67	3.4
£25,000	£75	3.6

How will I make the repayments?

Repayments will be collected through the Inland Revenue and will be deducted from your pay packet at source. Probably all you will know about it is an entry on your pay slip.

Will I have to pay back more than I borrow?

In real terms, no. The interest rates on loans are linked to inflation, so while the actual figure you pay will be higher, the value of the amount you pay back is broadly the same as the value of the amount you borrowed. The interest rate in the year to August 2007 was 2.4%; the rate from September 2007 to August 2008 was 4.8%; but by December, with the banking crisis taking a grip on the country, it was down to 3% and by January to 2.5%. Latest news: from 1st September 2009 to 31st August 2010 the rate will be 0%. So it does vary.

Will all students graduate with a huge debt?

Most students starting a course now will have to face up to the prospect of starting work with a debt to pay off, and this could be substantially more than the amount totted up under the Student Loans Scheme. According to the *NatWest Students Money Matters Survey*, school leavers in 2007 estimated that they would graduate with a debt of £34,740. Many of those students will graduate in July 2010 – I wonder how accurate their predictions were? Since they will be paying top-up fees for their full course their estimate could turn out to be a reality.

Our research amongst undergraduates this year shows that:

▶ 50% of students had overdrafts
▶ 60% had student loans
▶ 55% had a tuition fee loan.

A massive 86% expected to be in debt either to the bank or to the Student Loans Company, or possibly both, by the end of their course – by anything from a few hundred pounds to over £16,000. The most-quoted figure over £16,000 was £18,000, but £40,000–£50, 000 was not uncommon, especially among medical students.

It doesn't take much mathematical ability to work out what your debt is likely to be.

Take how much you pay for fees – this year £3,225. Multiply that by the number of years of your course and add a further amount for each year for inflation – the hike up from last year was around 2.5%.

Then take the amount of loan you receive (remember, not everyone can take the full loan), multiply that by the number of years of your course, add around 7% for each year for inflation, except for the final year, when you will receive less.

Add on your interest-free loan from the bank if you intend to use it (60% of our student contacts said they did) – which could be anything up to £3,000, depending on the generosity of your bank (see page 82) – and you will have some idea of what your debt is likely to be.

We estimated the worst debt on a three-year course outside London at nearly £26,000 and in London at over £34,000.

> ### it's a fact !
>
> Medical students seem to be the hardest hit, which is hardly surprising since the course is at least five years. Nearly a third of our student contacts at St George's, which is in London, anticipated a debt of over £30,000, and half of those thought it was more likely to be over £40,000. One 'poor' student from abroad expected to graduate to a debt of £150,000, which says something about the lengths to which students will go to get a good training.

The following example is for those unlucky students whose family income is around £50,775, and who would be entitled to take out the full loan. (Below £50,020 you would receive a portion of the grant and your loan would be cut. Above £50,775 your parents would be expected to chip in, so your loan would also be cut.)

	Outside London		In London	
Fee loan	£3,225 × 3 + 2.5%	£9,916	£3,225 × 3 + 2.5%	£9,916
Maintenance loan	£4,950 × 3 + 7%	£15,889	£6,928 × 3 + 7%	£22,238
Bank: free overdraft		£3,000		£3,000
Total		£25,805		£34,354

Note: this table does not take account of interest on loan, or slightly less loan given in final year.

The fact is, no two students' expenditure and income are ever the same, but it's good to be aware of the worst scenario.

Estimated student debt

Percentage of students surveyed	Anticipated student debt
14%	None
4%	£0–£1,000
3%	£1,001–£2,000
7%	£2,001–£4,000
6%	£4,001–£6,000
6%	£6,001–£8,000
7%	£8,001–£10,000
8%	£10,001–£12,000
7%	£12,001–£14,000
6%	£14,001–£16,000
32%	Over £16,000

Great News! Loan Repayment Holiday for Students

Students who started their course since 2008–2009, and will therefore start their loan repayments in or after April 2012, will be eligible for a loan repayment holiday of up to five years at any time after they graduate. This means you can put your repayments on hold at any time of your choice, which could be a great help if you want to buy a house, go travelling, or have got into debt. As we publish, this only applies to English-domiciled students. The rest of the UK is still thinking about the idea.

▶ Check out Chapter 10 on budgeting – it might save you a few sleepless nights.

▶ Compare current bank overdraft rates for newly qualified graduates.

cash crisis

Do the pay-back rules ever change?

They are reviewed every year to make sure graduates can realistically pay back what they owe. The payback threshold has been £15,000 for the last few years.

Will I be able to pay it all back?

As well as the possibility of graduating with a massive debt, most students graduate to a fairly substantial salary. Starting salaries for graduates with good second-class honours degrees in a blue-chip company in 2009 were expected to be around £25,000 (median figure – *AGR*

Winter Review 2009). If you are earning around £2,000 a month, the repayments won't seem quite so grisly. But will you find a job? Are you going to be a 2:1 success story? Many graduates start work on salaries of less than £16,000. At the time of writing, the employment market for graduates in the UK is likely to be the worst it has been for many years.

The graduate market is currently very volatile, so what it will be like in three or four years' time, when this year's first-year students graduate, is anyone's guess. But it's worth remembering that if you can't find work, the Student Loans Company will wait for repayment; the banks, however, may not be so sympathetic, though most do offer special overdraft facilities to graduates, which you should investigate.

I'm a graduate with £25,000 student loan debts to clear: is my new employer likely to pay this off?

When the loan scheme first came in, many employers thought they might need to offer the 'carrot' of paying off students' loans if they wanted to attract the best graduates. Whether the government was hoping that employers would step in and clear students' debts in this way was a question often discussed in the national press.

In fact, at least one major company did draw up contingency plans for a 'golden hello' scheme, and a number of companies we contacted said they were watching the market and their competitors very closely.

Then the 1990s recession hit the UK hard, graduate openings were in short supply, and graduates were competing for jobs rather than employers competing for graduates.

Facts and Figures

▶ Vacancies for graduates fall for first time since 2003 with a projected decrease of 5.4% in 2009.

▶ Banks expect massive 28% cut in number of vacancies.

▶ Engineering sector bucks the trend with expected 8.3% rise in jobs, but there may be a shortfall of graduates to fill them.

▶ Graduate salaries frozen for the first time.

▶ Employers urge struggling graduates to research jobs and prepare for interviews more thoroughly than ever as competition intensifies.

(AGR Winter Review 2009)

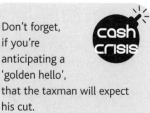

Don't forget, if you're anticipating a 'golden hello', that the taxman will expect his cut.

cash crisis

Women face unequal opportunities: you are likely to earn £1,000 a year less than your male counterparts, and this is apparent within three years of leaving university, according to a major survey on graduate experience published in January 2008 by the Higher Education Statistics Agency (HESA). Whatever happened to equal opportunities?

Employers put all ideas of 'loan pay-off schemes for students' on the back burner. However, market trends and influences change very rapidly. Good-quality graduates were in short supply again and employers were quite genuinely concerned about the amount of debt graduates have. So the 'golden hello' quietly materialised. 'Quietly' because few employers were keen to call it that. By 2008 around a third of AGR members reported that they offered a 'golden hello' to graduates, with a median level payout of £2,000. (*AGR Winter Review 2008*) You might think, in these troubled credit-crunch times, when everyone is predicting a cut-back on graduate opportunities, the golden hello would be a distant memory, but according to the *AGR Winter Review 2009*, so far employers have not cut back and the golden hello figures remain much the same, at least for those lucky enough to find employment.

Where are the big graduate starting salaries to be earned?

Median starting salaries in 2008 by type of organisation	
Law firm	£37,000
Investment banking/fund managers	£35,000
Banking/financial services	£28,000
Consulting/business services	£28,000
IT	£27,000
FMCG company	£26,000
Accountancy	£25,750
Public sector	£25,000
Construction company or consultancy	£24,000
Engineering/industrial	£23,115
Retail	£22,700
Transport or logistics	£16,000

Source: *AGR Graduate Recruitment Survey, Winter Review 2009*

Can I get out of repaying student loans?

Yes:

▶ if you never earn more than £15,000 a year

▶ if you become permanently disabled

▶ if you die!

▶ after 25 years the loan will be written off.

Is bankruptcy an option?

Not any longer. A few years ago we reported that some 9,000 students and graduates were considering making themselves bankrupt to avoid debt. New laws making it easier to become bankrupt were being introduced, and in straightforward cases you could probably clear your debts within 12 months.

The government, it would seem, were hot on their heels, moving rapidly to close this obvious loophole in its system of student finance, and today the Student Loans Company tells us that making yourself bankrupt is not an option for clearing your student loan debt. Well, at least your good reputation will be intact.

Is the Student Loans Scheme better than borrowing from the bank?

Most banks and some building societies will give students overdraft facilities on special terms, usually including an interest-free £1,000–£3,000 overdraft

It's Official . . .

. . . the great British entrepreneurial spirit is not dead and only slightly dampened by rising student debt. The number of students planning to set up their own business after qualifying remains consistent at 4%, or around 30,000 students. Even in the current economic downturn, as employers' graduate intake targets are reduced, many students are considering self-employment.

Prominent entrepreneur Lord Karan Bilimoria, the founder of Cobra Beer, started his business in the last major recession. He said recently that opportunities still abound for determined graduate entrepreneurs.

However, student debt is likely to slow down their plans: while 75% of students with ambitions to go it alone would either scale back or defer their plans until their debts were paid off, a brave (possibly unwise) quarter would carry on regardless.

If you see yourself as a potential entrepreneur, register for free mentoring and support at www.flyingstartonline.com. If you have the right ideas, they will help you on your way.

(Survey commissioned by the National Council for Graduate Entrepreneurship (NCGE) in conjunction with Barclays, 2006.)

facility (see below). This is intended mainly to help you during that difficult period when your loan hasn't yet arrived or you've run out of cash at the end of the term. The overdraft is wiped out as soon as the loan cheque arrives. It is better to use the bank's 'interest-free' facility if your financial problems are temporary or you are certain you will be able to pay the overdraft back once you graduate. Most banks won't start charging interest on student overdrafts immediately you graduate, giving you time to get a job. This can be several months, but check it out with your bank. Banks also offer students longer-term loans at competitive rates, which should be investigated.

But, in general, banks are not the best bet for long-term borrowing for students – the Student Loans Scheme is, since the interest rate is no more than inflation, and pay back is related to your salary and ability to pay. (See details on pay-back arrangements on page 75.)

It's worth remembering, however, that to get a loan you have to have a bank or building society account. As mentioned, if you already have an overdraft with your bank, as soon as the loan hits your account it will automatically be used to pay off the overdraft, so you might not find that you have any more cash in hand to spend, though you'll certainly have more peace of mind.

The bank is the student's friend

For most students the best thing the bank offers is the interest-free overdraft. But remember:

▶ to get the interest-free overdraft facility you must tell your bank you are a student

▶ if your overdraft goes over the set interest-free limit you will be charged interest

▶ you may be able to negotiate a larger interest-free overdraft, but don't rely on it

▶ use the bank's interest-free limit rather than build up debt on a credit card.

Interest-free loans offered by banks to students in 2008–2009

	Abbey	BOS	Barclays	Halifax	HSBC	Lloyds TSB	Nat West	RBS
1st year	£1,000	£3,000	£1,000	£3,000	£1,000	£1,500	£1,250	£2,750
2nd year	£1,250	£3,000	£1,250	£3,000	£1,250	£1,500	£1,400	£2,750
3rd year	£1,500	£3,000	£1,500	£3,000	£1,500	£1,500	£1,600	£2,750
4th year	£1,800	£3,000	£1,750	£3,000	£1,750	£2,000	£1,800	£2,750

Which is best, a big or small overdraft facility? The bigger the overdraft facility, the greater the temptation to overspend and the more you will have to pay back. On the other hand, a smaller overdraft facility may mean you go over the limit sooner and you start paying bank charges. You decide!

See what else the banks offer in Chapter 10, page 266.

Health Check

I'm sick and myopic, and I've got toothache – can I get free treatment?

As a student you don't actually qualify for any help, but as someone on a low income you could qualify for free or reduced:

▶ dental charges

▶ glasses

▶ eye tests

▶ prescriptions.

Form HC1 is the starting point, available from high street opticians, the Benefits Agency or the Post Office. That will probably send you off on a trail leading to form HC2 or HC3; if you haven't received either of these items you will need form HC5, and don't forget to ask the chemist for receipt form FP57 (EC57 in Scotland) to claim for free prescription charges. If you are confused – and who isn't? – then leaflet HC11 (*Are you Entitled to Help with Health Costs?*) will put you straight on the NHS in general and HC12 on costs – both are available from your Benefits Agency or by phoning 0845 850 1166 (local rates).

Try to get things going before treatment begins, or at least before you need to pay up.

Otherwise, make sure you keep all bills and receipts, as evidence of costs. If after filling in HC1 you are told you are not entitled to any help and you think you are, give the Department of Health Benefits agency another try. It could be that the computer is 'confused' as well – it has been known! It can be a long process but it's often worth the effort.

For immediate medical advice, phone NHS Direct on 0845 4647.

It's serious – I could be off sick for weeks. What should I do?

If you become seriously ill and are likely to be off sick for months then you should obviously let your university department know, but also your LA and the Student Loans Company, since your student loans might be affected if you are off for more than 60 days.

Thrift Tips

'Spend time in the library in winter as it's warm and saves on heating bills.'
2nd year Politics and History student, Aberystwyth

'Take all the food you can at breakfast, which is free, and eat it for lunch.'
1st year Medical student living in halls of residence at Dundee

'If you think £1 is nothing, try saving one a day for a year. £365 is two months' rent.'
2nd year Electronics student, Robert Gordon University

Further information

Who to contact/what to read

Contact student helpline 0845 607 7577 for financial information including information on your loans.

Full information about fees, maintenance grants and loans is given in the following free booklets, which you would be well advised to get and study:

For students in England: *Student Finance England – A Guide to Financial Support for Higher Education 2009/10* (which is the source for the loan statistics in this chapter). Tel: 0800 731 9133. Website: www.studentfinancedirect.co.uk. Braille and cassette editions also available.

For students in Scotland: *Student Support in Scotland: A Guide for Undergraduate Students 2009/10*, available from any Scottish university or the Student Awards Agency for Scotland (SAAS), 3 Redheughs Rigg, South Gyle, Edinburgh EH12 9YT. Tel: 0131 4768212. Email: saas.geu@scotland.gsi.gov.uk. Website: www.student-support-saas.gov.uk.

For students in Northern Ireland: *Financial Support for Students in Higher Education 2009/10*, Student Support Branch, Department for Employment and Learning (Northern Ireland), Rathgael House, Balloo Road, Bangor, Co. Down BT19 7PR. Tel: 028 9025 7710; (for booklet) 0800 731 9133. Website: www.delni.gov.uk.

Can't face all this debt?

There's always the Open University. More and more young people are choosing the Open University study-at-home way. With more than 250,000 undergraduate and postgraduate students enrolled, the OU is the UK's largest university. It offers 580 courses, covering 12 subject areas and leading to 100 different qualifications. These range from certificates, to foundation degrees to full undergraduate and postgraduate qualifications. The cost of an open degree is around £3,500, a Bachelor's (Honours) degree around £4,000, and an MBA through the EQUIS accredited Open University Business School around £11,000. Compare that with the costs of a three-year degree in a conventional university – estimated figures are now reaching £33,000.

Most students in our universities would probably argue that the OU route is not so much fun, but then debt isn't a bundle of laughs either. For information check their website (www.open.ac.uk) or phone 0845 300 6090. You can also access free materials and resources before committing to a fuller programme of study by visiting www.open.ac.uk/recession.

For students in Wales: *A Guide to Financial Support for Higher Education*, National Assembly for Wales, Higher Education Division 2, 3rd floor, Cathays Park, Cardiff CF10 3NQ. Tel: 0845 602 8845. Websites: www.studentfinancewales.co.uk; www.learning.wales.co.uk.

Lowest drop-out/failed to get a degree rates

Royal Academy of Music	0%
Royal Northern College of Music	0.9%
St George's Hospital Medical School	1.1%
Cambridge	1.2%
Oxford	1.2%
Glasgow School of Art	1.9%
University of St Andrews	2%
Stranmillis University College	2.2%
Liverpool Institute for Performing Arts	· 2.5%
Cumbria Institute of Arts	2.7%

Source: *HESA performance indicators for UK universities and colleges – full-time study for courses started 2005/2006 (predicted), published September 2008*

Highest drop-out/failed to get a degree rates

Bell College	24.4%
UHI Millennium Institute	24.0%
Bolton University	21.7%
Napier College	17.9%
University of Glamorgan	17.5%
University of Paisley	17.1%
Writtle College	16.7%
St Martin's College	15.6%
North East Wales Institute of Higher Education	15.6%
University of Ulster	15.2%

Source: *HESA performance indicators for UK universities and colleges – full-time study, for courses starting 2005/2006, published September 2008*

CHAPTER 4

Am I a special case?

This chapter looks at the funding and extra help that is available for students in special categories. In some cases this is in addition to the funding outlined in the previous chapter; in others there is a completely different system; for yet others, sadly, there is no funding at all.

- ▶ Scotland, Wales and Northern Ireland (page 88)
- ▶ Where is the best place to live and to study in the UK?   (page 94)
- ▶ Students from abroad (page 94)
- ▶ Courses with a difference (page 101)
- ▶ Attending a private higher education institution (page 105)
- ▶ Healthcare courses (page 105)
- ▶ Specialist courses (page 108)
- ▶ Additional help for special groups (page 110)
- ▶ Studying abroad (page 114)
- ▶ Information about fees, maintenance grants and loans (page 122)

Scotland, Wales and Northern Ireland

Not all regions of the UK follow the same student funding system. Scotland, for example, decided to introduce its own no-fees funding solution for its own students soon after the new Scottish Parliament was set up. Now Wales has decided to take a more independent line.

Scotland: what's the deal?

In brief:

▶ if you live and study in Scotland you pay **no fees** for your university education, and because of EU regulations, this also applies to non-UK EU students

▶ students from the rest of the UK who study in Scotland do pay fees but less than in the rest of the UK

▶ Scottish students attending universities in England, Wales and Northern Ireland pay fees of up to £3,225 p.a.

▶ as in the rest of the UK, those paying fees will be able to get a loan to cover their fees

▶ all students studying in or outside Scotland can apply for a maintenance loan

▶ non-repayable bursaries will be given to students from low-income families. These will replace part of the loan so you will not incur too much debt

▶ the graduate endowment, previously paid by Scottish and EU students who study in Scotland, has been abolished: a saving to students of over £2,000

▶ better-off Scottish parents are assessed to contribute more than in the rest of the UK.

I'm a Scottish student studying in Scotland

If you are a Scottish student studying in Scotland you are eligible for:

Student's loan	Min.	Max.
Living in parental home	£605	£3,665
Living elsewhere (amount depends on family income and bursary; loan rates for final-year students are slightly lower)	£915	£4,625
Non-repayable Young Students' Bursary (means tested on family income of up to £34,195; YSB replaces part of loan)	Up to £2,640	
Additional loan for young students where family income is £21,760 or below	Up to £605	

Note: Loan money for Scottish students studying in Scotland is paid out monthly.

Extra loan for longer courses

If your course is longer than 30 weeks and 3 days you can claim for additional loan:

Living in parents' home	£54 per week
Living elsewhere	£83 per week

I'm a part-time student: will I get any help?

Yes, a £500 part-time HE fee grant is given to new and existing part-time students who earn £22,000 or less and were studying 50% or more of a full-time degree course. See chart on page 101.

I'm a Scottish student studying outside Scotland

If you are studying in the UK but outside Scotland you will have to pay the full fees demanded by the university for your course, up to £3,225 p.a.

To help finance your studies you are eligible for:

Student fee loan to cover fees (not means tested)	Up to £3,225	
Non-repayable means-tested bursary (on family income up to £34,195; full bursary given where family income £18,825 or less)	Up to £2,150	
Student maintenance loan	**Min.**	**Max.**
Living away from home in London	£915	£5,710
Studying elsewhere	£915	£4,625
Studying outside Scotland but living at home	£605	£3,665
(The maintenance loan is based on family income and bursary received; loan rates for final-year students are slightly lower)		
Additional loan for students from low-income families (on family income up to £21,760)	£590	

You may be eligible for a bursary from your university: see page 48.

Extra loan for longer courses:

If your course is longer than 30 weeks and 3 days you can claim for additional loan:

Living in parents' home	£54 per week
Living elsewhere	£83 per week
London	£106 per week

What parents in Scotland are expected to pay

This table will give some idea of what Scottish parents could be in for.

But remember, students in families where the residual income is up to £34,195 should be receiving an income-assessed Young Student's Bursary.

Residual income	Assessed contribution
£24,275	£45
£25,000	£126
£30,000	£681
£35,000	£1,237
£40,000	£1,792
£45,000	£2,348
£50,000	£3,012
£55,000	£3,631
£60,000	£4,400

Note: figures for a spouse are slightly higher.

Families with a residual income below £24,275 are not expected to contribute.

A deduction of £195 will be made from the assessed contribution for every dependent child other than the student. No parent is expected to contribute more than £5,710 p.a. for one child studying in London or £4,625 p.a. if the student is living away from home and studying anywhere else, and £3,665 p.a. if the student is living at home, however much they earn. These figures are based on the full loan minus minimum loan that a student can take out. If there is more than one child at university the maximum contribution a parent can be expected to make is £8,000 p.a., regardless of how many offspring they have at university. Although Scottish parents may look with envy at parents in the rest of the UK, who will be assessed to contribute considerably less than those in Scotland, English students will be accumulating a great deal more debt than their Scottish counterparts.

Travel for Scottish students

If you are living away from home, three return journeys per year to your place of study can be claimed for, plus additional term-time travel to and from your institution. (This does not include students whose parents live outside the UK.) The first £159 of any claim will be disregarded. Only the most economical fares will be allowed. (Cost of student railcard or bus pass may also be reimbursed.)

How do I apply for financial support in Scotland?

Last year over 80% of Scottish students applied online, and ministers have agreed that this makes it the preferred method. That's on www.saas.gov.uk/studentsupport. If you prefer the paper method go to 'Guides and Forms' and download what you need. Alternatively phone 0845 111 1711 or 0845 111 0243. Or you can email saas.geu@scotland.gsi.gov.uk, or write to – or even visit – The Student Awards Agency for Scotland, Gyleview House, 3 Redheughs Rigg, Edinburgh, EH12 9HH.

I'm a student from outside Scotland studying in Scotland

If you are from outside Scotland you will pay a set fee of £1,820 p.a. This may seem like a lot less than the £3,225 students are paying in other parts of the UK, but the reasoning is that Scottish degree courses last for four years whereas degrees in the rest of the UK generally last for three. If you multiply £1,820 by four you'll see you're paying a lot less than the £9,675 some students will have to find. But Scottish universities are under no obligation to pay bursaries to students from lower-income families and they are unlikely to do so. The rest of your funding will follow the English pattern, so see Chapter 2 for details on fee loans (page 45), maintenance grants (page 48) and maintenance loans (page 53). For fees for Medicine, see page 105.

Wales: what's the deal?

I'm a Welsh student studying in Wales

The Welsh Assembly, like the Scottish Parliament, has decided to take an independent line on fees. While UK students from outside Wales will have to pay in full the top-up fees asked by universities, students who normally live in Wales and choose to study in Wales, along with EU students, will receive a fee grant of £1,940 p.a. to offset part of the fee. This is not means tested, does not have to be repaid and will have the effect of keeping the fees Welsh students pay in Wales down to £1,285 p.a. You are the lucky ones: make the most of this facility, because there is talk of doing away with it for next year's students. Changes are rarely retrospective, so you can expect to receive a fee grant throughout your course. To cover the portion of the fees you do have to pay, you can apply for a fee loan (see page 45)

I'm a Welsh student studying outside Wales

If you normally live in Wales but are studying outside Wales, the picture is not so rosy. You will not be entitled to a fee grant and will have to pay the fees demanded by the university of your choice – up to £3,225 p.a. You will be entitled to take out a loan to cover fees (see page 45).

All Welsh students

All Welsh students from lower-income families, wherever they study, will be able to apply for a Higher Education Assembly Grant of up to £2,906 to help with maintenance. This is means tested and, while it operates in a similar way to the grant in England, it has a much lower family income cut-off threshold.

Household income	Grant
£0–£18,370	£2,906
£18,370–£39,793	Partial grant depending on family income
Over £39,793	No grant

You can also apply for a maintenance loan.

		Full year max. available
Students living away from their parents' home and studying:	in London	£6,648
	elsewhere	£4,745
Students living in their parents' home		£3,673
Studying overseas		£5,658

For every £1 of grant received, the amount of maintenance loan will be reduced by £1 up to £1,285. Approximately 28% of loan is means tested on family income above £39,793. You may also be eligible for a bursary from your university: see page 48.

I'm a part-time student in Wales: will I get any help?

Yes. See pages 101 and 103.

I'm a student from outside Wales studying in Wales

Students who come from outside Wales and study at Welsh universities can be asked to pay fees of up to £3,225 and you will have to pay whatever the university demands. You will not be entitled to the fee grant given to Welsh students. You will be able to apply for a fee loan to cover the full cost of fees (as in England, see page 45). In fact, your financial package will be the package offered to all English students (see Chapter 2). Under this scheme more students will be eligible for maintenance grants as more family income is allowed (up to £50,000) before the maximum income threshold is reached. Student loans for English students are also slightly higher.

In addition, like all students studying in Wales, you may benefit under the Welsh Bursary Scheme. Students who receive the maximum maintenance grant

(Assembly Learning Grant in Wales), regardless of where they come from in the UK, will be eligible for a minimum bursary of £319 a year. This is instead of the university bursaries given in England. Welsh universities, like English universities, may choose to give higher bursaries (see page 49).

I'm Welsh: how do I apply for student funding ?

You can apply for support online by logging onto www.studentfinancewales. co.uk, or you can make a paper application by contacting your local authority for a form or downloading a form from 'Forms and Guides' on the Student Finance Wales website. As with the English application procedure (page 62), once you have registered you will be given an ART ID and password so you can track your account online.

Northern Ireland: what's the deal?

I'm a student from Northern Ireland: what funding can I get?

Northern Ireland generally follows the same funding system as in England (see Chapter 2), but each year there are more differences. For example, the basic grant (£3,406) is higher in Northern Ireland than in England, but the family income cut-off point for receiving a grant is lower, at £40,238, whether you study in Northern Ireland or anywhere in the rest of the UK.

Maintenance grants and loans in Northern Ireland – assuming student is living away from home and not studying in London

Income	Grant	Maintenance loan	Total
£18,820	£3,406	£2,953	£6,359
£20,000	£3,147	£3,014	£6,161
£25,000	£2,048	£3,274	£5,322
£28,349	£1,292	£3,453	£4,745
£30,000	£1,128	£3,617	£4,745
£35,000	£601	£4,144	£4,745
£40,238	£50	£4,695	£4,745

1. The maintenance grant is £500 higher than in England at £3,406. It is non-repayable and, of course, means tested. But, as you will see from the chart above, the amount of loan that students from lower-income families are able to take out is also reduced.

2. Cut-off point for grant is when family income reaches £40,238.

3. If you are planning to study at a publicly funded college in the Republic of Ireland you will not have to pay tuition fees. However, the college will make a registration charge of €900 (2008–2009 figures).

4. Extra help if in a sticky situation: Support Funds are available through your university in Northern Ireland. These operate in a similar way to the Access to Learning Fund in the UK. See page 71 for details.

I'm a part-time student in Northern Ireland: will I get any help?

Yes. See page 101.

How do I apply for student funding?

You can apply online from March 2009 at www.studentfinanceni.co.uk or request an application form from your ELB. You do not have to wait until you have a confirmed place on a course to apply. Return the application form, making sure you provide all the information requested.

Deadlines for applications: New students who choose **not** to supply financial information, 24 April 2009. Other new students, 26 June 2009.

Where is the best place to live and to study in the UK?

Check our comparative funding table, pages 95 and 96

Students from abroad

What will it cost, and who will pay?

EU students

EU students will be treated on a similar basis to their UK counterparts regarding fees.

- ▶ If studying in England or Northern Ireland you will be expected to pay up to £3,225 p.a. towards your fees.
- ▶ If studying in Wales you will pay £1,285 p.a. and will receive a fee grant of £1,940 to pay for the rest of your fees (see page 91).
- ▶ If studying in Scotland you pay no fees.

Confused by who gets what? This table may help.

Student support	English students in England & Wales	Welsh students in Wales	Welsh students in England/NI	NI students everywhere except Scotland	Scots in Scotland	Rest of UK in Scotland	Scots in Eng/Wales/NI
Fees	Up to £3,225 p.a.	£1,285 (rest of fee £1,940 p.a. covered by fee grant)	Up to £3,225 p.a.	Up to £3,225 p.a.	None	£1,820 p.a. (£2,895 for medicine)	Up to £3,225 p.a.
Fee loan	Up to £3,225 p.a.	£1,285 p.a.	Up to £3,225 p.a.	Up to £3,225 p.a.	None	£1,820 p.a. (£2,895 for medicine)	Up to £3,225 p.a.
Maintenance grant	Up to £2,906 p.a.	Up to £2,906 p.a.	Up to £2,906 p.a.	Up to £3,406 p.a.	Up to £2,640 p.a.	Up to £2,906 p.a. (up to £3,406 if from NI)	Up to £2,150
Full grant – earning up to:	£25,000	£18,370	£18,370	£18,820	£21,760	Eng £25,000 Wales £18,370 NI £18,820 p.a.	£21,760 (2008/09 figure)
Earnings threshold for grant	£50,000	£39,793	£39,793	£40,238	£34,195	Eng £50,000 Wales £39,793 NI £40,238 p.a	£34,195
Max. maintenance loan – London	£6,928 p.a.	N/A	£6,648 p.a.	£6,643 p.a.	N/A	N/A	£915–£5,710
Max. maintenance loan – elsewhere	£4,950 p.a.	£4,745 p.a.	£4,745 pa	£4,745 pa	£915–£4,625 p.a.	Eng £4,950 Wales/NI £4,745	£915–£4,625

(Continued)

Student support	English students in England & Wales	Welsh students in Wales	Welsh students in England/NI	NI students everywhere except Scotland	Scots in Scotland	Rest of UK in Scotland	Scots in Eng/Wales/NI
Live at home	£3,838	£3,673	£3,673	£3,673	£605–£3,665 p.a.	Eng £3,838 Wales/NI £3,673	£605–£3,665 p.a.
Extra maintenance loan	NO	NO	NO	NO	£605	NO	£605
Uni bursary if receiving grant	Min. £319 p.a. (average on full grant £1,000)	Min. £319 p.a. if on full grant	Min. £319 p.a. (average on full grant £1,000)	Min. £319 p.a. (average on full grant £1,000)	NO	NO	Min. £319 p.a. (average as English students)
Family contribution for one child	Up to 28% of loan not given – max £1,732 approx. p.a.	Up to 28% of loan not given – max. £1,186 p.a.	Up to 28% loan not given – max £1,662 p.a.	Up to 28% loan not given – max £1,660 p.a.	Max £3,710 p.a. (£3,060 p.a. if student living at home)	Eng max. £1,237 p.a. up to 28% of loan not given; Wales/NI £1,186	Max. £4,795 London, £3,710 elsewhere

All EU students will be able to take out a loan to cover their fees and then pay it off gradually once they graduate.

EU students are not entitled to apply for a maintenance loan or a maintenance bursary and will not receive a maintenance grant.

'I am French so studying in England is really expensive as there is not much help available. I will have to borrow money from my bank in France because I'm worrying about money. But at least I should have a job when I graduate, and the experiences I'm living are priceless!'

1st year Natural Sciences student, Durham

'Please give EU students loans and sponsorship – we need help too!'

Christopher, Physics student, Oxford

Non-EU 'overseas' students

Even though most UK students pay fees, the full cost of a course is subsidised by the government. Students from countries outside the EU will be charged the full cost of the course and can legally be charged higher tuition fees than UK students – so for a first-degree course you can think in terms of:

▶ classroom-taught: £9,000 p.a.

▶ science/lab-based course: £10,700 p.a.

▶ clinical course: £22,100 p.a.

Facts and Figures

More EU students than ever (18,745) started degree courses in our universities in 2008, up 3.7% on the previous year. And the number of students from non-EU countries was up 7.1% to 30,240.

(UCAS figures)

(Figures are median for the year 2008–2009, released by Universities UK.)

You will not be eligible for a fee loan, a maintenance loan or grant or any help with funding. Some universities do give bursaries to overseas students, and some charities have special funds for overseas students. See Chapter 8, page 206.

Fee rates for postgraduates can be higher (see page 220). Most universities and colleges do have a designated overseas adviser whom you could ask for help.

Non-EU students wanting to gain work experience in this country after they graduate will now find they can stay longer – up to two years.

Facts and Figures

The proportion of graduates recruited from ethnic minorities by AGR UK employers was 21% in 2008, down on the previous year's figures. Almost a quarter of these – 23.4% – were Indian, 12.6% were Chinese and 9.3% black African.

AGR Graduate Recruitment Survey 2009 Winter Review

Where to find help

For details on living in the UK, try the educational enquiry service at the British Council Information Centre (tel: 0161 957 7755; email: general.enquiries@britishcouncil. org; write to the British Council (Bridgewater House, 58 Whitworth Street, Manchester M16BB); or contact UKCISA (website: www. ukcisa.org.uk; Advice Line tel: 020 7107 9922, open 1p.m.–4p.m. Monday–Friday). Their Council for International Education handles around 10,000 enquiries from students a year. Otherwise, try the British Council, High Commission or Embassy in your own country.

Refugees and asylum seekers: what help is there?

Very little!

If you have the right qualifications, and can afford it, you are free to apply to any UK university. But any funding, and how much you must pay, will depend on your immigration status and how long you have been in the UK. Most refugees and asylum seekers do not qualify for funding and are considered 'overseas' students, which means they may well be charged the overseas fee rate. (See page 97, 'Non-EU "overseas" students'). Also see the ruling for students from former British colonies, above. If you're living and studying in Scotland your situation may be slightly different.

If you have already lived in the UK for three years, funding concessions are occasionally available, but don't expect it.

Facts and Figures

Students from the former colonies of Britain and some non-EU European countries will pay the same fees as students in England – generally £3,225 p.a.

However, if you are granted full refugee status, you will be eligible for the same funding as UK students – see Chapter 2. If you have already started your degree studies and your immigration status changes it is important to tell your university as soon as possible. You must apply for any support within four months.

So where can refugees and asylum seekers not entitled to funding find help?

Top 10 countries sending students to study in the UK

Country	2009	2008	Change
Ireland	5,425	4,780	13.5%
China	4,965	4,485	10.7%
Cyprus	3,094	2,619	18.1%
Germany	3,042	2,713	12.1%
Hong Kong	2,991	2,954	1.3%
France	2,648	2,196	20.6%
Malaysia	2,399	2,174	10.3%
United States of America	2,323	2,209	5.2%
Singapore	2,218	1,777	24.8%
Poland	1,800	1,946	−7.5%

Source: UCAS application figures for 2009

▶ Some universities offer bursaries to students from overseas – see *University Scholarships, Awards and Bursaries*, published by Trotman. Also check individual university websites and prospectuses.

▶ There are many trusts and charities in this country that have funds to help students from overseas – see Chapter 8.

▶ Scholarship search databases can be found on www.educationuk.org and www. hotcourses.com.

▶ For more information check out the following websites:

  ▷ www. britishcouncil.org.uk

  ▷ www.egas-online.org.uk/fwa/datapage.asp

  ▷ www.ukcisa.org.uk

  ▷ www.refugeecouncil.org.uk

  ▷ www.educationaction.org

  ▷ www.hotcourses.com

  ▷ www.educationuk.org

  ▷ www.direct.gov.uk

  ▷ www.refugeeaccess.info

'You think you've got it hard. As an overseas student I get no government support and I'm working my ass off to support myself.'

Connie, a Physics student at Imperial College London, who earns £84 a week during term time and £175 a week during vacations as a sales assistant

Further information for international students

EU students

▶ For information on tuition fees for European Union students, plus other information, contact: Student Finance Online, www.direct.gov.uk/studentfinace-EU; Student Services European Team, PO Box 89, Darlington, DL1 9AZ. Tel: 0141 243 3570 (Monday–Friday 9a.m.–5.30p.m.). Email: EUTeam@slc.co.uk.

▶ UK Erasmus, 28 Park Place, Cardiff, CF10 3QE. Tel: 029 2039 7405. Email: Erasmus@ britishcouncil.org. Website: wwwbritishcouncilorg/erasmus.

▶ Leonardo da Vinci: check with your university or college.

▶ *Investing in the Future – Financial Support for EU Students*, from Student Finance England Publications Department. Tel: 0800 731 9133.

Students from abroad studying in the UK

Studying and Living in the UK is a British Council publication which provides detailed information about life in the UK for international students. It should answer many of your general questions on subjects like accommodation, living costs, study options, cultural issues and much more. Download from www. educationuk.org/downloads/study_live_uk.pdf.

See also:

▶ Education UK, the British Council's one-stop-shop website for information on UK education, www.educationuk.org

▶ UKCISA (the Council for International Student Affairs), www.ukcisa.org.uk

▶ VisitBritain (the official website for tourism in Britain), www.visitbritain.com

▶ UCAS Instructions for Completion of the Application Form by International Students. Free from UCAS with your application form

▶ British Council Information Centre: a useful contact for funding enquiries. Tel: 0161 957 7755. Email: general.enquires@britishcouncil.org. Or access the website (www.educationuk.org) giving full information about courses. Or you can write to the British Council at Bridgewater House, 58 Whitworth Street, Manchester M1 6BB.

▶ *A Guide to Studying and Living in Britain*: full of practical advice. Published by How To Books. Available from Grantham Books, tel: 01476 541080.

Courses with a difference

I'm a sandwich student doing an industrial placement: will I have to pay fees during my industrial placement?

Yes. Whether it is a thick or thin sandwich placement, all students will have to pay fees. Those who spend an entire year of a course on an industrial/sandwich placement at home or abroad will pay reduced fees. However, students will find that universities can set their own figure, with a maximum of £1,612.50 –50% of the current fee. But why, you might ask, do you have to pay fees when you are not enjoying the advantage of university? This is said to be a contribution towards the cost to the institution of administrative and pastoral arrangements relating to the placement. If the placement is for less than a full year, full fees will be charged, up to £3,225 p.a. You may apply for a fee loan (see page 45) and also for a maintenance loan (see page 53). If you are on a full year's industrial training you will only be eligible for the reduced rate of loan, which is approximately half the full rate of loan – see rates below.

	Full year (approx. figures)
London	£3,464
Elsewhere in UK	£2,475
Parental home	£1,919
Overseas	£2,826

I'm a part-time student: will I get any help?

Yes, up to £1,470 p.a. in England, more in Wales.

Grants and Fee grants for part-time students

Course	England and N. Ireland fee grant	England and N. Ireland course grant (max. available)	Wales fee grant	Wales course grant (max. available)	Scotland fee grant (2008–2009)
50–59% of the full-time course	£805	£260	£635	£1,075	Up to £500
60–74% of the full-time course	£970	£260	£765	£1,075	Up to £500
75%+ of the full-time course	£1,210	£260	£955	£1,075	Up to £500

ConstructionYouthTrust

The Construction Youth Trust is a registered charity that aims to help remove barriers that young people face when entering the construction industry. These barriers include financial, gender, ethnicity, lack of aspiration and lack of understanding of the wealth of opportunity that the construction sector provides both at craft and professional level.

We deliver our mission through a range of programmes which include:

- individual bursaries
- support and guidance for ex offenders and the homeless
- mobile classrooms in deprived communities
- paid and unpaid work placements
- industry awareness sessions for school and college based students

The Trust's mission is keenly focused on the disadvantaged. Our charity takes a leading role to promote diversity and equality of opportunity in the construction sector through our innovative projects. We aim to use our skills of brokerage and solutions developer to enable disadvantaged individuals and communities to access employment opportunities in construction at both craft and professional level.

Our support from major construction companies and our understanding of the sector as a whole enable us to be very effective in supporting young people on their journey to work. The Trust works closely with ConstructionSkills (the Sector Skills Council for construction). Our Trustees have strong links with the industry, our Patron is HRH the Duke of Gloucester and our President is Sir Michael Latham.

Three projects described below highlight the work of the Trust:

- An example of a programme supporting young people into the professions is Capital Xperience, which provides work experience for 6th Formers from East London. The aim of the programme is to give the students an understanding of the professional opportunities the sector provides in order for them to make an informed decision about which course to study at university. The communities these students come from are some of the most deprived in the country.

- Our Budding Brunels programme is another programme that focuses on the professional opportunities of the sector by delivering sessions in schools. This programme involves site visits and presentations by young people already working for key employers in the sector.
- Our bursaries focus on financial need and provide small grants to individuals to support them in their learning at craft or professional level.

"Construction provides such exciting opportunities for young professionals and the Trust is keen to support talented young people in their journey to work"

-Construction Youth Trust Director, Christine Townley BSc CEng MICE

**If you would like to learn more about the Trust please email
cyt@cytrust.org.uk
and a member of the Trust would be pleased discuss
how we can help you or the young people you work with.**

Part-time students doing 50% or more of a full-time course can apply for an income-assessed fee grant towards fees and a course grant to help with travel and books of up to £1,435 in England and £2,030 in Wales depending on intensity of course and income. Both are means tested.

There are around 500,000 part-timers in higher education in England, and the government expects around 85,000 to benefit from this financial package.

I'm going to take a foundation course: will I get funding?

Some courses include a preliminary or foundation year. These are designed to prepare students for study in their chosen subject if their qualifications or experience are not sufficient to start a degree-level course of study. The same support is available to students on a foundation year as for undergraduates if – and this is crucial – the following conditions are met:

Facts and Figures

The number of students applying for foundation degrees by January 2009 was up by 15.2% to 26,732 (UCAS figures).

Note: some universities charge lower fees for foundation courses.

► the foundation year is an integral part of the course

► the course as a whole is eligible for student support

► you enrol for the whole course and not just the foundation year.

For full details of funding, see page 62 (England), page 88 (Scotland), page 91 (Wales), and page 93 (Northern Ireland).

I'm taking a second undergraduate degree at Oxbridge: is there any help?

If you are thinking about studying a second undergraduate degree at either Oxford or Cambridge in one of the disciplines listed below, you could be eligible for a College Fee Loan (CFL). You will need to hold a UK honours degree from a publicly funded institution to be eligible. A CFL information leaflet and application form is available from your college.

Eligible courses:

► medicine (undergraduate and four-year graduate accelerated)
► dentistry
► veterinary science
► architecture
► social work
► a course for which graduates are eligible for a healthcare bursary (see below).

I'm going to do a distance learning course: is there any help?

Yes: if you are on a 'designated' full-time distance learning course you can apply for a fee grant of up to £1,210 a year and a course grant of up to £260 a year (finding depends on family income). If you are disabled you may also qualify for allowances for disabled students (see page 112).

Attending a private higher education institution

Students attending a private higher education institution that has been designated by the DIUS should be able to take out a loan to cover fees of up to £3,225. It may not be enough to completely cover your fees, as these can be higher than in other types of university. You may also be able to take out a maintenance loan and could be eligible for a maintenance grant. The course could cover any topic – theology and complementary medicine, for example. See also the information on dance and drama, page 109.

Healthcare courses

What's the package for those taking nursing and midwifery courses?

You will not have to pay fees and will receive a non-repayable, non-means-tested bursary, provided you have been accepted for an NHS-funded place. If you receive a bursary you will not be able to apply for a student loan.

Bursary rates for nursing and midwifery DipHE

Based on 45 weeks' attendance.

England and Wales, from April 2008:

▶ studying in London: £7,629
▶ elsewhere: £6,531
▶ living in parental home: £6,531.

Scotland, from August 2008: £6,411.

Northern Ireland, from September 2008: £5,910.

I'm taking an allied health professional course: what support is there for me?

The UK health authorities pay the fees of full- and part-time pre-registration students on courses in: audiology, chiropody, dental hygiene, dental therapy, dietetics, occupational therapy, orthoptics, physiotherapy, prosthetics, radiography, and speech and language therapy. A maintenance bursary is available, but means tested on family income. It is, however, a bursary and not a loan, so what you get does not have to be paid back. You will also be able to apply for the lower-rate student loan to make up the balance of your living costs, and you may be eligible for help from the Access to Learning Fund (see Chapter 3, page 71).

Bursary and loan rates

	Bursary rates			Reduced loan rates for 2009–2010	
	England & Wales 2008–2009	Scotland 2009–2010	N. Ireland 2008–2009	England/ Wales/N. Ireland approx.	Scotland
London	£3,225	£3,020	£2,835	£3,263	£2,800
Living away from home	£2,672	£2,455	£2,300	£2,324	£2,265
Living in parents' home	£2,231	£1,865	£1,875	£1,744	£1,740

Extra allowances may be available for extra weeks of study, and also for older students, overseas students, single parents, those who have dependants, or students who incur clinical placement costs.

Medical and dental students: is there any extra help?

Medical and dental students who are on standard five- or six-year courses will be treated as any other student in that area for the first four years of their course and will have to pay the fees required.

Those from outside Scotland who are studying in Scotland will be charged standard fees of £2,895 p.a. Scottish students studying in Scotland will not be charged fees. See page 91 for fees in Wales.

In your fifth and any subsequent years, funding will be provided by the NHS, which means your tuition fees will be paid and you will be eligible to apply for a means-tested NHS bursary and a reduced maintenance loan from the Student Loans Company (see details under 'I'm taking an allied health professional course', above).

If you live in England and want to study in Scotland, Wales or Northern Ireland the NHS Student Grants Unit will assess and pay your bursary.

If you live in Scotland, Wales or Northern Ireland and want to study in England you should consult the relevant national authorities.

Graduates taking the four-year accelerated course in medicine for graduates should see Chapter 9, page 245.

'I've known a couple of medics who joined the army for a year, interrupting their five-year course, in order to earn money to help with the costs of doing their degree.'
2nd year Medical student, St George's

A medical student's story
'When you get to your first year of clinics (fourth year) you are still expected to survive on not much more than undergraduates (i.e. the student loan). However, your days and weeks are longer, there are weekend/night shifts, and it's a 48-week year – so not much time to work. All through uni I had relied on a holiday job to keep me afloat. Now it was not so easy. I was maxed out on an already over-extended overdraft and the bank was threatening to charge me, while my landlord wanted the rent.

All I needed was £100 to pull me back from the brink. I applied to my university, but the dean of students could not be contacted and the finance office said I would have to wait seven days even for an appointment to be considered for "emergency" funds. So what did I do? Borrowed from a friend.'
4th year Medical student, UCL

NHS bursaries

▶ **England**: NHS Student Grants Unit, 22 Plymouth Road, Blackpool FY3 7JS. Tel: 01253 655655. Courses helpline for England: 0845 358 6655. Website: www.nhspa. gov.uk/sgu. www.nhsstudentgrants.co.uk.

▶ **Wales**: NHS Student Awards Unit, 2nd floor, Golate House, 101 St Mary's Street, Cardiff CF10 1DX. Tel: 029 2026 1495. Helpline 8045 358 6655. www.wales.nhs.uk.

▶ **Scotland**: Student Awards Agency for Scotland, 3 Redheughs Rigg, South Gyle, Edinburgh EH12 9HH. Tel: 0845 111 1711, 0131 476 8227. www.saas.gov.uk.

▶ **Northern Ireland**: Bursaries Administration Unit, Central Services Agency, 2 Franklin Street, Belfast BT2 8DQ, Tel: 02890 553661. Or contact the appropriate Education and Libraries Board (ELB) www.delni.gov.uk

Specialist courses

This section covers information on teaching, social work, and dance and drama courses.

What's the deal for trainee teachers?

If you already have a degree and are considering a postgraduate initial teacher training (ITT) course, turn to Chapter 9, page 241, for details of the incentive package that is being offered. You could be in for a nice surprise.

There are no special incentives for undergraduates any more. Undergraduate trainee teachers receive the same funding as other students – sorry!

Trainee teachers in Wales

In addition to the normal funding for undergraduates, in Wales there's a special deal called the Secondary Undergraduate Placement Grant, which is available on an annual basis to support you during school-based teacher training. £1,200 will be paid to undergraduate students who are on a secondary initial teacher training course specialising in one of the secondary priority subjects (which are: design and technology, information and communication technology, maths, modern languages, music, religious education, science and Welsh).

This information applies to 2009–2010 and is subject to change in future years. The grant is paid in two instalments by ITT providers: enquiries about your eligibility should be directed to the ITT provider with which you wish to study.

Small hardship grants are also available for those who get into unforeseen difficulties that might prevent them completing their course. Postgraduates: see Chapter 9 page 242 for more funding information.

I'm taking a degree in social work: can I get a bursary?

The Social Work Bursary

The Social Work Bursary is available to students ordinarily resident in England studying on an approved undergraduate course (full or part time).

The bursary is non-income assessed, which means that earnings, savings and other sources of income are not taken into consideration. It includes a basic grant, a fixed contribution towards practice learning opportunity-related expenses and tuition fees. Financial awards are dependent on individual circumstances.

Undergraduates – what you will get (figures are for 2009–2010, based on a 52-week period).

Full-time students subject to top-up fees:	
London-based HEI	up to £4,975
Elsewhere-based HEI	up to £4,575
Part-time students:	
London-based HEI	up to £2,487.50
Elsewhere-based HEI	up to £2,287.50
Full time students not subject to fees:	
London-based HEI	up to £3,475
Elswhere-based HEI	up to £3,075

Graduates: see page 224.

For full details on eligibility criteria and funding availability visit www.ppa. org.uk/swb or email your enquiry to swb@ppa.nhs.uk. Alternatively, call the Bursaries customer service team on 0845 610 1122.

I want to study dance and drama: will I get funding?

If you are offered a state-funded place on a higher education course you should be eligible for the same funding as students on degree courses. RADA, the Guildhall School of Music and Drama, the Central School of Speech and Drama, Bristol Old Vic Theatre School, Rose Bruford College and many other institutions fall into that category. (See Chapter 2.)

A majority of accredited dance and drama courses at private HE institutions offer some form of funding to help with fees and living expenses. While higher education courses in dance or drama no longer offer Dance and Drama Awards (having introduced the 'state-funded places' scheme), awards are given by some 20 performing arts schools. Competition for all these awards is very fierce – not all students who achieve a place will receive an award.

If you are offered a place as a private student by your college and it is not state funded you will have to pay the full cost of the private tuition fee. For those who do not receive an award, a three-year course (including living costs) could set you back £50,000. However, you should still contact your local authority for details of how to apply for help as a private student on a designated course, as some funding might be available. Not all accredited courses attract government funding, so if funding is essential, check the status of a course before you start applying. The booklet *A Guide to Vocational Training in Dance and Drama* is full of useful information, including a full guide to funding. Tel 0845 602 2260 or see www.direct.gov.uk/.

Additional help for special groups

I'm a mature/independent/married student: is there any special funding or advice for me?

An independent student is someone who no longer lives with their parents, has been working for at least three years, or is over 25. As an independent student you are entitled to the general funding package for students (see Chapter 2 or the beginning of this chapter if you're based in Scotland, Wales or Northern Ireland). Independent English students can earn up to £25,000 before losing any of their funding entitlement. For students from Northern Ireland the figure is £18,820, and in Wales £18,370. If you are married, or living with someone in a stable relationship, your partner's income may well be means tested if you apply for a maintenance loan/grant. There is no age limit on taking out a fee loan, and the cut-off point for taking a maintenance loan is now 60 years.

Facts and Figures

The number of mature students (aged 25 and over) starting a degree in UK universities in 2008 was 51,443, up a massive 21.7% on last year.

(UCAS figures)

If I become a student will I still receive benefits such as income support?

In order that Income Support or Housing Benefit can be paid, students receive a non-repayable Special Support Grant. This works in a similar way to the maintenance grant (see Chapter 2, page 49) – it is given to low-income families. If you receive the special support grant you will not be eligible for the maintenance grant.

I have children to support: are there any other allowances, grants and bursaries I could apply for?

▶ A non-repayable special support grant of up to £2,906 a year is available for new full-time students who are eligible for benefits such as Income Support or

Housing Benefit while they are studying. Main beneficiaries are likely to be lone parents, other student parents and students with disabilities. The grant is based on household income and does not have to be paid back. If you're eligible for the special support grant you will not be eligible for the maintenance grant. This will not affect any university bursary you are offered.

▶ The Parents' Learning Allowance: up to £1,508 p.a. for help with course-related costs for students with dependent children. Income is assessed.

▶ Childcare Grant: up to £148.75 a week for one child and £255 for two or more. Amount given based on 85% of actual childcare costs. Paid in three instalments by the Student Loans Company. Does not have to be repaid.

▶ Child Tax Credit: available to students with dependent children and paid by the Inland Revenue. Students receiving the maximum amount will be entitled to free school meals for their children. The amount you get will depend on circumstances. Call 0845 300 3900 for more details or visit www.inlandrevenue.gov.uk/taxcredits and check out how much you could get.

▶ Adult Dependants' Grant: up to £2,642 p.a. for full-time students with adult dependants. Paid in three instalments.

▶ Access to Learning Fund: see page 71. Universities generally look very favourably on mature students when allocating access funds.

Scotland

Please note: help for parents in Scotland and the amounts available are different from those listed here.

I'm disabled and I want to go into higher education: can I get extra help?

There are a number of ways you can get extra help, depending on your disability. If you follow up every lead offered here, it's going to take time, but the results could be worthwhile.

What's the starting point for somebody who has a disability?

First choose your course, then choose the university or college where you would like to study. Next check out the college facilities, and their ability to cope with your specific disability, by:

1. writing for details of facilities
2. visiting suitable institutions
3. having a 'special needs' interview with the institution.

Then fill in your UCAS application.

When should I start getting organised?

It's a good idea to start getting organised in the summer term of your first A level year, as you may have to revise your choice of institution several times.

What financial help can I expect from my local authority?

Like most students on full-time higher education courses in this country, as a disabled student you would be eligible for the full financial support package for students described in the previous chapter.

I am severely disabled: can I get a student loan?

Yes. As an undergraduate you would be eligible for a student loan. In fact, the regulations laid down when the Student Loans Company was set up allow for the loans administrator to delay the start of repayment for people with disabilities, and any disability-related financial entitlements you receive will be disregarded when calculating your repayment amounts. Phone the Student Loans Company helpline free on 0845 607 7577.

Can I apply to the Access to Learning Fund?

Yes. Each institution decides its own criteria for payments – there are no set rules. You might find being disabled gives you more entitlement (see details on page 71).

What extra money is available for disabled students?

There are Disabled Students' Allowances (DSAs) for full- and part-time students, which offer support to those with a disability or specific learning difficulty such as dyslexia.

There are four Disabled Students' Allowances.

1. Up to £20,520 per year for non-medical personal help – e.g. readers, lip-speakers, note-takers (up to £15,390 if studying part-time).
2. Up to £5,161 for the whole course for specialist course equipment – e.g. computer, word processor, Braille printer, radio microphone, induction loop system (whether studying full- or part-time).
3. A general Disabled Students' Allowance – up to £1,724 p.a. (up to £1,293 for part-time study) for minor items such as tapes, Braille paper, extra use of phone.
4. Extra travel costs incurred as a result of your disability.

Distance learning

Full-time undergraduates who cannot attend their course because of their disability will be eligible for full-time student support in addition to DSAs. (See page 104.)

Can I get help with travel?

The loan for students includes a set amount for transport costs (£303) – as a disabled student you can claim for extra travel expenses incurred over this amount if your disability means, for example, that you are unable to use public transport and must travel by taxi (see point 4 above).

What about Social Security benefits?

Most full-time students are not entitled to benefits such as Income Support and Housing Benefit. However, such benefits can be available to students in vulnerable groups such as people with disabilities, but the situation is complicated. The people to put you in the picture are your Jobcentre/Jobcentre Plus or Skill: the National Bureau for Students with Disabilities (see below); alternatively phone the Benefits Inquiry line on 0800 882200; minicom users 0800 243355. Opening hours: 8.30a.m.–6.30p.m. Monday–Friday; 9a.m.–1p.m. Saturday.

Can I get a Disability Living Allowance?

Yes. This allowance is available to you as a student. It provides funds on a weekly basis for those who need help with mobility – e.g. the cost of operating a wheelchair or the hire or purchase of a car. It also covers those who need care and assistance with any physical difficulties such as washing or eating, or continual supervision. The allowance will not affect your Disabled Students' Allowances in any way. See previous question for people to contact.

Further information for specialist groups

Mature students

▶ *Returning to Education: A Practical Handbook for Adult Learners*. Published by How To Books. Available from Trotman, tel: 0870 900 2665 or visit www.trotman.co.uk/bookshop.

▶ *Mature Students' Directory*. Published by Trotman; to order, tel: 0870 900 2665 or visit the website www.trotman.co.uk/bookshop.

Disabled students

▶ Students' Welfare Officer at your university or college, students' union, local Citizens' Advice Bureau.

▶ Skill: National Bureau for Students with Disabilities. It runs a special information and advice service, open Tuesday 11.30a.m.–1.30p.m. and Thursday 1.30p.m.–3.30 p.m., tel: 0800 328 5050, and also publishes a number of useful leaflets (free to students) and books for disabled people, available on website. Or from Skill, Unit 3, Radisson Court, 219 Long Lane, London SE1 4PR. Textphone: 0800 068 2422. Email: info@skill.org.uk. Website: www.skill.org.uk. Fax: 020 7450 0650.

- ▶ Benefits Agency or JobCentre/JobCentrePlus: address should be in your local telephone directory.
- ▶ Royal National Institute of Blind People (RNIB), RNIB Education and Employment Network, 105 Judd Street, London WC1H 9NE. Main line 020 7388 1266. Helpline open: 0303 123 9999 Monday–Tuesday/Thursday–Friday 9a.m.–5p.m., Wednesday 9a.m.–4p.m. Messages can be left on the answer phone outside these hours. Email: helpline@rnib.org.uk. Website: www.rnib.org.uk.
- ▶ Royal National Institute for Deaf People (RNID), 19–23 Featherstone Street, London EC1Y 8SL. Tel: 0808 808 0123. Textphone: 0808 808 9000. Fax: 020 7296 8199. Email: informationline@rnid.org.uk. Website: www.rnid.org.uk.
- ▶ *Bridging the Gap: A Guide to the Disabled Students' Allowances*. For copies, tel: 0800 731 9133. Textphone: 0800 328 8988. Fax: 0845 603 3360. Also available from www.studentfinancedirect.co.uk.
- ▶ *The Disabled Student's Guide to University*, published by Trotman. To order, tel: 0870 900 2665 or visit www.trotman.co.uk/bookshop.

Studying abroad

I have to spend part of my course studying abroad: will I get extra help?

Yes, but it will be a loan. If you study abroad for at least 50% of an academic quarter (which normally means a term) you are eligible for an overseas rate of loan, which for 2009–2010 is:

- ▶ England: max. £5,653 (Wales and Northern Ireland may vary slightly)
- ▶ Scotland: highest-cost countries £1,215–£6,720; high-cost countries £1,095–£5,655; all other countries £915–£4,625.

Don't forget, unless you are on an Erasmus exchange (see page 115), if you spend a year away in another country you will still have to pay reduced fees. These are set by your university up to a maximum of £1,612.50 (50% of the normal fee). You will be able to take out a loan to cover these.

Scottish students who normally study in Scotland will pay no fees. Welsh students who normally study in Wales and receive a fee grant will find around 60% of the fee demanded is paid.

My course abroad is longer than my course in the UK: can I get more money?

Yes. The rate given is worked out on a year of only 30 weeks and three days. If you need to stay longer, you can increase your loan.

The rate for 2009–2010 is up to £115 per week (up to £150 per week in Scotland).

'*Students who have a compulsory study period abroad can get into serious financial difficulties. Nobody warns you of the cost of this before you choose a course such as European Studies and Modern Languages.*'

3rd year French and Russian student

It's going to cost me a lot more to fly to Tokyo than to take a train to Leeds: can I get any help with travel?

Yes, but not for the full fare. Your loan already includes some travel element (£303 in England/Wales, Northern Ireland), and this will be taken into consideration in calculating how much you receive. It is probably best to let Student Finance England calculate what you are entitled to. Remember when putting in for costs to give all the facts – the journey from your home to the airport costs something, too. (Arrangements differ in Scotland, where the disregard amount is £159.)

Student dilemma: the loan allowance for students studying abroad in 2009–2010 was set before the value of the pound started to fall, and has not been changed to cover this. Students studying abroad may find they are even more hard up than in previous years.

Is there any other help for students who want to study abroad?

Two organisations have been set up to assist students wanting to study in the EU:

▶ Erasmus (sometimes known as Socrates-Erasmus), the European Community Action Scheme for the Mobility of University Students, is designed to encourage greater co-operation between universities and other higher educational institutions in Europe. Under this scheme, students taking courses, including foreign languages, in other European countries may be given a grant towards extra expenses while studying abroad for a period of three to 12 months. These could include travel expenses, language courses, or living and accommodation costs. If you're part of this scheme you should also be exempt from paying the reduced fees that sandwich students taking a year out have to pay. For more details phone 029 2039 7405, email erasmus@britishcouncil.org or visit www.britishcouncil. org/erasmus.

▶ The Leonardo da Vinci scheme provides opportunities for university students and recent graduates to undertake periods of vocational training of up to 12 months with organisations in other member states; placements are largely technology based. While individual employers will provide any salary, the Leonardo scheme can make a contribution towards language tuition and expenses. For more details phone 020 7289 4157.

Who to contact

Funding from these organisations is arranged mainly through your university or college. They should have full information and should therefore be your first point of call. Otherwise, contact the European Commission, 8 Storey's Gate, London SW1P 3AT, tel: 020 7973 1992.

What happens if I get sick while studying abroad?

Don't wait until you get sick: take out health insurance cover before you go. (See information about travel insurance on page 174.) Your local authority will probably reimburse the costs of health insurance, providing they consider it 'economical'. Check out the situation with them first. If you are going abroad as part of your course, seek advice from your university; they will know the score. You may have to pay a social security charge. (See page 118, 'Focus on three popular places for studying abroad'.)

Remember, above all, to hold on to your receipts. Without these you are unlikely to get reimbursement from your local authority.

If you have to take out medical insurance, you can also get help to cover the cost of the insurance.

Can I study for my whole degree abroad?

You can, but it's not going to be cheap because you won't be entitled to a student loan, unless you are studying at the University of London Institute in Paris. As it is part of the University of London, the institute's three-year French course can be studied in Paris, but you would be treated as any UK student and would be eligible for UK funding. This means you could be eligible for a maintenance grant, the maintenance loan at the overseas rate (which this year is up to £5,653) and could be offered a university bursary. The downside is you would have to pay UK fees of £3,225 per annum (2009–2010 figure). If you go to an EU country and study at a non-UK institution, as a resident of the UK you will be treated like the students in that country and will normally pay no tuition fees. In most European countries higher education institutions do not charge tuition fees; if tuition fees are charged, they are generally set at a nominal rate.

But a number of universities do have registration fees, and there are additional health and personal insurance costs, students' union fees and other expenses to consider.

Many countries have special concessions for their students, e.g. concessionary rates for meals, transport and accommodation. As an EU student you would benefit from these.

The most expensive part of your stay will be maintenance costs, and because you are not taking any part of your course in the UK, you will not be eligible for the student loan or maintenance grant.

Will my EU university give me a bursary or scholarship?

Unlikely. As EU students find when they come to the UK, you will be treated like a home student as far as fees, entry and other costs and concessions are concerned, but you are not covered by their funding package, and bursaries and scholarships for first degrees are not easily found.

What will it cost me to live abroad?

Living costs vary depending on where you are studying. As in the UK, capital cities are more expensive places to live than country towns.

When it comes to the price of food in the EU, the UK is among the more expensive places. If you are thinking of studying further afield than Europe, the cost factor is appreciably higher as it is unlikely that you will get your fees covered for a full degree course, and travel will be a major expense.

Will studying abroad be very different?

Every country has its own particular approach to study and its own characteristics. In Europe, for instance, individual universities tend to cater for a greater number of students. Lectures, classes and seminars are more crowded and there is a greater dependence on printed course material. There is less contact between tutor and student and the system generally is more impersonal.

Another major difference is the exams. Often there is a greater reliance on oral examinations. In Italy, for example, the majority of the exams are oral. While this tends to give students additional self-confidence and make them more articulate, it is something new to UK students and something they need to get accustomed to.

European students are more inclined to attend their local university, and many live at home. As a result, universities do not provide the wide range of social and recreational facilities you would expect to find at a UK university. Students use the facilities of the local city or town, which can be expensive.

The universities of Europe are often situated in fine old towns and in regions you will want to explore, which again will be a drain on your (limited) resources.

'My third year was spent abroad, but I still had to pay half tuition fees – for what? It's outrageous!'

4th year Languages student, Durham

'The fourth year of my degree is in France. Even though I don't need a student loan at the moment, I have taken it out and put it in a high-interest account because I know I will want to travel once I get to Europe.'

1st year Chemistry student, Imperial College, London

Facts and Figures

Countries that attract the most students from abroad:

USA	22%
UK	12%
Germany	10%
France	9%
Australia	6%
Canada	5%

(OECD Education at a Glance 2007)

Focus on three popular places for studying abroad

(Please note: all figures are approximate.)

France

You need to prove you have sufficient resources to maintain yourself while studying in France. Minimum threshold level is about €5,160, with a minimum of €430 a month, but this will be barely enough to cover your living expenses. In reality you will need more like €600 a month

What are these expenses likely to be? (Figures for 2007–2008.)

▶ Annual cost of a course: €150– €900 in a public institution and €3,000– €7,000 in a private university.

- ▶ Accommodation: €150 per month in the university, €300 per month for a studio in the city.
- ▶ Food: €230 per month.
- ▶ Transport: €31 per month.
- ▶ Course charge: €92 per month.
- ▶ Telephone: €30 per month.

For the first month it is estimated that you will need around €1,500. This will cover:

- ▶ first month's rent: €150– €300
- ▶ deposit for lodgings (2 months): up to €600
- ▶ annual insurance for lodgings: €50
- ▶ social security: €180
- ▶ health insurance: €70– €285 depending on risk taken
- ▶ registration fee €150.

Scholarships: there are very few available. Try the Entente Cordiale Scholarships for postgraduates. Contact the French Embassy in London. Helpful website: www.cnous.fr.

Germany

A degree in Germany takes between four and six years, so you must anticipate a long stay. Each year is divided into two semesters. The first hurdle is registration: this gives you that all-important student card, which will entitle you to special rates on local transport, reduced rates for cultural events and use of the refectory. Tuition in universities is generally free, but a number of states have introduced fees of up to €500 per semester. Foreign students need to prove they have sufficient funds for their stay – around €770 per month (€7,716 p.a.) is about what German students have, but you can get by with less, certainly in the former East Germany. Rents vary – in the larger cities like Frankfurt and Hamburg the average is €310 a month. In smaller places – Dresden, Jena, Chemnitz, for example – the average is around €186 a month. Balance that against the fact that it is easier to find a job in a bigger city. Though EU students are allowed to work in Germany this is not a good way to fund your studies, as unemployment is high at the moment. Expenses will include:

- ▶ enrolment and administration fee, €100 per semester
- ▶ semester ticket: for travel (some universities), €50.

Average monthly expenses:

- rent (including additional charges): €250
- food: €160
- clothing: €60
- transport (car/public transport): €86
- health insurance: €60
- telephone/internet/TV licence: €50
- work/study materials: €37
- total: €703.

Books, depending on course, could be €200–€250 a semester.

Scholarships: German institutions do not generally award scholarships and grants, and if given they are generally based on academic ability. The most extensive scholarship programme is organised by the German Academic Exchange Service (DAAD), but this is only for postgraduates. Try www.study-in-germany.de/english/grants. Try also: www.daad.de/deutschland/foerderung/stipendiendatenbank.

United States

Students are responsible for paying both their fees and their living expenses. These vary enormously between individual colleges and depending on whether they are state run or privately run. Tuition fees average around $17,452 for out-of-state students at public four-year institutions and $25,143 at private four-year institutions. For two-year colleges tuition rates are around $6,000. Then there are books and equipment, adding sometimes as much as $2,000 p.a. On top of that you have living costs, which could add another $4,000–$14,000 to your bill each nine-month academic year. You will also need money for travel from the UK and back, health insurance and personal expenses.

Approximately two-thirds of full-time undergraduates receive some type of grant aid. While private universities tend to charge higher tuition fees they are more likely to have funding for international students or students with a household income of less than £30,000–£35,000. Some financial aid is granted: in most institutions it is based on academic merit, though some colleges may give funding based on need. Full scholarships are rare. Because of this, students often have jobs during term time and work their way through college. Students can work on campus for up to 20 hours a week, but this cannot be listed as a source of income for visa applications. Other forms of funding include scholarships for special talents such as athletics.

Contact the Fulbright Commission, 62 Doughty Street, London WC1N 2JZ. Tel: 020 7404 6994. Fax: 020 7404 6874. Email: education@fulbright.co.uk. See also their website: www.fulbright.co.uk. Special loans are available for all students: try www.fulbright.co.uk/media/pds/UGSudy/Undergraduate_ Scholarships_for_UK_Students.pdf

Many universities in the USA are vast and can resemble small cities, with their own post office, grocery stores and shopping centres; they can dominate the local community and its economy. The US does not have a system like UCAS, so all applications must be sent direct to individual colleges. This can be expensive: the application fee (non-refundable) is $50–$100 for each university, and you may be charged for prospectuses and test applications. So it is important to select the institutions you are interested in with care. A College Day Fair is held in London when you can meet over 100 representatives from US universities.

Can I get funding to study in the US?

Don't rule out studying in the US on the grounds of finance, even if you come from a low-income family. Yes, fees are much higher over there, but many of the hundreds of universities and colleges in the States are well endowed. There is a tradition in the US of alumni supporting their old college. So most offer bursaries and scholarships even to international students. Some awards are for academic performance, sport or music, but many are given for financial need. Even well-known top institutions such as Princeton, Stanford, Berkeley, Yale and Harvard all offer help for students from low-income families. This may cover fees and living expenses, or both, be a straight cash gift, or

Top US University Targets UK Students

Think Harvard, one of the America's leading universities, is beyond your financial reach? Think again. Harvard has a policy of giving students from low-income families generous financial assistance. In fact, students whose parents earn less than £31,500 ($60,000) a year could find they can study free. Harvard is keen to attract some of Britain's best and has launched a recruitment drive in some of our state schools. But Harvard is not alone: over 4,000 UK undergraduates and around 2,500 UK postgraduates were studying in the USA last year.

a guaranteed job to help you earn your way through. But of course, first you have to get there, and you have to get in. Every institution has its own website.

As we go to print, the exchange rates between the euro, the dollar and the pound make studying in the countries abroad most favoured by students more expensive than in the past, and this is something you should consider before you go.

Further information for students from the UK studying abroad

▶ *Study Abroad*, UNESCO publication, available from the Stationery Office. TSO, PO Box 29, Norwich NR3 1GN. Tel: 020 7873 0011.

▶ *Getting into US and Canadian Universities*, Margaret Kroto, published by Trotman. To order, tel: 0870 900 2665 or visit www.trotman.co.uk/bookshop.

▶ *You Want to Study Where?! Alternative Degree Destinations*, published by Trotman. To order, tel: 0870 900 2665 or visit www.trotman.co.uk/bookshop.

▶ *Jobs Wolrdwide*, Susan Griffith, includes over 50,000 jobs worldwide. Updated annually. Available from Trotman, 0870 900 2665

▶ UK Socrates–Erasmus. Rothford, Giles Lane, Canterbury, Kent CT2 7LR. Tel: 0122 776 2712. Fax: 01227 762711. Email: info@erasmus.ac.uk. Website: www.erasmus. ac.uk.

Information about fees, maintenance grants and loans

▶ England: *A Guide to Financial Support for Higher Education Students in 2009/10* (the source for the loan statistics in this chapter), Braille and cassette editions also available. For publications, tel: 0845 602 2260 (booklet: 0800 731 9133). Helpline, tel: 0845 607 7577. Website: www.direct.gov.uk/studentfinance.

▶ Scotland: *Student Support in Scotland: A Guide for Undergraduate Students 2009/10*, available from any Scottish university or the Student Awards Agency for Scotland (SAAS), 3 Redheughs Rigg, South Gyle, Edinburgh EH12 9YT. Tel: 0131 476 8212. Email: saas.geu@scotland.gsi.gov.uk. Website: www.student-supportsaas.gov.uk.

▶ Northern Ireland: *Financial Support for Students in Higher Education 2009/10*, Student Support Branch, Department for Employment and Learning (Northern

Ireland), Rathgael House, Balloo Road, Bangor, Co. Down BT19 7PR. Tel: 028 9025 7710 (booklet: 0800 731 9133). Website: www.delni.gov.uk/index.htm.

▶ Wales: *A Guide to Financial Support for Higher Education 2009/10*, National Assembly for Wales, Higher Education Division 2, 3rd floor, Cathays Park, Cardiff CF10 3NQ. Tel: 0845 602 8845. Website: www.studentfinancewales.co.uk, and www.learning.wales.co.uk.

CHAPTER 5

Paying your way

This chapter looks at the main reasons why students work, what they can do and what they can expect to earn.

Why do students work?

There are many reasons why students work, either before or during their study course. In this chapter we investigate some of those reasons and give advice on what sort of work you can expect to find; how to go about getting it; who to contact; and what to read. But the main reason why students work is to . . .

Make money to fund your degree

If you have read the first five chapters of this book, you will realise that what you are likely to get to finance you through university just won't be enough. A large number of students work, most from sheer financial necessity, and their aim is to earn as much as possible.

▶ Three-quarters of a million undergraduates (nearly half the UK student population – 42%) were thought to be in part-time employment when the new 2008–2009 academic year started.

▶ In total, they are likely to earn over £2 billion, a sum representing the total value of the UK theatre industry.

▶ Nearly 25,000 more undergraduates took up part-time employment during term time in 2008 than in 2007 – an increase the size of Oxford University.

▶ Over 40% are working to pay their way through university, saying it would be too expensive without additional income.

▶ Over the current academic year, 2008–2009 university students are expected to spend £10.8 billion on living and accommodation costs, compared to £10.3 billion in 2007, as the cost of living increases.

(NatWest Student Living Index 2008)

Should you/can you work during term time?

Most universities and colleges allow students to work during term time; in fact, many universities have set up job shops, so you could say they are actively encouraging it. But most suggest a limit on the number of hours you work during term – generally 15 hours a week, though some say 10–12 and others 16.

The university students' union is a great source of work, providing job opportunities in students' union shops and bars. How many students actually work during term time varies between universities. Many universities just don't know. However, the following universities suggest:

University	Percentage of students who work
Dundee	25%
Aberdeen, Bath, Glasgow, Sheffield, Surrey	30%
Brighton, Edinburgh, Staffordshire	35%
Coventry, Lincoln, Oxford Brookes, Slade	50%
Aston, Gloucestershire, Middlesex, Portsmouth, Northampton, Sheffield Hallam	60%
Sussex	70%
Hertfordshire	80%
Huddersfield (top of the list)	90%

Going against the trend are Oxford and Cambridge, where many (but not all) colleges actively forbid or strongly discourage students from working during term time, except perhaps if they work in the student bar. Since the Oxbridge term is just eight weeks and, as one lecturer pointed out, 'very intensive weeks at that', perhaps the colleges have a point. (For full and more up-to-date figures and information on individual universities, see the *Guide to UK Universities 2010*, published by Trotman.)

The tutor's view
'When it comes to work, academic staff attitudes vary from the positive to the negative. Obviously they would like it if students didn't have to work, but are realistic, especially with the introduction of fees. If you want to encourage students from diverse financial backgrounds, then you have got to be prepared to let them work.'

Co-ordinator of Student Work Place, the University of Manchester job shop

The students' view
'The necessity of finding part-time work means the quality of your college work suffers.'

PGCE student, Bangor

'Get a job with a good employer – for money, experience, skills and references.'

Final year Sociology student, Kent

'Part-time work teaches you discipline and keeps you from being in the bar every night.'

3rd year Sociology student, De Montfort

How important is it to get a job? Will it make a difference to my finances?

It certainly will, as the table on page 129 shows.

If you want evidence that students are being hit by the credit crunch, look at the previous year's figures for average weekly expenditure (the figures in brackets) – they tell a sorry story.

Plymouth looks like the best place to study – providing, that is, you find a job and don't mind putting in the hours – followed by Dundee. Students in Portsmouth seem to work just as hard as those in Plymouth, but they don't see quite the same rewards, while Exeter students work the least for about the same return as students in York, who work fewer hours.

But the real questions are:

1. Will the student finance package you receive (grant, bursary, loan, parental help) be enough to make up the extra cash needed? See previous chapters.

2. Will you find a job when there is so much unemployment?

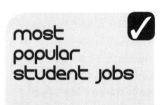

most popular student jobs ✓

Sales assistant
Waiter/waitress
Barperson
Student ambassador
Tutoring
Hospital administration

University job shops

Among the most important innovations in recent years are university job shops. They can be found in most universities throughout the UK. They all seem to operate on their own individual system but have one aim in common – to find work for students during term time and the holidays. Pay is never less than the minimum wage, which is currently £4.77 for 18–21-year-olds and £5.73 for those over 22. Information collected by the *NatWest Student Living Index Survey* in 2008 showed that students earned on average £6.49 per hour.

Close-up on three job shops

Job shops come under a variety of names. There is Joblink at Aberdeen, Student Employment Service at Edinburgh, WorkStation at University College London, CUBE at Coventry and PULSE at Liverpool. All seem to have different ways of working.

Students' average weekly budget

Town/City	Average weekly rent	Average total weekly expenditure	Average weekly earnings	Average hours worked per week	Extra cash needed per week
Aberdeen	£71	£197 (£135)	£98.80	16.7	£122.40
Belfast	£58	£205 (£147)	£102.40	15.5	£160.60
Birmingham	£67	£193 (£138)	£72.20	10.4	£187.80
Brighton	£76	£198 (140)	£120.30	12.4	£144.70
Bristol	£70	£183 (£130)	£107.10	14.4	£145.90
Cambridge	£87	£154 (£123)	£110.80	15.1	£130.20
Cardiff	£68	£200 (£131)	£85.40	14.2	£182.60
Dundee	£64	£155 (£135)	£98.60 (£113)	16.9	£120.40
Edinburgh	£77	£166 (£121)	£76.5	12.3	£116.50
Exeter	£80	£206 (n/a)	£66.70	9.9	£219.30
Glasgow	£76	£188 (£132)	£89	15	£175
Lancaster	£57	£213 (£112)	£88	12.6	£182.18
Leeds	£69	£171 (£129)	£99.30	15.3	£140.70
Leicester	£57	£221 (£109)	£88.40	14.2	£189.60
Liverpool	£80	£192 (£120)	£101.40	17	£148.60
London	£90	£221 (£159)	£103.20	15.4	£207.80
Manchester	£76	£168 (£130)	£64.50	11.8	£179.50
Newcastle	£63	£191 (£128)	£92.60	13.9	£161.40
Nottingham	£65	£191 (£148)	£84.40	14	£171.60
Oxford	£92	£198 (£132)	£87	13.7	£203
Plymouth	£69	£148 (n/a)	£114.60	18.4	£102.40
Porstmouth	£67	£189 (n/a)	£110.90	18.4	£145.40
Sheffield	£62	£132 (£156)	£75.20	14	£142.80
Southampton	£68	£174 (£137)	£59.30	10.9	£182.70
Swansea	£61	£180 (£116)	£63.70	15.4	£177.30
York	£68	£146 (£124)	£65.40	10.7	£147.60
All	£73	£192 (£130)	£92.89	14.3	£172.11

Source: Taken from the NatWest Student Living Index 2008

Cardiff

Cardiff University's Jobshop was one of the first student employment services established in the country. It offers both a student employment agency and a Jobcentre-style service and keeps registered students updated with new vacancies every day via email. Around 4,500 students register with the Jobshop every year and it provides a flexible service that enables them to balance paid work with their study commitments. All kinds of work are offered, from bar/waiting to clerical/admin, flyering and library shelving. The Jobshop provides casual staff for not only the university and students' union but also the growing number of local companies who are now taking advantage of the service.

Talking of the credit crunch, Jane Howorth of Cardiff University staff says they had a slow start to the academic year, 'but things are gathering momentum. But we have definitely had less in terms of permanent part-time vacancies, so you could say employers are seeking temporary rather than permanent part-time staff.'

Southampton

The University of Southampton's Careers Service has a free online vacancy service called e-jobs. Between 100 and 150 new vacancies come in weekly and around 8,000 students use the service. There is a wide range of part-time and casual opportunities listed on the site, as well as internship and placement opportunities. Types of work include retail, promotional and marketing activities, IT, admin support, care and catering. Asked if they would accept any kind of job, Angela Faux, who works in the Employer Liaison team at the Careers Service, said: 'We check all vacancies that come in. We have a vacancy code of practice and don't carry commission-only or pyramid-selling vacancies.' How are unsuitable vacancies kept off the site? Angela has her finger firmly on the delete key and commission-only jobs at the local casino were trashed pretty smartly.

Students who have registered apply for jobs direct. Employers can also access the system to advertise jobs. The service is open to all undergraduate and postgraduate students. Just log on to www.soton.ac.uk/careers and register for e-jobs via the blue 'e-jobs' button on the home page.

Talking of the credit crunch, Southampton says that while in the first term of this year, they saw an increase in jobs notified, they feel there is greater competition for vacancies and that employers are receiving more unsolicited approaches from students.

Manchester

Student WorkPlace is the specialist work experience unit of the University of Manchester Careers Service. It handles all types of student work, including part-time jobs, industrial placements and vacation work positions. Students can search vacancies online or register to receive appropriate vacancies by email. Around 200 jobs are advertised each month. Manchester students can also find information on over 20 company sponsors and a wide range of national and international work experience schemes. Student WorkPlace also provides advice on creative job hunting in the credit crunch, and writing applications for part-time work. Recent jobs included Arabic software translator, boating lake attendant, campus brand manager, cocktail bartender, editorial assistant, freelance reporter, HR assistant, part-time headhunter, mad scientist, marquee rigger, voiceover artist, private tutor and web developer.

Talking about the current job market, Scot Foley, Student Recruitment Manager at Student WorkPlace, says: 'With the credit crunch we find that not so many jobs are being advertised for part-time work, for example in retail, which is being hit by reduced consumer spending. Some are waiting to see what happens in the coming months, others have perhaps revised the number of people they want to take on, rather than stopping recruitment altogether.' And his advice to students is, 'There are still jobs out there but you have to be more proactive. Work hard on polishing your CV, develop your skills through voluntary work or unpaid projects if you have no work experience or can't find paid work. But most important, target your CV and show more than ever what skills you have which are relevant to the job: e.g. for a bar job, communication and working under pressure.'

Does your university have a job shop?

Check it out as soon as you arrive. Jobs go very quickly. Most students want or need to take jobs during the long summer vacations. Your university job shop or that of a university closer to home may be able to help you here.

Thrift Tips

'Potatoes and more potatoes – mixed with cheese, with ham, with butter – at least you're full.'
3rd year Egyptian Archaeology student, UCL

'Forget the gym – walk. You'll be fit and save a fortune.'
1st year Korean Studies student, Sheffield

'Cover your plates with cling film and save on the washing up.'
3rd year Forensic Science student, Wolverhampton

Try Slivers of Time

- Can't commit to regular hours of working, but need to earn money? Then Slivers-of-Time working could be just for you.

- Slivers-of-Time working is for anyone with spare hours to 'sell' to local employers. Ideal for students, this new way of working takes the idea of casual work a sophisticated step further and will give you immediate cash, a range of skills and a verified CV of successful short bookings.

- Work-seekers are called Sellers because they sell their time and skills and interested companies bid for them in an eBay-style auction. This is how it works. It's 5p.m. and you realise you have a couple of hours to spare that evening, say 6p.m. to 9p.m., so you enter that on to the Slivers of Time website and wait for a text message from an employer – or employers. If you are a good, reliable worker, you will get a higher rating and more jobs.

- The scheme was successfully piloted in East London in 2006. Since then a number of new areas have come online. The most recent include Kirklees, Westminster, South Liverpool, Hull, Cambridgeshire, Sheffield, Leeds, Exeter and Bristol and there are more in the pipeline. If your area doesn't come up on the Slivers of Time website, check with the local authority to see if they have a scheme in the pipeline. To find out more and get registered log onto www.sliversoftime.com

Cathryn's story

As an English student at Sussex University, Cathryn was looking for a well-paid summer vacation job. But what she found was an amazing experience and not what you might expect. She became the carer for a paraplegic. When asked why she wanted the job she answered, 'the money'. And in student terms it was good money: £6 an hour for a 24/7 week, every other week. Surprisingly, that was the right answer. Jacob, the young paraplegic, was just 23 and had recently graduated from Sussex University. He wanted someone who saw caring for him as a job, not a mission. Disabled for two years, having jumped into the wrong end of a swimming pool, he was now paralysed from the shoulders down. There was no time in Jacob's life for self-pity. He had a full social life and was an active member of a youth group. So for Cathryn this meant a hectic three months of meetings, social events and driving up and down to London: she even went with him to a summer camp in Wales. By the end, Jacob was a friend rather than a job, and still is. Through him she has met a whole new circle of friends. She earned around £3,500 over the summer and enjoyed every moment of it. She found the job through the Sussex University job shop, which, she says, has some fantastic and unusual well-paid jobs on offer. If caring isn't your scene, how does hot air balloon instructor – in France – grab you?

Term-time working can be fun, as Jono, a third-year student studying Innovative Manufacturing and Technology at Loughborough University, discovered when he joined the OTC.

Jono's story

'It was 3a.m., dark, cold and the middle of winter; I was sleeping in a ditch. A hand grabbed my shoulder and shook me violently – it was my turn to go on sentry duty, there was three inches of snow on the ground and we were under fire . . .

'If you want to earn money and have some fun, join the OTC (it's a kind of cop-out TA for students). There are field weekends once every five weeks, when you are paid over £80 to crawl around in the cold and wet from Friday evening to Sunday with a gun in your hand shooting at the enemy (blanks of course).

'All too often you'll be sleeping out in the open. If you're lucky, you can sling a hammock between two trees and kip down, but that's luxury. Snow isn't as bad as rain. One weekend it tipped it down for 48 hours non-stop, and it doesn't matter how waterproof your gear is: after 10 hours of throwing yourself on the ground and getting into trees, you are soaked to the bone. That's when you start wondering what on earth you are doing there. But

It's a Fact

Pay for students in the OTC is currently £37.48 per day for non-graduate Officer Cadets and £59.24 per day as a Graduate Officer Cadet/ Second Lieutenant (TA).

believe me, it is cracking fun. You feel you've achieved something. It's the camaraderie, the challenge, often the sheer absurdity of it all. There are some fantastic expeditions, like parachute jumping in Cyprus. There was just one drawback – I was on work experience at the time and missed it!'

What work are students doing and how did they find it?

Students seeking evening or weekend work during term time will probably find it easier in a large city than in a small town. London students should fare better than most – which is just as well, since they are among the most financially stretched.

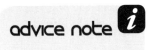

advice note

Don't leave it too late! If you want to work over the Christmas holidays, start planning early, even before you go up to uni – competition is high.

You are most likely to find work in bars, restaurants or general catering, dispatch-riding (must have your own wheels and a fearless mentality!), pizza delivery, office or domestic cleaning, childminding, market research, modelling, offices (temporary work), hotels, and of course shops and supermarkets.

Here are a few examples of what students have been doing:

Type of work	How found job	Pay per hour	University
Clapper loader, BBC Drama	Friend	£9	UCL
Teaching online, US university	Previous employer	£9	St Andrews
Private tutor	Friend	£25	Oxford
Uni ambassador	Uni	£7.25	UCL
Bike mechanic	Asked	£5.35	Huddersfield
Office manager, Shakespeare Co.	–	£6	Oxford
Zoo supervisor	Word of mouth	£5.02	Durham
Website designer	Offer to students	£10	Oxford
Nighclub	Job centre	£5.50	Essex
National Trust admin	Temp agency	£6.50	Lancaster
Interior design	Relation	£5.20	Kingston
Football club turnstile operator	Advert in programme	£7.50	Southampton
Cinema cashier	–	£5.28	Lancaster

Basketball coach	Interview	£10	Wolverhampton
Door supervisor	Rugby team	£8	Luton
Language teacher	Contacts	£12	Sussex
Party planner	–	£5 approx.	Hull
Singer – gigs	Word of mouth	£60	City
Piano teacher	–	£6.80 approx.	Robert Gordon
College bar	Signed up	£5	Oxford
Gym instructor	Gym member	£5.57	Wolverhampton
Ironing	Imagination	£5 approx.	De Montfort
Secret shopper	Job shop	£5.50–£11	Hertfordshire

Further information

Who to contact

- University job shop.
- Employment agencies.
- Job centres.
- Local employers on spec.

What to read

- Local newspaper job ads.
- *Summer Jobs Worldwide* (updated annually) published by Vacation Work. Tel: 020 8997 9000. See also www.trotman.co.uk.

Work experience and internships

What counts as work experience?

'All experience is good and can count as work experience,' according to Liz Rhodes of the National Council for Work Experience (NCWE). 'A placement in an industry where you are being considered for a career is of course excellent and a great way for you to find out if it's right for you, but even a job in the local restaurant, shop or office can help build key transferable skills – from dealing with people to prioritising and keeping a cool head in a crisis,' she says. Make the most of the opportunities and experiences that come up. You'll be surprised just how much you have learned and the challenges you've faced, and it could do wonders for your CV. Visit www.workexperience.org. uk for more advice on work experience, from different types of programmes to how to go about setting up the placement.

What is really meant by work experience?

In terms of students, work experience is the opportunities offered by different organisations for students to gain specific experience of working in an area that will help them with their degree studies, or with entrance into a career. Of course it helps that students are paid to do this work, so finding a placement during the vacations is a double whammy.

What is an internship?

Work experience by a different name. The word 'internship' came from the USA and was spread by multinational companies throughout Europe, where it is now widely used. In the States some internships are unpaid, so it is always worth checking. Sometimes the phrase 'vacation placement' is used.

Who provides work experience?

Many organisations that are unable to offer sponsorship or industrial placement do offer vacation work experience – banks, insurance companies, accountancy and law firms, for example.

Big companies such as BP, Shell, Credit Suisse, Barclays, Microsoft, National Grid, Exxon Mobil, etc. take on a number of students for vacation work each year. (At least they did, but in these troubled financial times, places may not be so easy to find.) Many of these companies offer placements abroad. Some of these placements are better than others. The NCWE holds an annual competition to find the company offering the best work placements. There are a number of different categories covering different sized organisations, charities and length of placements. Winners for 2008–2009 included Centrica (overall winner), Lockheed Martin, Microsoft, px Ltd, Madventure, MERU, Financial Services Authority, Tri-Synergy Ltd and CEI Collins Engineers Ltd.

How do you find a vacation placement?

Companies advertise in your university careers advice centre; or try www.workexperience.org, or www.prospects.ac.uk. Expect a fairly intensive interview, as many companies think vacation work might lead to a more lasting relationship, e.g. full-time employment after you graduate, and are looking at you with this in mind.

You may also find openings in areas where sponsorship is out of the question and industrial placements are difficult to find, such as personnel, marketing or publishing.

If you are considering the media, advertising or journalism you may well find securing paid work impossible. However, if you are prepared to work unpaid, just for the experience, then you might have better luck. Try some of the local radio stations, the many TV channels and TV production companies, local papers (especially the freebies) and the wide range of different magazines that are published. It will be a high-energy activity securing success, as you will need to write to individual editors giving details of how you could add value to their publication or programme. Ideally, select ones you know something about.

Work experience placements are not all one-sided: the employer gets something out of it, too – the chance to look at a possible new employee while providing you with real and interesting experiences and the opportunity to work on 'live' projects as part of a closely integrated and supportive team. But actually getting a work placement is incredibly competitive.

'Vacation placements and workshops are an excellent opportunity for you to learn first-hand what a particular career would involve,' says Caroline Beaton, Graduate Recruitment and Development Manager at law firm Clifford Chance. 'Choosing the right career and the right employer are important and often difficult decisions. There will be a whole range of options to consider and you will want to be as well informed as possible. Spending a couple of weeks with a prospective employer gives you a very good idea of what the work would involve and what kind of atmosphere you would be working in. In addition to vacation placements, there are also opportunities to attend workshops which can offer a more compact way of gaining an insight into a career as a lawyer.'

Clifford Chance offers 105 vacation placements of between two and four weeks during the spring or summer break, and currently pays £270 a week. There are also 100 places available on the firm's two-

Around half a million students look for work placements for the summer vacations. Competition is fierce. To avoid disappointment, start looking as soon as you have your university place. Work experience is becoming an important deciding factor on a student's CV, and an important aid to financial survival. Check out your uni job shop or the website www.prospects.ac.uk.

day winter workshops. As well as gaining an insight into law at Clifford Chance, students also benefit from unlimited use of outstanding facilities, including the staff restaurant, swimming pool and state-of-the-art gymnasium.

How will I find a placement?

Big employers

Large companies such as Procter & Gamble offer what they call summer internships to students on a worldwide scale. They see it as a fair means of assessing students' ability and hope eventually to recruit most of their graduates through their internship scheme. AkzoNobel (which now incorporates ICI) is another major company that offers summer internships and industrial placements, which provide students with an excellent opportunity to gain hands-on work experience. They also see their internships as a chance to assess students' talents and potential for their Graduate Development Programme. They say they look for drive and motivation in students who are team players with good interpersonal skills. Is that you? Your university careers office should have details of these and other programmes with major companies. Otherwise contact employers directly, or look on the net.

Small employers

Small companies can be contacted direct, or you could try Shell Step. This UK-wide scheme is designed to encourage small- and medium-sized employers to take on undergraduates for an eight-week summer placement to carry out a specific project which will be of benefit to both the employer and the student. Students have the opportunity to use their existing skills and the chance to develop new ones while experiencing life in the workplace. Opportunities are open to second and penultimate year undergraduates of any degree discipline.

You'd earn £210 per week. This is in the form of a 'training allowance' and so exempt from tax and National Insurance contributions. In 2008, over 600 projects were undertaken across the UK.

Money, of course, is important, but so too is getting the right job at the end of your degree course. The competition out there is very strong, even for top graduates, so you need to make your CV stand out. Taking part in a Shell Step work placement in an area relevant to your future career aspirations is certainly one way to achieve this.

Internships vs Work Experience

Will the new deal proposed by the government to save new graduates from the dole by offering them internships with major companies dry up the internship market for undergraduates? Only time will tell.

Heather Collier, Director of the NCWE, had this to say: 'Inevitably some companies are cutting back, but it's a question of striking a balance between cost savings in the short term and investing long term in the talent who would be in place and ready to aid company competitiveness when the upturn comes.

'Not sure whether the government initiative is going ahead at the moment. Advice for students is that fewer graduate opportunities means more competition for every undergraduate opportunity for work experience. Joining a university society would give them something to articulate at interview and make them stand out from the hundreds of hopefuls, as would of course any previous work experience. There are lots of good skills learned behind a bar or even waitressing – students shouldn't discount the value of anything they have done or learned outside of their studies.

'Salaries during work experience depend very much on the industry and location of the opportunity. They are very competitive in London, but in the North, typically £14,000–£16,000 pro rata.'

For details, visit the Shell Step website, www.shellstep.org.uk, where you'll find more information and an online application form for the summer programme, or contact your university's careers advisory service.

The following text gives details of what the three winning Shell Step students achieved in 2008.

Chris Haig, Warwick University

Chris was placed at Cressall, the world's foremost resistor manufacturer. They distribute internationally from a factory in Leicester, employing around 100 people. Chris's project was to design and create Standard Operating Procedures (SOPs). Without SOPs, there had been problems of inaccurate communication and training for key factory processes, leading to inefficiencies and waste.

Chris produced seven SOPs with many resultant benefits including slicker training and reduced wastage – this led to an estimated saving of over £6,000 per month. Chris also produced a specific SOP for a Saudi Arabian contract opportunity, which formed a key part of a successful bid worth half a million pounds.

Chris won the title of UK's Most Enterprising Student for Shell Step.

Claire Hoey, Manchester University

Claire worked for Croft Engineering Services during her placement. The project was to identify areas for improvement, then plan and implement actions for business development. A number of areas were looked at, including sales development, segmentation of marketing and new markets.

As a result of Claire's investigative work, she identified that the company would benefit from taking on a sales development consultant in order to market the products direct. A better understanding of their target market and customers was reached, which will in turn, enable better targeted marketing.

Marketing materials have been developed not only in English, but also in French and Italian, as well as revised entries in various business directories, all ensuring that the message about Croft and their products is clear.

Claire won the Judges' Commendation Award at the UK Shell Step finals.

Andrew McIntosh, York University

Andrew worked at Powerchex for his placement. The overall objective of his PR project was to get as much free publicity for the company as possible.

To this end Andrew wrote a number of press releases which he managed to get published in a variety of publications including the *Financial Times*, *The Times* and the *Telegraph* online.

Overall, he achieved promotional savings in excess of £170,000 and this exposure could potentially have been seen 160 million times.

As a result of both this and another project undertaken while Andrew was at Powerchex, the company has two new customers worth an additional £34,000 p.a. and there is a possibility of an exclusive £150,000 new contract with the London Olympic Committee.

Andrew was awarded the Runner-Up prize at the UK Finals of the Shell Step programme.

What Shell Step 2008 students thought of their Shell Step experience

▶ 96% thought their employability had improved as a result of participating in Shell Step.
▶ 97% said they would recommend the Shell Step programme to other students.

What Shell Step 2008 companies thought of their Shell Step experience

▶ 97% of SMEs thought the Shell Step programme met or exceeded their expectations.
▶ 96% of SMEs said the Shell Step project would have a positive impact upon their business's future performance.

Ethnic minorities

The Windsor Fellowship Undergraduate Programme

Windsor Fellowship is a unique charitable organisation that designs and delivers high-impact personal development and leadership programmes. It works in partnership with leading UK employers and educational institutions to ensure that talent from diverse communities is realised. The Leadership Programme for Undergraduates is a two-year professional and personal development programme for Black and Asian minority ethnic (BAME) undergraduates. It includes residential seminars, outdoor challenges, voluntary work, mentoring and a minimum six-week paid internship with a sponsor, providing a real-life insight into employment with leading organisations. Sponsors can vary by year but have regularly included Deutsche Bank, GlaxoSmithKline, John Lewis Partnership, Morgan Stanley, Friends of the Earth and several government departments such as the Department for Innovation, Universities and Skills, the Department of International Development and the Department for Work and Pensions. Application forms and further information about this and other programmes can be downloaded from www.windsor-fellowship.org.

'The foundation has been laid. I believe I have more edge than my counterparts and this is a fantastic position to be in at the beginning of one's career. Thank you!'

Zanele Hlatshwayo

'The WF experience has benefited me by making me more confident, giving me direction and skills needed for the working world as well as introducing me to like-minded people who have become my closest friends.'

Aarti Patel

Oxford University

Oxford University Careers Service offers much support for those looking for work experience. Its website has an extensive, searchable database with many types of work experience opportunities advertised on it at any one time. Opportunities include summer internships, part-time work, careers-related courses, longer placements, volunteer work and overseas work. This is backed up by a well-resourced information room with further details about the organisations concerned, and a wide range of other resources to assist those looking for suitable opportunities. A team of professional careers staff helps with students' work experience queries – ideal for those wanting tips to track down the more elusive work experience opportunities. The service also runs a work experience fair in November, which is useful for those looking for work experience. In addition, the Careers Service delivers via its website advice, guidance and information specific to work experience. Oxford University students and graduates who completed their courses up to four years ago can access all these services by registering online, free, at www.careers.ox.ac.uk.

It's a Fact

More and more students are getting top marks. A record number, 60%, of higher education students gained a first or an upper second degree in 2007.

(HESA statistics for 2007)

Most other university careers services offer similar services. Check with your own university careers service to see what is available. See also 'University job shops' on page 128.

Further information

Who to contact for work experience:

- ▶ local employers
- ▶ major employers
- ▶ course directors
- ▶ college noticeboards
- ▶ your university careers advisers
- ▶ university job shops
- ▶ STEP
- ▶ local employment agencies.

Surf the net

There are a number of websites that can help you find work experience. Here are just a few of the best.

- ▶ Prospects, www.prospects.ac.uk, the graduate careers website, which has a work bank section.
- ▶ National Council for Work Experience (NCWE), www.work-experience.org. Aims to support and develop quality work experience and encourage employers to offer more opportunities.
- ▶ Best part-time jobs: hotrecruit.co.uk; or through UCAS: www.yougo.co.uk.
- ▶ Just Jobs for Students: www.justjobs4students.co.uk, www.student-part-timejobs. com, www.activate.co.uk.
- ▶ And for something different: www.sliversoftime.com.

Making your work experience work for you

The supply of graduates continues to grow and, until now, the graduate labour market has been buoyant, but the credit crunch has changed all that. Many companies have cut their recruitment targets by as much as 17%, according to a High Flyers survey published in January, and some companies are withdrawing offers that have already been made to graduates. Whether this downturn will continue is difficult to predict. Let's hope that by the time the new 2009–2010 undergraduates graduate the pendulum has swung back.

In good times the areas with most vacancies are likely to be accountancy, professional services firms, engineering, industrial companies, investment banks and the public sector. Almost a fifth of all vacancies have been in buying, selling and retailing. London and the south-east of England are generally the graduate hot spots.

What are employers looking for?

Whatever the state of the employment market and whatever area of work interests you, getting that first foot in the door is incredibly competitive. All employers are seeking the best students, and with increasing numbers of graduates coming out of our universities the pool is getting larger and larger. It is not unusual to have 4,000 applicants chasing 100 places. Despite the number of graduates around, many companies surveyed said they were not able to find graduates with the skills they required to fill all their vacancies. Obviously companies can interview only a small proportion of prospective applicants. So how do they seek out the best? What are their criteria? And what do you need to have on your CV, in addition to a good degree and possibly work experience, to make you stand out from the crowd and turn an application into an interview? We asked some major employers.

'We find that candidates who have some work experience, or who have taken the opportunity to broaden their horizons by working in the community or even travelling, have normally had a greater chance to develop and practise the sort of skills we are looking for.'

Graduate Resourcing, Royal Bank of Scotland

'Initiative and follow-through; leadership; thinking and problem-solving; communication; ability to work with others; creativity and innovation; and priority setting. We look for evidence of these skills, which together we'll be able to develop further to run the organisation of the future.'

Human Resources Manager,
Recruitment, Procter & Gamble UK

'We are looking for the next generation of senior managers, the people who will drive our business forward in the future, so the kinds of qualities we are seeking – conceptual and analytical thinking, strong interpersonal skills, ability to influence and motivate others – can't all be demonstrated through a good academic record, important though it is. We want to know about other areas of achievement as well.'

Graduate Recruitment, AkzoNobel (former ICI)

Don't just sit back and think, 'I have a degree – everybody will want me', because the sad fact is they won't. The notion that students can walk into top jobs simply because they have a degree, even in good times, is a fallacy. Not everybody is a blue-chip high-flyer. So if you want one of those top jobs you have got to be proactive and start lining up the kind of skills and experiences that employers are looking for now – which is why getting the right work experience is so important.

Apply by 15 January 2010 for

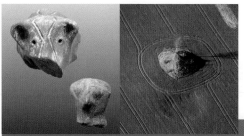

human development in landscapes
GRADUATE SCHOOL AT THE UNIVERSITY OF KIEL

A QUEST OF UNIVERSAL INTEREST IS TO UNDERSTAND HOW HUMANS AND SOCIETIES DEVELOPED OVER TIME IN INTERACTION WITH THEIR ENVIRONMENT. THIS IS THE THEME OF THE GRADUATE SCHOOL 'HUMAN DEVELOPMENT IN LANDSCAPES' AT CHRISTIAN ALBRECHTS UNIVERSITY IN KIEL. HERE, LANDSCAPE IS NOT DEFINED IN ITS PICTURESQUE SENSE, BUT RATHER AS A DYNAMIC SPACE OF SOCIAL, CULTURAL, AND ECOLOGICAL SIGNIFICANCE, WHICH DEVELOPS INTERACTIVELY WITH THE HUMAN SOCIETIES OCCUPYING IT. TO UNDERSTAND HUMAN DEVELOPMENT, WE NEED TO DETAIL THE INTERAC-TIONS BETWEEN HUMANS AND BOTH THEIR PHYSICAL AND THEIR PERCEIVED ENVIRONMENT. EVIDENCE FOR SUCH INTERACTIONS MAY BE OBTAINED FROM BOTH, DIFFERENT ENVIRONMENTAL ARCHIVES AND ARCHAEOLOGICAL OR HISTORICAL SOURCES. ACCORDINGLY, THE GRAD-UATE SCHOOL BRINGS TOGETHER EXPERTISE FROM THE NATURAL AND SOCIAL SCIENCES AND THE ARTS AND HUMANITIES TO REVEAL THE DYNAMICS OF HUMAN DEVELOPMENT - AND THUS OF LANDSCAPE AND LIVING.

The Graduate School 'Human Development in Landscapes', joins expertise from a wide range of disciplines, as represented by 15 institutes from five Faculties at Kiel University, the Schloß Gottorf Archaeological State Museum, and the Leibniz Institute of Science Education (IPN) and on a broad network of 29 international institutions.

AIM

The Graduate School aims to cover the complexity of natural, social, and cultural phenomena involved in the human development in landscapes. These phenomena include climatic and environmental changes, technical innovations, means of sustenance and settlement development, as well as social factors, such as the development of mentalities, social structures and creation of material culture as a result of the human relationship with nature. The school's aim is to educate highly qualified experts with a broad understanding of past human and environmental interactions. Our graduated students should posses advanced analytical skills and the ability to carry out independent research projects.

PROGRAMME

In order to achieve these goals, the post grade programme balances individual research and graduate interdisciplinary courses within three thematic clusters:

CLUSTER 1 | "SOCIETY AND REFLECTION"; CLUSTER 2 | "SOCIAL SPACE AND LANDSCAPE", CLUSTER 3 | "MOBILITY, INNOVATION AND CHANGE"

IN ADDITION, the programme offers an advanced training in communication and soft skills, analytical techniques and use of written sources. All students will have, despite their diverse background, individual tutoring and solutions tailored to their needs and interests. Furthermore international workshops and biweekly colloquia will provide the opportunity for frequent scientific interchange at an international level.

FELLOWSHIPS

The Graduate School publishes openings for grant applications every 2nd year, the next application period is scheduled for autumn 2009. For more information, please contact us.

Contact:
Prof. Dr. Johannes Müller (johannes.mueller@ufg.uni-kiel.de)
Dr. Mara Weinelt (mweinelt@gshdl.uni-kiel.de)
Postal address: Graduate School „Human Development in Landscapes", Olshausenstraße 40, CAU zu Kiel, D-24098 Kiel (Germany) Website: www.uni-kiel.de/landscapes

Christian-Albrechts-Universität zu Kiel

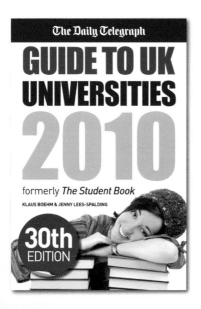

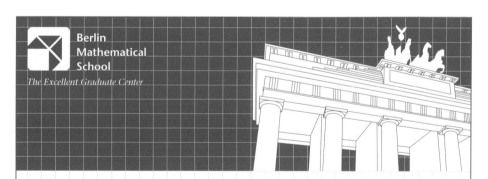

Graduate Recruitment Facts

Here are the findings of research carried out into 100 firms:

- recruitment targets have been cut by 17%
- there are 47% fewer graduate entry-level jobs in the investment/banking/finance sector
- panic on campus that this is shaping up to be one of the worst years in two decades
- graduates will face a more difficult time chasing jobs
- half of leading employers are lowering recruitment targets, which will mean a 6.7% reduction in job availability
- the biggest reduction in jobs will be in investment banking, retailing, accountancy and engineering
- half of employers have downgraded their graduate recruitment targets for 2009
- interviewed in December 2008, only 13% of finalists are confident that they will land the job they want

after graduation. Half think they will have to take any job offered

- a third of employers confirmed they had reduced their graduate recruitment budget for 2008–2009.

Finally:

- graduate jobs in the public sector increased by 51% in 2007
- the armed forces have stepped up recruitment by 17% over the last two years
- graduate starting salaries were expected to rise to an average of £27,000 – a rise of 5.9% – that's if you can find a job.

(Findings of the High Flyers survey, published January 2009)

However, the AGR Summer Review reported that graduate employment is at its lowest for five years and the median graduate starting salary for 2009 is static at £25,000. More AGR findings on page 148.

Job check

Always keep your future career in mind when you head for holiday and even term-time jobs. That's the advice of the National Council for Work Experience. Skills learnt from time spent working can make a great contribution to your CV and help convince a future employer that you are better than the competition. Whatever and wherever the job – supermarket, pub, the student union – make the most of the opportunity to enhance your employability. To help you, here is the NCWE checklist.

- Set some personal objectives for the period of employment before starting a job: what do you want to get out of it, beyond the pay packet?

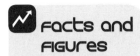

Facts and Figures

Looking further ahead, what is likely to make you happy in 10 years' time? Based on research carried out with 25,000 university applicants:

► having a job that is interesting (82%)

► spending time with family (68%)

► owning a home (46%)

► spending time with friends (46%)

► being in a long-term relationship (45%)

► having a job that contributes to society (40%)

► having a job that pays well (39%)

Future Leaders Survey, conducted by Forum for the Future and UCAS and sponsored by Friends Provident

check

► motivation and enthusiasm
► team working
► oral communication
► flexibility and adaptability
► initiative/being proactive.

► Don't be afraid to ask questions and take notes when being briefed by your boss at the outset. Better to ask now and be clear than make mistakes later.

► Keep a note of challenges you overcome each day and any problem solving required. This demonstrates initiative and prioritising skills.

► Grab any chance to take on more responsibility: undertaking new tasks is a sure way of developing new talents.

► Do the best job you possibly can for self-satisfaction and the possibility of being asked back for the next vacation – maybe even for a permanent position in the future.

► Ask for feedback from your boss and the people you work with – there may be room for improvement – and note successes and achievements: these are what you need to put on your CV.

► Make suggestions – just because you're a holiday worker or work experience student doesn't mean you don't have good ideas, and your colleagues will always appreciate seeing things from a new perspective.

► Keep a diary of your thoughts throughout the placement. This will help you to add your achievements to your CV and will show you how far you've come.

► Ask for a reference from your boss; it will stand you in good stead for moving on to a permanent job.

► Work hard, but take the time to get to know your colleagues and enjoy the work atmosphere. After all, you may be spending every day there for a while!

Stop press!

► www.getalife.org.uk provides up-to-the-minute information on employment issues for students and graduates.

▶ www.prospects.ac.uk/chat is a communications channel enabling students to put their careers questions to big-name recruiters.

▶ Prospects also has a 24-hour chat room, where job-seeking students and graduates who wake up in a cold sweat in the middle of the night need not be in anguish alone. See www.prospects.ac.uk/links/gradtalk.

What to read

▶ *Prospects Pocket Directory*: hundreds of jobs for students and graduates – from your university careers service.

▶ *Hobsons Careers Directory*: careers service or public library. To order, tel: 0870 900 2665 or visit www.trotman.co.uk.

Industrial placements

Will I get one?

The idea of the four-year sandwich course that includes an industrial placement was never envisaged as a financial lifesaver, but many students find that a year in industry, with a good salary, helps them to clear their debts while they gain invaluable experience. But with more higher education institutions developing more sandwich courses, finding good industrial placements is becoming increasingly difficult. This is felt mostly where courses are fairly new and the institutions haven't yet built up a good rapport with industrial concerns. When applying to universities, it is worth checking out the extent and quality of the industrial placements offered to students. There are essentially two sorts of sandwich courses: those where you take a year out – usually the third year – to work in industry; and courses in which you alternate six months at university with six months at work.

advice note

'Dress for success' is the advice to job-seeking students from Prospects. Whether attending an interview, recruitment fair or assessment day, creating a favourable impression is important. Getting the right look shows you understand the employer's business.

Facts and Figures

Can it be true?
A quarter of top graduate programmes will pay new recruits more than £30,000 when they start work. The most generous salaries are those on offer from investment banks (median figure £38,000), law firms (median figure £37,400) and management consulting firms (median figure £31,000). The highest published graduate starting salary in 2009 was £40,000, offered by Aldi for their graduate development programme. Aldi also provided its recruits with an Audi A4 car. Nice work if you can get it!

High Flyers: The Graduate Market 2009 report

Salary Check

- ▶ Graduate vacancies fall for the first time since 2003 with an expected decrease of 5.4% on 2008.

- ▶ Starting salaries frozen: median starting salaries in summer 2009 expected to remain at £25,000.

- ▶ Top median starting salaries of £37,000 were paid for legal work and investment banking in 2008.

- ▶ Top starting salaries in legal firms were £38,000 in 2008. Median figure £37,000.

- ▶ General management has dropped to bottom of the AGR salary league table for graduates.

- ▶ 21% of graduate recruits joining 43.2% of AGR companies who responded to survey came from minority ethnic backgrounds.

(Association of Graduate Recruiters Winter Review 2009)

In the beginning, industrial placements were mainly for courses in engineering, but increasingly courses in business studies, retail, computer sciences and languages include an industrial placement year. Aberystwyth has taken this a step further with its YES scheme.

What is the YES scheme?

Aberystwyth University has pioneered an initiative to give any student in the university who is not already on a sandwich course the opportunity to take an industrial year out. The scheme is called YES (Year in Employment Scheme), and currently over 40 students at Aberystwyth are saying YES to the opportunity. They come from a range of disciplines: arts, economics and social sciences, information studies, international politics and the sciences. You can choose a placement that is relevant to your degree subject, such as accounting, marketing, scientific research, events management, environmental conservation work, or use the time to experience work in an area that is totally new to you, such as human resources, retail management or production management.

You can even work abroad: YES students have recently worked in Europe, Australia, New Zealand, Africa and the USA. Students also work with major employers in the private, public and voluntary sectors such as IBM, KPMG, the Environment Agency, Perkins Engines and the Centre for Ecology and Hydrology. Salaries vary from around £8,000 up to £18,000, although some voluntary placements may only pay expenses. With everybody now having to pay fees, earning money for a year during study is a definite bonus.

Aberystwyth is adamant – with some justification – that the skills learned during the year out have enhanced both degree performance and employment prospects. The latest figures from the university show that students who have undertaken work experience gain employment after graduation more quickly than students who have not participated in any form of work experience. Joanne Hiatt, YES Project Officer, believes that 'YES provides an opportunity for students to develop their employability skills whilst earning money and having some fun!'

Emma's Story

Emma is a final-year geography student at Aberystwyth. This is how she spent her year out.

'Hi

'I should have been panicking over my finals as a third year, but there I was in Sheffield having a great time peering into drains and studying the birdlife on our landfill site – and believe me you can learn a lot from a red-legged partridge and fieldfare.

'I had decided to take a year out to do a year in industry. And was lucky enough to get a job working at Outokumpu Stainless, a steel works in Sheffield as an environmental placement student in their environment department. It was a job packed with interest, based mainly around environmental management and monitoring. I also had to be willing to talk to lots of different people at various different levels of the company from managers down to the people on the shop floor (steel makers).

advice note

Graduate recruitment in the UK is heading into a chilly period, with widespread vacancy reductions and a salary standstill, reports the *AGR Winter Review*. Here are some suggestions to enhance your employment chances from AGR employers:

► research the company before applying
► apply early
► be prepared to relocate mentally by broadening your job criteria
► be positive – graduates who are indecisive are not hired
► get experience to enhance your soft skills, e.g. volunteering or a gap year
► get into work somehow – temporary paid employment is better than no employment.

Taking extra qualifications after graduation was not given the thumbs up.

'I lived in a shared house close to where I worked. I didn't know my other housemates until I moved in, but it worked well. It cost me £364 per month, which is not cheap, but worth it. I made lots of friends in the company, but they mostly lived outside Sheffield, so we didn't socialise much in the evenings. There were other students in other departments and a company social was organised for us all. While in Sheffield I spent a lot of time walking and exploring the Peak District.

'I was paid £12,000 for the year and managed to save around £200 a month, enough to run a car.

'I know dipping into boreholes and testing water treatment processes may not suit everyone, but I really enjoyed my placement and would certainly recommend a year out to everyone.

'Cheers,

'Emma'

When is the best time to do a year in industry?

If you take your year in industry at 20 you are going to earn substantially more than you would at 18, so it could help pay off your debts – you will also know more about your topic so the experience can be more valuable. But if you take a year out before you start at university, the money you save will help to ease your finances once you start managing on student funding, and the experience will help with your studies.

Another point to consider: most universities charge fees during a year out in industry, and though these are much reduced – around 50% of the current fee. If your industrial placement is taken as a gap year either before or after university you won't have to pay this.

Could an industrial placement lead to sponsorship/employment?

Sometimes a year in industry is an integral part of a sponsorship scheme (see Chapter 7 for full details). If it is not, a successful period of work experience can result in your employer offering to sponsor you for the rest or the whole of your degree. With some three-quarters of employers who recruit new graduates providing work experience, there is no doubt that the student who has spent a successful placement with an employer is in a good position regarding future employment. An industrial placement provides the opportunity for you to get to know your employer and your employer to get to know you. It will help you to develop work-related skills that employers value.

The Year in Industry: Work, Earn, Win

Get Ahead

If you are looking for paid work experience in industry, which could really help your future career and possibly lead to university sponsorship, the Year in Industry (YINI) are the people to contact.

The Year in Industry is a nationwide programme run by the education charity EDT. Working with internationally renowned companies, YINI offers work placements that are challenging, rewarding and deliver real business experience to help you stand out from the crowd.

All YINI placements give you the skills and knowledge employers are looking for, the experience will help you make the most of university – and you get to earn while you learn.

What YINI can do for you

A work placement with YINI will:

- ▶ give your CV the competitive edge
- ▶ let you try out your degree or career choice

- ▶ give you 'real work' experience
- ▶ pay while you learn
- ▶ help you make the most of university
- ▶ help set you up for life with contacts, experience and opportunities.

In some instances, placement companies have gone on to sponsor YINI people through university, and even offer them jobs at the end of their degree.

Who will I work for?

YINI only works with companies who are committed to giving you real business and industry experience. Its partners range from leading FTSE 100 companies to small innovative start-ups.

What kind of job will I do?

YINI has placements for students interested in all areas of engineering, science, IT, e-commerce, business, marketing, finance and logistics.

You will become a trusted member of the team, be given your own responsibilities and be expected to deliver results. The satisfaction you get will be huge.

Applications for placements should be made as soon as possible. The earlier students apply, the more opportunities are available.

Placements follow the academic year and students earn competitive salaries during their placement. An administration fee of £25 is payable after application and acceptance onto the scheme. For further information, contact: The Year in Industry National Office, University of Southampton, Hampshire SO17 1BJ. Tel: 023 8059 7061. Fax: 023 8059 7570. Email: info@yini.org.uk Website: www.yini. org.uk.

What the students say

'I met great people, worked in a fast-moving and friendly team and it gave me a much clearer idea of the kind of career I want after graduating. As a result of my experience I am a much more confident person than when I left school a year ago.'

William Jackson, Natural Sciences, Cambridge, worked for 1 Ltd

'The projects I worked on were very challenging, but the feeling of satisfaction after they were complete made it all worth while.'

Emma Stephenson, Aeronautical Engineering, Glasgow, worked for Shell

'By doing a YINI placement I was given roles and responsibilities that would never usually be offered to a person of my age and experience. I know that I will carry the skills that I've learned to my degree course, allowing me to gain a lot more out of the university experience. I know how to apply my knowledge from the classroom to the workplace and I am now more aware of managing my money.'

Nicol Perryman, Mathematics, Newcastle, worked for Permoid Industries

Further information

Thinking about taking a sandwich course?

The internet is the place to look. There are a number of electronic resources that can help in the search for sandwich courses or other work placements.

- ▶ Sandwich courses are indicated with '4SW' on the Universities and Colleges Admissions Service (UCAS) site: www.ucas.com.
- ▶ ASET (Association for Sandwich Education and Training) is the national body for work-based learning practitioners. It's an educational charity that promotes

best practice for work placements, as well as providing support and advice for all professionals who work in the field. Contact: ASET, The Work-Based and Placement Learning Association, Department for Innovation, Universities and Skills (DIUS), W11 Moorfoot, Sheffield S1 4PQ. Tel: 0114 221 2902. Fax: 0114 221 2903. Email: aset@asetonline.org. Website: www.asetonline.org.

▶ The National Council for Work Experience (NCWE) has useful information on a range of work experience opportunities. Website: www.workexperience.org. If you want advice on work experience they are the people to ask.

Around 112,000 students went on sandwich placements each year, according to ASET.

Who to ask about placements

If you are not a sponsored student, contact your careers department at university. It will have a list of possible employers who might offer placements.

Contact employers directly – don't forget the smaller companies, which might have just one placement but don't advertise in case they get deluged.

What to read

▶ *Engineering Opportunities for Students and Graduates*, published by Professional Engineering Publishing Ltd, available free from IMechE, c/o Marketing & Communications Department, 1 Birdcage Walk, London SW1H 9JJ. Email: marketing@imeche.org.uk. Don't forget to include your address.

▶ *Everything You Wanted to Know about Sponsorship, Placements and Graduate Opportunities*, regularly updated and published by Amoeba Publications. Available from Trotman, tel: 0870 900 2665, or visit www.trotman.co.uk/bookshop.

Facts and Figures

Credit crunch reassurance

▶ Research shows that graduates are more likely to be employed than those with the next highest qualification and are more likely to return to employment following periods of unemployment or economic inactivity. (Universities UK)

▶ Recent figures from HESA show that unemployment among recent graduates continues to fall.

▶ Graduates in the UK also enjoy one of the highest financial returns of any OECD country. (Universities UK)

CHAPTER 6

Taking a gap year

This chapter looks at all the opportunities open to those who opt to take a gap year before or during university.

- ▶ Why take a gap year? (page 156)

- ▶ A gap year to raise money (page 156)

- ▶ A voluntary work gap year (page 159)

- ▶ A gap year for travel abroad (page 169)

- ▶ The student travel scene (page 172)

Why take a gap year?

Taking a gap year after A levels is becoming increasingly popular: each year around 230,000 students are thought to take a year out. After 13 solid years on the academic treadmill many young people just feel that they need a chance to recharge their batteries. Most universities will accept deferred entry; some institutions actively encourage it. But don't assume that deferred entry is an automatic right. You must always ask, and if the course is popular, you may be refused.

It's a fact

520,000 UK residents take a gap year each year (not all students) and it's estimated that by 2010 that number will increase to 2 million, with the total expenditure reaching £11 billion (source: Mintel). Gaptravelguides.co.uk claims that a staggering 70% of students aim to take a gap year and 75% of people are seriously considering taking a career break as a means of broadening their horizons and experiencing new cultures. As yet, it is not known what effect the current economic downturn will have on these figures.

Many young people use their gap year to gain a skill or experience in a specific organisation as well as to make money. Often this results in them having a ready-made job to walk into during vacations, once they have started their degree course. Others just want fun and new experiences or the chance to do something to help others. Here we look at three very different kinds of gap year: to raise money, to do voluntary work and to travel.

A gap year to raise money

If your aim is to save money, your best bet is to work as close to home as possible, where bed and board are likely to be at a very advantageous rate – if not free – and to avoid travel costs. In the past there were always plenty of jobs going in shops, restaurants and pubs, and you might still be lucky. Go for the multiple outlets, such as Next, Tesco or a pub chain. You will then have street cred, and may be able to find a part-time term-time job in your university town.

Since you have a whole year to work and a clutch of A levels to offer, you might be able to find a job with better pay and which stretches your ability more. But be realistic: you are not going to earn great bags of gold. A gap-year student could expect to earn at least the minimum wage, which is £4.77 per hour for 18–21-year-olds (£4.83 from October 2009) and £5.73 per hour for those aged 22 and over (£5.80 from October 2009). But you might be offered more. One student we interviewed was earning £15 an hour, but that was teaching abroad. Save just a quarter of that and you will be thankful for it once you start at uni – the first term is very expensive. Of the students we contacted who had taken a gap year, 54% said they had managed to save on average £2,000. If, on the other hand, you are thinking of using your savings to travel, keep an eye on exchange rates. As we print, the exchange rates for the pound against the dollar and the euro are very low, and your money may not go very far.

A gap year isn't only about earning money: many students see it as a chance to gain useful experience towards their career, to gain skills or to help others.

What students did in their gap year

- ▶ Joanne worked for a supermarket driving a fork-lift truck, but managed to get heavily into debt before she even started an equine science course at Aberystwyth.
- ▶ Ruth travelled in Nicaragua for six months, but still managed to save £600 for uni working in a pub. She is studying Latin American studies at Essex.
- ▶ Lucky Ryan split his time between working in a ski resort and surfing in Australia before his engineering course at Cambridge.
- ▶ Christopher worked in a sausage shop, where he learned how to mix up a 'mean banger'. It paid for driving lessons, got him his wheels and gave him a £2,000 bank balance when he started a course in business administration at the University of the West of England.
- ▶ Kerry started her year working in Disneyland near Paris. She then worked at Eurocamp in Italy and Camp America in Northern California. She didn't save a bean but had a great time. She went on to study maths at Liverpool.
- ▶ Giles worked as an associate director on a film project before studying politics at Hull.
- ▶ Jordan went to China to study martial arts at a school near Si Ping City but saved remarkably little. He is now studying Chinese language and history at Sheffield.
- ▶ Conni took a job as a classroom assistant in the dance and drama department of a school and sometimes helped out with PE – useful experience for her degree course in dance and sport at Wolverhampton University.
- ▶ Edward spent his year singing in gigs and is still wowing the revellers in clubs around London while financing his music degree at City University.
- ▶ Kate had a fun-packed year, spending five months volunteering in Nepal, five months working and two months travelling around Canada before taking up theological studies at St Andrews.
- ▶ Laura taught English in Qatar before starting her own English studies at St Andrews.
- ▶ Rebecca travelled to Japan and Australia, where she taught. She is now at Lampeter.
- ▶ Peggy lived and worked in a school in New Zealand, returning to start her studies at St Andrews after a year.

▶ Rachel devoted her year to others, working as a carer for the elderly for five months and then for a charity as a volunteer. She is now at St George's studying medicine.

▶ Before going up to Oxford, Tim worked for DEFRA and then for a charity in South Africa.

▶ Lily worked as a trainee behaviour support worker in schools, which was good experience for her course in applied criminology at Huddersfield.

▶ Globetrotting Laurel undertook volunteer conservation and community work in Kenya and then worked as an office assistant in an American summer camp. She is now studying zoology at Durham.

▶ Anna's gap year was a glorious mix of holidaying in Australia and Canada and skiing in Switzerland, and working as a nursery nurse. She is now studying developmental biology at UCL.

▶ Sapphire worked hard for 11 months in research at Merck Neuroscience Research Centre before taking a month off in Kenya. She is now studying medicine at UCL.

▶ Mark took a Diploma in Art Design Foundation Studies course but still managed to save £1,000 towards his course in interior architecture at Nottingham Trent University.

▶ Julia 'A' went to Calcutta with the Baptist Missionary Society, where she worked with street children, and lived with the Mother Teresa nuns. She is now studying law at Reading.

▶ Julia 'B' took a job in a factory to get enough money to join a volunteer conservation project in Australia. On her return she worked at a scientific research centre to gain experience and save money – around £3,000 – for her degree in natural sciences at Durham.

▶ Rory was on duty at the Odeon cinema for six months, then blew everything he'd saved on a fabulous six-month trip to Australia. He is now studying English at Durham.

Students talk in more detail about their gap years on page 164.

Further information

Who to contact

▶ Year Out Group – see page 159.

▶ Banks, insurance companies, accountancy firms – many offer work experience; always worth a try.

▶ Shops, supermarkets, chain stores – try to find an organisation with a number of local outlets, and one that offers a training scheme.

▶ Teaching – you don't actually need any training to take up a temporary position as assistant teacher or matron in a preparatory school. As an assistant matron you could find yourself darning socks and getting the kids up in the morning. As an assistant teacher you'd probably be involved in organising sport and out-of-school activities, coaching and supervising prep and classes when staff are away. Current rates of pay are in line with the minimum wage with a small amount deducted if food, accommodation, etc. are included. Term ends in July, so you would then have two months' travelling time. For gap year vacancies try Gabbitas Educational Consultants, Carrington House, 126–130 Regent Street, London W1B 5EE. Tel: 020 7734 0161. Websites: www.gabbitas.co.uk andwww.teacher-recruitment.co.uk.

A voluntary work gap year

How would you like to undertake projects in Africa, Mexico or Peru, while having the experience of a lifetime? Go on an Art History Abroad course to Venice, Florence, Bologna? Work and travel in the USA? Help the needy – homeless people, young offenders, children with special needs? Take a Trekforce or Greenforce expedition with the chance to help international conservation projects in such far-flung places as Belize and Guyana? Do you see yourself working to save endangered rainforests, wildlife or coral reefs, or perhaps developing some theatre techniques? All or any of these are possible.

Year Out Group

Once you've made the gap year decision, the Year Out Group is a good starting point if you are seeking adventure or a great experience.

The Year Out Group is an association of 38 leading year-out organisations that was launched in 2000 to promote the concept and benefits of well-structured year-out programmes, to promote models of good practice and to help young people and their advisers select suitable and worthwhile projects. All the organisations have agreed to adhere to a code of practice and appropriate operating guidelines. Projects last from a few weeks to a year and are available in the UK or overseas. For many of them you will have to finance yourself (this is considered part of the challenge) – but others do pay quite well. It is wise to start your planning early and to do it in as much detail as possible. In a full gap year there is time to work to earn money as well as to work on a project that is worthwhile, exciting and which could change your life forever. Each year, Year Out Group produces a booklet called *Planning your year out?*, which provides information on planning a well-structured gap year. The booklet is sent to all schools, colleges and careers offices each autumn and can also be downloaded from the group's website. To learn more about the members of Year Out Group and the opportunities they offer, read on. You can also contact them directly or via the Year Out Group website, www.yearoutgroup.org, from which you can also request a copy of the booklet.

So what's on offer?

▶ Africa & Asia Venture – combines teaching and coaching sports, plus community projects, with adventure in Africa, India, Nepal, Thailand or Mexico. Tel: 01380 729009; email: av@aventure.co.uk; website: www.aventure.co.uk.

▶ African Conservation Experience – opportunities to work on game and nature reserves in southern Africa. Tel: 0870 241 5816; email: info@ConservationAfrica.net; website: www.ConservationAfrica.net.

▶ Art History Abroad – courses including a Grand Tour. Tel: 01284 774772; email: info@arthistoryabroad.com; website: www.arthistoryabroad.com.

▶ Blue Ventures – projects and expeditions that enhance global marine conservation and research. Tel: 020 8341 9819; email: madagascar@blueventures.org; website: www.blueventures.org.

▶ BUNAC work and travel programmes – USA, Canada, Australia, New Zealand. Volunteer programmes in Africa, Asia and Latin America. Tel: 020 7251 3472; email: enquiries@bunac.org.uk; website: www.bunac.org/yog (see also BUNAC, page 170).

▶ Camp America – join the staff at a summer camp. Tel: 020 7581 7373; email: enquiries@campamerica.co.uk; website: www.campamerica.co.uk.

▶ CESA – language courses abroad. Tel: 0120 921 1800; email: info@cesalanguages. com; website: www.cesalanguages.com.

▶ Changing Worlds – offers volunteer and paid placements worldwide. Tel: 01883 340960; email: ask@changingworlds.co.uk; website: www.changingworlds.co.uk.

▶ Coral Cay Conservation – coral reef and rainforest conservation in the Philippines, Tobago and Papua New Guinea. Tel: 0207 620 1411; email: info@coralcay.org; website: www.coralcay.org.

▶ Cross-Cultural Solutions – volunteer work with carefully selected partner programmes in Africa, Asia, Eastern Europe and South America. Tel: 0845 458 2781; email: infouk@crossculturalsolutions.org; website: www.crossculturalsolutions.org.

▶ Flying Fish – full range of courses to help you upgrade your water sport and winter sport qualifications. Tel: 0871 250 2500; email: mail@flyingfishonline.com; website: www.flyingfishonline.com.

▶ Frontier – conservation and volunteer projects worldwide. Tel: 020 7613 2422; info@frontier.ac.uk; website: www.frontier.ac.uk.

▶ Gap Year Diver – diving training from beginner to divemaster plus learning, cultural, conservation and adventure activities in Egypt, Costa Rica, Venezuela, Fiji and the Bahamas. Tel: 0845 257 3292; email; info@gapyeardiver.com; website: www.gapyeardiver.com.

▶ Global Vision International – conservation and humanitarian projects in over 30 countries. Tel: 01727 250250; email: info@gvi.co.uk; website: www.gvi.co.uk.

- Global Xperience – international volunteer placements, sports qualification courses in six continents. Tel: 0871 221 2929; email: sports@globalexperience.com; website: www.globalxperience.com.

- Greenforce – join a conservation project and help scientific understanding. Tel: 020 7470 8888; info@greenforce.org; website: www.greenforce.org.

- i to i – work worldwide in media, health, building, teaching, conservation, community work. Tel: 0870 442 3042; email: info@i-to-i.com; website: www.i-to-i.com.

- International Academy – winter sport instructor courses in Canada and New Zealand. Tel: 029 2066 0200; website: www.theinternationalacademy.com; email: info@theinternationalacademy.com.

- Lattitude Global Volunteering – assist in schools, hospitals, on conservation projects and outdoor projects in 34 countries. Tel: 0118 959 4914; email: volunteer@lattitude.org.uk; website: www.lattitude.org.uk.

- The Leap – volunteer and paid work placements in Africa, Asia, South America and Australia. Tel: 01672 519922; email: info@theleap.co.uk; website: www.theleap.co.uk.

- Madventurer – volunteer projects as part of a team or as an individual in Africa and elsewhere. Tel: 0845 121 1996; email: team@madventurer.com; website: www.madventurer.com.

- Nonstop Adventure – winter sport instructor courses in Canada. Water sport experiences from UK. Tel: 0845 365 1525; email: info@nonstopski.com; website: www.nonstopadventure.com.

- Outreach International – volunteer projects with local communities in Mexico, Costa Rica, Sri Lanka, Cambodia and Ecuador. Tel: 01458 274957; email: info@outreachinternational.co.uk; website: www.outreachinternational.co.uk.

- Oyster Worldwide – paid and voluntary work in Canada, Tanzania, Nepal, Chile, Brazil and Romania. Tel: 01892 770771; website: www.oysterworldwide.com.

- Peak Leaders – winter sport instructor courses and more in Canada and elsewhere. Tel: 01337 860079; email: info@peakleaders.com; website: www.peakleaders.com.

- Personal Overseas Development – volunteer projects in Nepal, Peru, Tanzania, Thailand. Tel: 01242 250 901; email: info@thepodsite.co.uk; website: www.thepodsite.co.uk.

- Projects Abroad – projects in Africa, Latin America, Asia, Eastern Europe. Tel: 01903 708300; email: info@projects-abroad.co.uk; website: www.projects-abroad.co.uk.

- Project Trust – worthwhile volunteer placements in 26 different countries. Tel: 01879 230444; website: www.projecttrust.org.uk; apply online info@projecttrust.org.uk.

- Quest Overseas – projects and expeditions in South America and Africa. Tel: 01273 777 206; email: info@questoverseas.com; website: www.questoverseas.com.

- ▶ Raleigh – challenging community and environmental projects overseas. Tel: 020 7183 1270; email: info@raleigh.org.uk; website: www.raleighinternational.org.
- ▶ Real Gap Experience – a variety of programmes in over 30 countries. Tel: 01892 516164; email: info@realgap.co.uk; website: www.realgap.co.uk.
- ▶ Travellers – voluntary teaching, work experience and conservation projects on many continents. Tel: 01903 502595; email: info@travellersworldwide.com; website: www.travellersworldwide.com.
- ▶ Trekforce Worldwide – project-based expeditions and volunteer placements in Central and South America. Tel: 0207 866 8110; email: info@trekforce.org.uk; website: www.trekforce.org.uk.
- ▶ VentureCo – expeditions offering language training, conservation and community projects in challenging environments. Tel: 01926 411122; email: mail@ventureco-worldwide.com; website: www.ventureco-worldwide.com.
- ▶ Village-to-Village – a project-driven charity providing volunteer placements in northern Tanzania involving teaching, sustainable agriculture, HIV/Aids awareness training and other local initiatives. Tel: 01274 235558; email: enquiries@village-to-village.org.uk; website: www.village-to-village.org.uk.
- ▶ Worldwide Experience – conservation and community projects in southern Africa and elsewhere. Tel: 01483 860560; e-mail: info@worldwideexperience.com; website: www.worldwideexperience.com. Provides valuable advice on planning.
- ▶ Year in Industry – places potential graduates in leading industrial companies in the UK. Tel: 023 8059 7061; email: enquiries@yini.org.uk; website: www.yini.org.uk.
- ▶ Year Out Drama – develop your theatre skills while working with professionals. Tel: 01789 266245; fax: 01789 267524; email: yearoutdrama@stratford.ac.uk; website: www.yearoutdrama.com.
- ▶ Year Out Group – the association that has brought together all the leading year-out organisations mentioned here. Provides valuable advice on planning your gap year. Tel: 01380 816696; email: info@yearoutgroup.org; website: www.yearoutgroup.org.

Voluntary work abroad in developing countries is not as easy to find as it once was, especially if you have no recognised skill, and many organisations seek people over 21. Some projects will pay maintenance costs, and sometimes give pocket money, but it is not unusual for volunteers to be asked to pay their own fares.

Conservation work is much easier to find, both in the UK and abroad. Most of it is completely voluntary and unpaid. You might even be asked to contribute to your food and accommodation. You could become involved in projects for the National Trust, the Royal Society for the Protection of Birds, on the restoration of cathedrals, working with disabled people and underprivileged children, painting, decorating – it's amazing what some students turn their hands to.

While the financial returns from both voluntary and conservation work are likely to be zero, in terms of your CV it could be of considerable value. Employers are impressed by the altruistic and enterprising qualities needed for voluntary work.

You could also try:

Long-term volunteering

The National Trust

If you are looking to fill a gap year, change career or gain work experience, and have six months or more to spare, then you could join the National Trust's full-time volunteering programme. As a full-time volunteer you could get involved in many different activities at Trust properties throughout England, Wales and Northern Ireland. You could work alongside a warden or gardener; assist house staff with aspects of running and preserving historic buildings and help with learning and events co-ordination. Training is provided and accommodation may be available. There's no pay, but out-of-pocket expenses are covered. For further information, contact the central volunteering team on 01793 817632, visit the National Trust website at www.nationaltrust.org.uk/volunteering or email volunteers@nationaltrust.org.uk.

You can also volunteer for National Trust Working Holidays. Fruit picking and costume conservation are just two of the more unusual opportunities on offer. The Trust runs more than 400 conservation working holidays a year throughout England, Wales and Northern Ireland for as little as £70 for a week's full board and lodging (from £45 for a weekend). They take place at beautiful Trust locations and are open to volunteers aged 16 and over. For a current brochure write to Working Holidays, Sapphire House, Roundtree Way, Norwich NR7 8SQ, phone the brochure line on 0844 800 3099, email working.holidays@nationaltrust.org.uk or see their website: www.nationaltrust.org.uk/workingholidays.

Archaeological digs

It won't earn you a fortune – more likely nothing (subsistence pay is rarely given) – but it can be fascinating work. See the special section included in every issue of *British Archaeology*, published six times a year by the Council for British Archaeology, St Mary's House, 66 Bootham, York YO30 9BZ, tel: 01904 671417. The supplement gives full details of current UK digs. For subscription rates (including student reductions) and forms see the CBA website at www. britarch.ac.uk/shop/index.html. But the magazine should be available in public libraries and selected retail outlets. For full details of membership and details of digs in your area, see the CBA website, www.britarch.ac.uk/briefing/field.asp.

Alternatively, contact the county archaeologist for your district: details available from www.torc.org.uk/orgsearch.asp, under 'local government archaeologists'. For archaeological digs abroad phone the Institute of Archaeology to contact Archaeology Abroad on 020 7504 4750.

BTCV

BTCV runs around 252 conservation holidays worldwide throughout the year. Prices start at about £60 for a weekend in the UK. Projects include pond maintenance, tree planting, step building, hedge laying, scrub clearance, drystone walling and community development. Contact BTCV, Sedum House, Mallard Way, Doncaster DN4 8DB. Tel: 01302 388 883; email: information@ btcv.org.uk. You can browse and book online at www.btcv.org/shop.

In the case studies below, four students talk about their gap year and the skills they gained.

Sophie's year

'I started my year as a clapper loader on the BBC drama *Casanova*. A friend, who is a film cameraman, was working on the drama and needed an assistant. Take 1 Scene 1 – my role was to operate the clapperboard and then load and re-load the camera with film. It was hard work – a six-day week of 50–60 hours. Often we were on the road by 4.30a.m. to ensure we were at the next location before the day's filming began. We (cast and crew) even spent two weeks filming in Croatia. But what an experience! I was rubbing shoulders with the stars – David Tennant (of *Dr Who* fame), Matt Lucas (of *Little Britain*) and Peter O'Toole – and earning fantastic money – £485 a week for 10 weeks' work. I also worked on a couple of music videos – nobody famous yet!

'Then it was straight off to the Amazon for another amazing experience. I joined a team working with the Kichwa tribe in Ecuador to save the rainforest. To explain: lying between two national parks in Ecuador is a corridor of pristine virgin rainforest beneath which is thought to be a large reserve of oil and gas. The aim was to keep the oilmen out by establishing that this was an area inhabited by rare species. We travelled – mostly by canoe – to a remote area 200 nautical miles into the rainforest. There we met and lived with the tribespeople. Living was very rudimentary, a thatched shack raised from the ground to keep dry. I ate snake and stingray – not recommended – and you never went anywhere alone or without a whistle and compass. Step a few metres off a path and you were lost. We discovered a rare baby howler monkey, some extremely rare species of birds and trees. I can't profess to be an ardent eco-warrior, to be honest I went for the experience, but what we achieved was very rewarding.'

Sophie is now studying human sciences at UCL.

Skills gained:

▶ living the dream
▶ being away from restrictions
▶ learning to cope/addressing fear whatever the drama, e.g. a cockroach in your bed
▶ knowing yourself.

Laura's year

For her gap year, Laura decided to join her parents in Qatar, where they had just moved. Her original plan was to do work experience with the Al Jazeera news organisation. When that fell through, she got work with an English language school just five minutes' walk from home. In Qatar everyone is keen to learn English.

Teaching was a new experience for Laura: 'Don't worry, we'll give you a full course of instruction,' they said. One day of learning the ropes and Laura was trying to control a class of boisterous six-year-olds. 'I'd been thrown in at the deep end, and I was not happy. They were very sweet, very chatty, and very determined, if they didn't want to do something, you couldn't make them.'

She found teaching adult classes suited her better. Everyone in Qatar has a smattering of English – gained from TV, films, pop music, the web – so even with no Arabic herself she could make progress and she learned a lot about their culture. All teachers have to speak English, so she also found herself travelling out into the country to teach teachers – now that was a challenge.

She was well paid – £15 an hour, very different from the £5.83 she currently earns as a waitress in Scotland. During her gap year Laura saved £5,000 towards her first year at the University of St Andrews where she is studying English.

Skills gained:

- ► the joy of teaching
- ► self-confidence
- ► ability to adapt to different cultures.

Will's year

Will worked like crazy as a manual labourer for the first four months of his year to earn enough money to take a French language course in Grenoble – which he did, and learned to ski at the same time.

However, getting his course sorted out proved difficult. The company he found on the internet to organise his trip let him down in many ways. And that set him thinking – 'I'm sure I could do it better.'

Back in the UK and studying law at Durham, he decided to have a go at setting up a web-based company of his own that would send people on French language courses to Grenoble.

This was completely new territory for Will. He had never run a company before. With the help of Neil, an economics graduate of Sheffield University, and another friend based in Grenoble, he set up and registered his company, calling it Apprendre. He negotiated with the course providers, and developed a website to advertise the programmes offered. Check it out: www.apprendre.co.uk.

Skills gained:

- ► setting up a business
- ► dealing with people
- ► marketing
- ► negotiating.

Edward's year

Edward's gap year began to take off four weeks after the end of A levels when a friend contacted him to say he had a record contract with Universal as a singer-songwriter and needed a backing group. Would he like to join? No need to ponder the idea – this was far better than stacking shelves in the supermarket. Edward had known his friend Ben Earle since he was six, when they were both choristers at St George's Choir School, Windsor and sang daily in Windsor Castle. But this was a very different kind of music.

Edward was to play keyboard and provide backing vocals. What an opportunity! It was mostly recording sessions with the occasional gig. He earned £100 a week to be on stand-by at a moment's notice, plus expenses of around £20 a day. He met many stars, such as KT Tunstall and Amy Winehouse.

'At the same time I was working to get my own break as a solo singer-songwriter. What I needed was performance exposure, and I found it through mike nights at local pubs and a couple of times on local radio.' He also built on his classical music experience and was asked to sing as a tenor with Keble College, Oxford. To eke out his earnings he worked as a barman in his local. So when his friend and Universal parted company, Edward had plenty to fall back on.

Now in his first year at City University studying music, he has moved on from mike nights, and has done a number of solo gigs at different venues in London, including the Troubadour in Old Brompton Road, where the likes of Jimmy Hendrix and Joni Mitchell once played, and the Ginglick, Shepherds Bush. Earnings around £60 an hour – when you can get it.

Will Edward make it in the pop world? Judge for yourself. Tune into slicethepie.com, select investment (you don't have to) and hear Edward perform. The recordings may have been done in less than 90 minutes in a friend's bedroom, but when we last looked he was top of the pops with slicethepie visitors.

Skills gained:

▶ confidence
▶ belief in his own ability
▶ working an audience
▶ handling difficult situations.

10 tips for a gap year

1. Decide what you want to do with your year – work, travel, both – make a plan and stick to it.
2. If you have a university place either ask for deferment or secure your place before going travelling.
3. Work locally and live at home, you'll save more.
4. Make sure you travel with a reputable organisation – the Year Out Group (see page 159) is a good start.
5. Work out the cost before you go – with some voluntary projects it's you who pays. Factor in socialising, food, clothes, topping up your iPod when budgeting.
6. Check health regulations and take out health insurance. Get necessary vaccinations. Do you need a work permit and visas?
7. Make sure you have a return ticket or enough money to get home.
8. Arrange accommodation before you go.
9. Limit luggage to the amount you can carry yourself.
10. Don't run up credit card/bank debts: you'll do plenty of that once at uni.

Further information

What to read

▶ *The Gap-Year Guidebook*, published by John Catt Educational Ltd. Available from Trotman, tel: 0870 900 2665 or visit www.trotman.co.uk/bookshop.
▶ *A Year Off . . . A Year On?*, published by Lifetime Careers. Available from Trotman, tel: 0870 900 2665 or visit www.trotman.co.uk/bookshop.

► *Opportunities in the Gap Year*, published by the Independent Schools Careers Organisation. Available from Trotman, tel: 0870 900 2665 or visit www.trotman. co.uk/bookshop.

► *Working Holidays Abroad* – try grape picking, yacht crewing, driving, tour guiding, beekeeping – there's information on 101,000 jobs in 70 different countries. Available from the Central Bureau, Seymour Mews House, Seymour Mews, London W1H 9PE.

► *Your Gap Year*, Susan Griffith, published by Trotman. To order, tel: 0870 900 2665 or visit www.trotman.co.uk/bookshop.

A gap year for travel abroad

What employer is going to give you time off to travel the world? None. You will never, ever get a chance like this again. So if you have a yen to travel, make the most of your time, and budget wisely. Many gap year students, especially those who take their gap year after their studies, do it to travel. Some work before they go and see it as a great holiday. Others work their way around from country to country.

When you start to investigate the student travel scene, you'll discover that there's plenty of help available. The paths to the Far East, the kibbutz and Camp America are well worn. There is a plethora of publications and organisations, cheap travel firms, ticket concessions – even government advice – handed out to get you safely there and back. If that makes it all sound rather overplayed, pioneers can be accommodated.

Backpacking and inter-railing are always journeys into the unknown. Things rarely turn out exactly as you had envisaged. That's the excitement. As for working your passage, most students do a wide range of jobs in a variety of countries before they get back home again. Skiing instructor, courier, au pair, grape picker, summer camp assistant – the *Guide to Student Money* has found them all.

Further information

Who to contact

The Year Out Group (see page 159) has more than 30 organisations eagerly looking for willing students in order to help fulfil their travel dreams.

► AIESEC runs an International Exchange Programme – the Work Abroad Programme – which provides the opportunity for undergraduates and recently qualified graduates to work for companies and other organisations throughout the world.

Placements can last from two months to 18 months. Typical placements are for marketing and business studies (Management Placement), IT and engineering (Technical Placement), teaching (Education Placement) and voluntary and NGO work (Development Placement). AIESEC operates in 106 countries and is represented in 23 universities across the UK. Check out its website, www.aiesec. co.uk, or contact AIESEC United Kingdom, 29–31 Cowper Street, London EC2A 4AT. Tel: 020 7549 1800.

► Au pair/nanny: try adverts in the *Lady* magazine and *The Times*; also see the *Au Pair and Nanny's Guide to Working Abroad*, published by Vacation Work, available from Trotman, tel: 0870 900 2665; or visit www.trotman.co.uk/bookshop.

► BUNAC – to meet the cash crisis facing many students, BUNAC (British Universities North America Club) organises various paid work and volunteer programmes for students and young people interested in working in the USA, Canada, Ghana, New Zealand, South Africa, Australia, Costa Rica, Cambodia, China and Peru (see information on the Year Out Group on page 159). Those working on the Summer Camp USA and KAMP programmes will find that their air fares are paid in addition to all food and accommodation. Every year, BUNAC awards three scholarships of up to £1,000 each to help applicants cover the costs of taking part in a BUNAC work-abroad programme to the USA or Canada. To enter the Green Cheese Scholarships, all you need to do is submit a humorous piece of original creative writing based on a travel-related topic. You're free to write about anything at all – whether it's a trip to the other side of the world or a journey you made closer to home. Entries should be no more than 1,500 words. Contact your university/college or BUNAC, 16 Bowling Green Lane, London EC1R0QH. Tel: 020 7251 3472. Fax: 020 7251 0215. Email: enquiries@bunac.org.uk. Website: www.bunac.org.

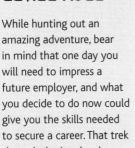

advice note

While hunting out an amazing adventure, bear in mind that one day you will need to impress a future employer, and what you decide to do now could give you the skills needed to secure a career. That trek through the jungle when a wild beast slunk off with the rations might provide the ideal answer to the question, 'Have you ever been faced with a challenge when your swift actions saved the day?' Even losing your tickets need not be a complete disaster and dismissed as incompetence, but turned into a useful episode of resourcefulness. Get the picture – always keep your CV in mind.

Try the internet: enter 'student gap year' in your favourite search engine and you'll have an amazing choice – Ultimate Gap Year, Mad Gap Years, 100s of Gap Year Ideas, Global Gap Xperiences, Mad Adventures and the Gap Year Directory – which tells you what to do, where to go, and has a range of special travel offers and much more besides.

What to read

All these titles are published by Vacation Work and are available from Trotman, tel: 0870 900 2665; or visit www.trotman.co.uk/bookshop.

- *Directory of Jobs & Careers Abroad.*
- *International Voluntary Work* – gives details of over 500 organisations that recruit all types of volunteers for projects in all parts of the world. It's the A–Z of voluntary work.
- *Live and Work in . . .* France, Spain and Portugal, Italy, Germany, Belgium, the Netherlands and Luxembourg – a series of books giving details of temporary and permanent work in various countries.
- *Summer Jobs USA, Summer Jobs Abroad.*
- *Teaching English Abroad* – guide to short- and long-term opportunities for both the trained and untrained. Eastern Europe, Greece, Turkey, Japan – the choice is vast and varied.
- *Working in Ski Resorts* – details on a variety of jobs from au pair to disc jockey and snow cleaner.
- *Work Your Way Around the World* – offers authoritative advice on how to find work as you travel, with hundreds of first-hand accounts. Find out how to become a barmaid, kiwi-fruit packer, ski guide or jackaroo.

If you can't afford the books suggested in this chapter, look in your local library. Nearly all the books mentioned here should be found in the reference section of your local public library, and if they are not your library might well order them for you. A group of you might think it worthwhile buying some of the publications mentioned.

'Students have the time and the opportunity to travel and experience the "ideal" of freedom. You won't get that chance again.'

Loughborough University student, back from Africa

Thrift Tips

'It is much more economical to pay rent with bills included. It may look more expensive initially, but works out cheaper in the long run.'
3rd year Performing Arts student, Derby

'Work in a fast-food take-away and eat your favourite junk food for free.'
4th year English student, Cheltenham

'Choose flatmates the same size – it extends your wardrobe.'
1st year Animal Management student, Bradford

The student travel scene

It's all very well to whet your appetite for travel, but how are you going to manage to get to that exotic destination? This section looks briefly at the student travel scene.

As a student, can I get cheap travel abroad?

Yes: there are a number of travel organisations that operate special schemes for students. In fact, you will find they are vying for the privilege to send you off on your travels, often dropping the price in the process. If you decide to take the cheapest, make sure it is a reputable organisation, with ABTA (Association of British Travel Agents) membership. It's better to be safe than stranded.

How do I go about getting cheap travel?

If you are already a student, your college's student travel office is the best place to start. There you'll find experts who will understand your particular needs and financial restraints, and are ready to give you advice.

If you are taking a gap year, or your college has no travel office, try STA Travel, which is one of the biggest names in the student travel business. You can check them out on www.statravel.co.uk., tel: 0871 230 8569. If you prefer face-to-face contact, they have some 35 branches in or close to universities throughout the UK.

There are on-campus STA Travel offices at: Bath University, Birmingham University, Durham University, University of London Union, Leeds University Union, Manchester University, Sheffield University and the University of Warwick. High street branches near universities include: Aberdeen, Belfast, Birmingham, Bournemouth, Brighton, Bristol, Cambridge, Canterbury, Cardiff, Dundee, Edinburgh, Exeter, Glasgow, Kingston, Leeds, Leicester, Liverpool, London, Manchester, Newcastle, Norwich, Nottingham, Oxford, Portsmouth, Preston, Reading, Sheffield and Southampton.

STA Travel offers a great choice of adventure trips, conservation and volunteer projects, accommodation, language courses. As Thomas Grist of STA Travel says:

'Whether you want to coach rugby in Fiji, take an African safari, inter-rail around Europe or simply need a cheap flight home, STA Travel can help you get there.'

Also big on the student travel scene is the International Student Travel Confederation (ISTC) with 500 offices in 120 countries (including 33 in the UK) and some 10 million students and youth travellers on the move. Their website, www.isic.org, is a must for any would-be adventurer. Make sure you have an ISIC card: it gives you an entrée to an amazing range of around-the-world opportunities. See details below.

What should I join before setting off?

▶ ISIC: £9. The International Student Identity Card (ISIC) offers you thousands of discounts in the UK and around the world. From high street stores to hotels and hostels, weekend breaks (not specifically, unless you take their SY airfare), flights, buses, trains, restaurants, guidebooks, entertainment, attractions, museums, galleries, CDs and travel gear, gym memberships, software, eating out. You can also get low-cost international calls and texts in over 100 countries, free voicemail and an international travel emergency helpline via the ISIConnect phone and SIM card. ISIC is available to all full-time students. See the ISIC website for details of where you can get your card or try STA Travel.

▶ IYTC Youth Card: £7. If you are not a full-time student but are aged 26 or under, the International Youth Travel Card (IYTC) is for you. It offers fantastic discounts and ISIConnect services, available through ISIC (see above).

▶ YHA: £9.95. YHA (England and Wales) Ltd offers access to UK and international youth hostels. Changes made to membership rules a couple of years ago mean that you don't even have to be a member to use their youth hostels. Non-members just pay a £3 a night supplement, or £1.50 per night for under 18s. However, you do need a membership card to use all Hostelling International (HI) member hostels in other countries. An annual card is now down to £9.95. A two-year card costs £16.50 and a three-year card £20.95 (if you are under 26). There are more than 4,000 HI Hostels across 80 countries. They all have assured standards for hygiene and safety. An annual card for those over 26 costs £15.95, but couples can buy a joint annual card for £22.95. To join call 0870 770 8868 or visit www.yha.org.uk. Address: YHA, Trevelyan House, Dimple Road, Matlock, Derbyshire, DE4 3YH.

▶ Young Person's Railcard: 16–25 card £24. This entitles all young people aged 16–25 to a third off most rail fares in the UK. Did you know that it also covers the London all-zone One-Day Travel Card? See leaflet for travel restrictions and useful discounts. (Mature students of 26 and over in full-time education also included.)

---

advice note ⓘ

The web is a great source for cheap travel and excellent deals for students, but make sure you are dealing with a reputable firm. Never pay full fare on bus, coach, train or plane. Take advantage of rail and coach cards, bucket shops selling bargain tickets, classified ads, chartered flights, stand-by fares, advance bookings and deals offered by student travel companies. Some of the budget airlines are giving the most fantastic deals.

▶ Student Coachcard: £10. This entitles all students aged 17 and over to a third off National Express and Scottish Citylink fares; also some continental and Irish services – check with your local coach station or Victoria Coach Station, London, or phone National Express Call Centre on 08705 808080.

Cards to carry checklist

Young Person's Railcard	£24
Coachcard	£10
ISIC	£9
IYTC under-26 card	£7
YHA card	£9.95

What is InterRail?

InterRail gives you the flexibility to see Europe the way you want to – you can go where you like, when you like. Your InterRail pass gives you unlimited travel on the extensive network that covers over 30 European countries. Choose a one country pass from £32 or a global pass from £158. It is available to European citizens and anyone who has been resident here for six months. Available from STA Travel (pop into a branch, call 0871 230 8569 or click www.statravel.co.uk).

Further information

Who else could I consult?

The national tourist office or board. Many countries have a national tourist office or board in this country. Most are based in London. London telephone directories can usually be found in the reference section of your local library.

What to read

The 'Rough Guide' series and the 'Lonely Planet' series cover almost every country and provide a useful insight into an area. Cost varies according to the country covered; try your local library.

As a student, do I need insurance?

Yes! Don't leave home without it. Travel insurance is often the last thing you think about, but it's the first thing you'll need if things go wrong.

Some work camps and voluntary agencies arrange insurance for those taking part in projects. Check this out, and check what it covers. There are certain reciprocal arrangements for medical treatment in some EU countries: you will need to apply for a European Health Insurance Card (www.ehic.org), but remember – this may not cover all medical expenses, and your property won't be covered if it's stolen.

STA Travel offers three levels of cover and three geographical areas of cover to suit every trip, whether your bag is bungee jumping, white water rafting or snowboarding, or even soaking up the sun, from at little as 32p a day. (This assumes you are under 35 years of age and taking out European Budget cover for a period of 24 months.) Contact STA Travel on 0871 230 8569 or www. statravel.co.uk, or visit one of their branches.

Some banks offer travel insurance and you may get a good discount as part of the student package – see Chapter 10, page 268.

Endsleigh's travel products are also designed to reflect the lifestyles of their customers, especially students, and they suit all types of holiday and travel experience. It offers a choice of cover options including basic, essential and comprehensive benefits in the UK, Europe or worldwide. Contact Endsleigh Insurance on 0800 028 3571, www.endsleigh.co.uk.

Just a few examples. Feed 'student travel insurance' into your search engine and a host of names will come up. Be warned: read the small print before committing yourself. You don't want to be stranded on the other side of the world with a broken leg because of a legal loophole.

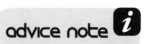

advice note

Find out about any rail passes offered by individual European countries. STA Travel should be able to help you out – 0871 230 8569 or www.statravel. co.uk.

Thrift Tips from Oxbridge

'Enter competitions you see. Sell things you don't need. Use tea bags twice.'
Economics student

'Ebay.co.uk is fantastic for selling anything.'
Veterinary Medicine student

'Get involved in student marketing and police ID parades – means a little cash to make life easier.'
Chemistry student

'Mystery shopping! www.gapbuster.com: quick good money.'
English and Drama student

Most popular full-time first degree courses with students starting in 2008

	Number of students studying subject
Law by area	17,042
Design Studies	15,902
Psychology	14,833
Management Studies	11,134
Computer Studies	10,707
Business Studies	10,575
English Studies	9,839
Combined Business and Administration	9,306
Sports Science	8,885
History by period	8,082

Note: if the figures for pre-clinical medicine (8,013) and pre clinical dentistry (1,209) had been combined (as in the past) they would have come in at number eight.
Source: Figures provided by UCAS on student returns for 2008

CHAPTER 7

Sponsorship

This chapter is a brief guide to getting sponsorship, and what to expect from it.
The major topics covered here are:

Sponsors and sponsorship

Probably the best and most comprehensive way of raising extra finance to help you through higher education is sponsorship. It gives you money during term time and paid work during the vacations.

In this chapter we turn the spotlight on sponsorship, on the changes to the sponsorship market that have been taking place recently, and on some of the companies most likely to offer sponsorship.

What is sponsorship?

You've heard of big companies sponsoring events such as the London Marathon, the FA Cup and cricket test matches. It means that they back the event with money. In the same way, an organisation could sponsor you through university.

Fast facts on sponsorship

Who gives it?	Major companies
When?	• For a full course
	• After first year of study
	• After industrial placement
	• For final study year
To whom?	**Degree and HND students**
Most sponsored subject	Engineering
Most likely sponsors	Manufacturing and production companies
What it's worth	£2,000 approx. p.a. bursary £1,208 per month approx. work periods
Other plus points	Work experience – industrial placement, additional skills.
Will it secure a job?	Helpful, but no guarantee

Who gives sponsorship?

▶ Employers – mainly large companies, banks, accountancy firms, etc. (see also the Power Academy, page 180).

▶ The three armed forces (see page 192).

- ▶ Ministry of Defence – Defence Engineering and Science Group (DESG) www.desg. mod.uk (see page 181).
- ▶ Professional bodies, e.g. the Institution of Mechanical Engineers (IMechE) (see page 204).
- ▶ Universities, on behalf of employers.

Sponsorship of university students has been going on for many years. It was originally started to attract more young people into engineering. Even today, engineering is the major area where sponsorship can be found.

Why do companies give sponsorship?

The reasons most often given by employers are: to have access to high-quality students before they graduate, with the hope of future employment; to assess students over a longer period as potential employees; to develop a student's skills and have an input into their training; to publicise the company as a potential employer among other students. Or in their own words:

'Opportunity to see trainees in work situations before graduation.'

'Input of fresh ideas into the company.'

'Gives students a chance to look at us and us a chance to look at them before job offer made.'

How does sponsorship work?

There are no hard-and-fast rules – every company devises its own scheme. In principle it works like this.

As a sponsored student you would get training, work experience and financial help while at college – to varying extents, depending on the company scheme. You might be asked to work for a whole year in the company either before or during your course; you might be expected to work only during the summer vacations.

In return, the sponsor gets the opportunity to develop close ties with 'a potentially good employee' and to influence your development. There is generally no commitment on either side to employment after the sponsorship. However, since the company has invested a considerable amount of money in you as a student, it is unlikely not to offer you a job.

Check out the Power Academy

The Power Academy is an engineering scholarship fund launched in 2004 for students studying an IET-accredited (Institute of Engineering and Technology) degree course at a partner university. It is backed by the Institution of Engineering and Technology, seven universities and 16 companies in the power industry. There are over 60 scholarships available in 2009 to students studying at the University of Bath, University of Cardiff, Imperial College London, University of Strathclyde, University of Manchester, University of Southampton and Queen's University, Belfast, for the full length of their course.

The sponsorship offers:

▶ £2,200 annual bursary

▶ payment towards university fees

▶ £220 book allowance

▶ summer vacation work

▶ free membership of the IET

▶ annual seminar for all PA-sponsored students.

Why such generosity? The Power Academy was set up because there is a shortage of good power graduates coming out of our universities, and the industry could be facing a crisis. It is anticipated that 25% of the power industry's current engineering workforce will retire over the next 15 years, and there are not enough good people around to fill the vacancies. So it looks as if there could be some good jobs available in the future.

The companies involved include CE Electric, E.ON, EDF Energy, National Grid, Scottish and Southern Energy, Scottish Power, Western Power Distribution, EA Technology, Siemens, ABB, AREVA T&D, Atkins Power, RWE npower, Rolls-Royce, UKAEA and NIE.

To find out more, log on to www.theiet.org/poweracademy.

What would sponsorship mean to me?

There are many types of sponsorship. Generally, a sponsorship will include a bursary given while you are studying, and paid work experience, which is usually at the going rate for somebody of your age. In financial terms, it would probably mean that you would be around £40–£80 a week better off than your contemporaries during term time, with guaranteed work for at least eight weeks during the summer. But it's not just about money – the work experience and training are valuable assets, too.

The question of cash

Looking at it purely in cash terms:

▶ £1,500–£3,500 annual bursary, average £2,000 approx. Given during academic study. For manufacturing and production students it could be higher. The armed forces give higher rates still, but they have a different kind of arrangement.

▶ Salary £1,200–£1,500 monthly, but could be more. This is what you could expect to earn when working for your sponsor. However, salaries are generally age related, so a third-year student would earn appreciably more than a pre-university student.

Employers' additional costs

From the employer's point of view, the costs don't stop there. Generally a sponsorship includes training, which may well mean several weeks at their training centre. Some companies provide a personal tutor for students. There are also courses and meetings to arrange work experience. All this takes time, and time costs money. Every time somebody stops to tell you how to do something, it's work time lost to the employer.

Will my sponsorship bursary affect what I get as my financial support package?

Any scholarship or sponsorship you receive should not be included when calculating how much loan, grant and uni bursary you can have. Money earned during vacations is also not included. So for a normal sponsorship the answer is probably no.

Ministry of Defence DESG sponsorship scheme

▶ The aim of the DESG (Defence Engineering and Science Group) Student Sponsorship Scheme is to help you explore the variety of careers available in the Ministry of Defence while gaining valuable work experience.

▶ There is no commitment to work for the MoD on graduation, but obviously they hope that you will.

▶ A bursary of £1,500 p.a. will be given while studying.

▶ 10 weeks' guaranteed work experience at a MoD establishment in the UK is given during summer vacations; pay based on an annual salary of £14,025. (Salary review in August.)

▶ Work placements are designed to give valuable experience to engineers and scientists, so expect a challenging project that will make a real difference to the team you are working with.

▶ All students will be assigned a mentor who will help them select summer placements and provide advice on professional development.

▶ The scheme is open to those studying an approved engineering or science degree in a UK university and who are likely to achieve a 2:2 degree or better. (See their website for subject list.)

▶ Check www.desg.mod.uk/downloads/sponsorship_fact_sheet.pdf for more details and www.desg.mod.uk for online application form and to sift through the exercises.

Application for sponsorship

How do I get sponsored?

1. You apply to a company that offers sponsorships. These are generally offered to students doing specific subjects.
2. You are offered sponsorship after a period of work experience.
3. Your university has contacts with employers.

What subjects are most likely to attract sponsorship?

Engineering outstrips any other subject, with the largest number of sponsorships being found in the manufacturing and production sector. However, there are opportunities for civil engineers in the construction industry.

Many employers look for subjects with a close link to their own business activities. Good examples are food science, quantity surveying and polymer technology. So if you feel you are studying a degree relevant to a company's business it is worth a try.

Any discipline: a few organisations, especially in the financial sector, will sponsor people on any degree course, but you have to have an interest in finance.

When could I get sponsorship?

► After A levels or BTEC for a full degree or HND course.

► After a gap year spent with a company between A levels and higher education.

► After your first year of study.

► After a successful period of work experience or an industrial placement year.

► For your final year of study.

While sponsorships are still given to A level students for their full three to four years of academic study, more and more companies are choosing to sponsor students later in their degree course, when a commitment to the subject has been established. Work placements and sponsorships are now considered to be one of the best graduate recruitment tools by large employers.

'The sponsorship market has changed. Companies have certainly cut back on numbers and many offer only a final-year sponsorship, but I think it has reached its trough. Many of the smaller organisations that only want one or two sponsorship students are now going straight to the universities of their choice and asking for who they want. This is largely to avoid having to deal with the thousands of applications which advertising in our publication would engender. There are some good sponsorships around which are well worth going after.'

The University Schools Liaison Officer of IMechE

What to expect when applying for sponsorship

The application form

These are more likely to be online than paper forms and you need to think carefully when filling them in, because you only get one chance. Mess it up, and your application will go no further.

Employers are – quite naturally – looking for the brightest and best students to sponsor; they want to have the pick of the potential high-flyers at an early stage. If you are applying for sponsorship before you start university, you may only have GCSE results, possibly some AS level results and a head teacher's report to show what you are capable of. This can be tough on those who wake up academically after GCSE or who really excel only in their one chosen subject. But good employers are more aware than you might expect; selection is not on academic qualifications alone.

Sponsors are looking for signs of those additional qualities needed to succeed in your chosen career: leadership potential, the ability to grasp ideas quickly and to work in a team. They want ambitious, innovative, get-up-and-go people who can think for themselves and get things done. So if your GCSE grades slipped a bit – or, as one student we interviewed put it, 'you look like Mr Average on paper' – think through what else you have been doing. Playing in the football or hockey team; helping out at the local club; hiking across Europe; getting a pop group together – it could help to redress the balance. Remember: the application form is the first weeding-out process and you are up against stiff competition. This is no time for false modesty – you've got to sell yourself for all you're worth.

The interview

Interviews vary enormously. Some companies give a full-scale assessment with psychometric testing and tricky questioning, and watch how you respond to certain situations. Others are much more laid back and go for a straight interview. Whatever the process, if you are an A level student it will probably be something quite new to you. Don't worry. The company will be fully aware of this and will not ask you to do something you are not capable of. Remember, too, that your competitors will be in much the same position.

Still, don't expect an easy time at an interview.

How Alex got her sponsorship

Alex is 21 and in her fourth year at Manchester University. This is her story.

'Out of the blue a letter arrived from Manchester University saying Procter & Gamble were offering sponsorships and would I like to apply? Would I! I had applied to Manchester University to study chemical engineering with chemistry; I had a provisional place, but A levels were still several months away. If I was interested, I had to apply direct to P&G – online.

'Having filled in my application form, I was then asked to complete a "personality test", again online.

'Next I went to Manchester to take yet another test, this time "critical thinking". This was in two parts – an English section and a lateral thinking section. I was told it was the same test given to graduates wanting to join the company. It was not exactly difficult, but certainly challenging. I think if you didn't have an engineer's mind you might struggle. We were told the results right away.

'Two weeks later I was back in Manchester for an interview. I was very nervous and a bit scared. By now I had learnt this was a new sponsorship programme being set up and that there were just two or possibly three sponsorships available – 25 students had applied. My chances of success were slim.

'I had never done anything like this before. It was a one-to-one interview with the head of the sponsorship programme. Most of the questions were based on how you would cope in difficult situations and leading a team – and they wanted examples. Fortunately I had been on the Duke of Edinburgh's Award Scheme, so I had plenty of examples of leadership. But it was tough. You had to think on your feet, and concentrate hard.'

Alex was successful. In her first year she received a bursary during her academic year and then worked for P&G at a plant in Essex for around 11 weeks during the summer. She was engaged on the environmental side and undertook her own project. Having paid for her accommodation in Essex, she used some of the money she earned, about £4,200, to pay off her university debts of around £2,000. Of her work experience she says: 'It was brilliant, the P&G people were very welcoming and supportive. I learnt a lot about day-to-day life and issues of working in a process plant as well as developing my technical knowledge. I also made some good friends.'

The following summer Alex worked at P&G's Manchester plant, so she could stay in the house where she currently lives. She undertook two projects: one involved looking at new equipment, and the other gave her experience in day-to-day production on the plant. The highlight of her internship was a business trip with another employee to Poland where she had a fantastic few days in Warsaw. The internship lasted 10 weeks and she earned £1,650 a month. She used the money to have a good time, go on holiday and pay off her overdraft. For her final vacation she was given the option by P&G to have the summer off and not do an internship, which she took, and travelled in India and Spain. She now has the promise of a graduate job with P&G in process engineering management starting in September on a salary of a minimum of £28,500, all as a result of her sponsorship. She feels she is lucky. As she says: 'Chemical engineering jobs do seem to be more difficult to obtain this year.'

What Alex received:

1st year   Bursary of £1,500 p.a. (she used this to cover her fees and books)

10 weeks' guaranteed work experience during the summer (she did 11 weeks)

Pay of £1,650 a month – £4,200 in total

Entrée to the P&G staff shop – 'Anyone fancy a Pringle'?

2nd year   Bursary of £1,500 p.a.

10 weeks' guaranteed work during the summer at £1,650 a month

3rd year   Bursary of £2,000 p.a.

4th year   Bursary of £2,000

Graduate job starting in September

Estimated total: £14,900

Work experience

Students gain amazing experience during placements, but make sure it is the right experience for you. It is important not to be so mesmerised by the bursary money that you don't consider what the company offering sponsorship does and whether it can provide experience that will help your career. The downside to a sponsorship is that during your degree all your work experience will be in one company and, because of this, it can shape the direction of your future career. When you go for your interview ask about the experience and training you can expect and the skills you will acquire.

Thrift Tips

'Get a bike.'
1st year Geography student, St Andrews

'Swap socialising for work so you don't drink.'
2nd year Politics/Philosophy student, Durham

'Make roll-ups out of cigarette butts.'
2nd year English student, Sussex

Terms and conditions

How much time do I have to spend with my sponsor?

Some sponsors demand you spend a year working with them either during your course or for a gap year before university. Others give you the choice. Most stipulate summer vacation work of six to eight weeks. Students often ask for more and may do Easter vacation work as well. Engineering firms are generally more demanding and the sponsorship is more likely to be geared to a sandwich course, so you could be looking at a full year in industry plus two summer vacation placements.

Planned vacation work

Some companies will hold special vacation planning sessions. These are usually during the Easter vacation and can last anything up to a week. During these sessions you would plan with your sponsor how you want to spend your summer vacation time.

Comment: sponsors occasionally allow their sponsored students to gain experience in other companies during vacations, as they feel that it will help to broaden their mind and knowledge. But most are loath to do so, for obvious reasons.

It's a fact

Employers recruit from students who undertake work experience with them. Employers offer work experience/sponsorship as part of their recruitment strategy.

Am I obliged to join my sponsor after graduating?
Are they obliged to employ me?

No, you are not obliged to join your sponsoring company after graduating, unless it says so in your contract. Equally, they are not obliged to offer you a job. But there is no doubt that companies are taking a tougher stand these days, and seeking value for money from their sponsorships. For example:

advice note *i*

The armed forces are slightly different from other employers; they have always included service as part of their sponsorship schemes.

▶ some companies will stop your bursary payment for the final year if you don't agree to join them after graduating

▶ a few companies demand reimbursement of their sponsorship money if you don't join them. You would have been informed of this before you agreed to a sponsorship

▶ some companies only give sponsorship for the final year after a job offer has been accepted.

Can my sponsor terminate my sponsorship?

Sponsorship is a legal contract. Look at the terms carefully. Most agreements will have a clause that allows the employer to withdraw if your academic performance is unsatisfactory. There may be other clauses you should watch out for.

What exactly is meant by academic performance?

If you fail the odd exam, you're probably all right, but if your end-of-year results are so bad that you have to repeat the year, you may find that your sponsor is no longer interested.

Other aspects to consider

How do I choose a sponsor?

'Be practical – go for the cash' was one student's advice on selecting a sponsor. Certainly cash is something to bear in mind, but there are many other factors to consider.

▶ Compare salaries for work experience and bursaries: the plus on one might cancle out the minus on the other.

- Check out the training for engineers – is the training accredited by the appropriate institution? – and the experience: is it a well-organised programme of development or are you just another pair of hands?
- Talk to students on the scheme: find out about projects undertaken; how many sponsored students joined the company as graduates?
- Where would you be located? Do they provide accommodation if away from home? Are there opportunities to gain experience abroad?
- Finally, ask yourself: is this the kind of company where you would want to make your career?

> **advice note** ℹ
>
> - Make sure any literature you are reading on sponsorship is up to date – school and college careers libraries are notorious for displaying last year's information.
> - Look at your contract in detail and, above all, check the small print.
> - Question your sponsor; they will respect you for that.

When should I apply for sponsorship?

- Full degree course sponsorship: some companies offer sponsorship for your full degree course. Applications for these schemes should be made early in your final school year, and at least by the time you send in your UCAS form.
- Second-year degree course sponsorship: some sponsors like to see commitment to your course before offering sponsorship. Applications should be made early in your first year at university. Ask your department head for likely sponsors.
- Final-year degree course sponsorship: increasingly, employers are offering sponsorship to students for just the final year of their degree course. Often this will be offered after a successful industrial placement year or summer vacation period. Employers offering sponsorship at this stage will expect students to agree to join them after graduation.

Jono's sponsorship

I went to Loughborough to study mechanical engineering, but a week after getting there I was asked if I would like to be a guinea pig. They were starting up a completely new course called Innovative Manufacturing and Technology. If I took the course I would get sponsorship – a bursary of £500 a year for the first two years and then £1,000 for the next two years. It wasn't the money that decided me: the course was really interesting;

I liked the idea of doing something so new. There were only three students on the course. Another feature of the course was that the sponsorship came from a mix of companies, so you received a wide range of work experience and work in a number of different companies such as Perkins, Bentley, Morgan, Caterpillar – all good names.

What's the competition for sponsorship?

Phenomenal. All sponsors say that applications outstrip sponsorships available, and it is getting worse – so get in early. The earlier you apply the better. Applications for full course sponsorship should have been made by the time you send in your UCAS form.

What is a sponsor looking for?

A straw poll of sponsors suggested that sponsors favour students with:

- good A level (or equivalent) grades
- maturity
- potential
- ambition
- evident team skills
- sense of humour
- hard-working attitude

- ability to get a good second-class degree
- interest in their degree topic
- ability to assimilate information and learn quickly
- a spark that sets you apart from the rest
- business awareness
- interpersonal skills.

Which comes first: UCAS or sponsorship?

They both come at once, which makes for complications. However, both sides are aware of this, so a system has been worked out.

First you should discover whether a sponsor you are interested in requires you to gain a place on a particular course – if so, you should name that course on your UCAS form.

However, it could happen that an employer you had not originally been very interested in offers you a sponsorship with the proviso that you gain a place on a course not named in your selection on your application form. While UCAS does not generally allow students to make alterations to their original application, in the case of sponsorship they usually relax this rule.

What about deferred entry?

Another complication is whether you want deferred entry or not. If you get sponsorship, your sponsor may require you to do a pre-degree year in industry, but at application time you may not know this. If in doubt, apply for the current year. It is always easier to ask a university to defer your entry rather than bring it forward. On some courses, especially popular courses such as law, deferment may be more difficult to arrange.

Will my university find me sponsorship?

If you are accepted on to a course either conditionally or unconditionally, it is always a good idea to ask the course director if they know of any sponsoring companies. Often they will have a list. Some students will find that they are automatically offered sponsors to apply to, and on some courses that are actually sponsored by employers, the sponsors are involved in the selection procedure. College prospectuses may give you some guidance. A number of universities advertise sponsored courses in *Engineering Opportunities for School Leavers, Students and Graduates* – for details see 'What to read' at the end of this chapter.

Not all sponsors advertise

If you look down the list of sponsors in most sponsorship books, you will be surprised how many large companies appear not to offer sponsorship or work experience, yet in fact they do. Many companies just don't bother to advertise – the requests flood in anyway. Others have special relationships with selected schools or universities. So just because a company doesn't advertise sponsorship, that shouldn't stop you from asking.

Facts and Figures

▶ Median starting salary paid to graduates in 2009 – £25,000 p.a., unchanged from last year. (*AGR Graduate Recruitment Winter Review 2008*).

▶ 334,890 first-degree students – a record number – graduated from higher education institutions in the UK in 2007/08. (HESA release 2009)

▶ Typical sponsors are large firms with 1,000–9,000 employees. (ASET figures)

▶ Approximately 120,000 students in the UK are enrolled on sandwich courses. (ASET figures)

Don't forget the smaller companies

If you're thinking in terms of your CV, it must be admitted that a well-known name will carry more weight than a smaller company. But with a smaller, little-known company there is less competition. Perhaps more important, you are likely to be treated as an individual. You may well be the only sponsored student they have and you can develop your own training and experience package. Of course, if they have no experience of sponsored students, they may not know what you are capable of and what experience you should be getting. So you could find you have to stand up for yourself.

Is it best to apply to local companies?

It is always best to apply to a company that interests you. Nevertheless, some companies do prefer to take on local people. From their point of view, there is no accommodation problem when it comes to work experience, and statistics show that many students want to return to their home town to work when they complete their studies. So the company is more likely to keep the sponsored student as an employee.

Will sponsorship be good for my CV?

Yes, but with reservations: 73% of the companies we asked said sponsorship was a plus point. The others felt that it made little difference. A careers adviser at Bath University said that, while sponsorship on your CV shows that you have been 'selected', it was the work experience that would be seen as the important element on a CV.

Of course, prospective employers will probably ask why you didn't join the company that sponsored you, so you will need to have a well-phrased answer. Most employers realise that a decision made at the age of 18 may not look so right when you are 22. It's always worth remembering that your would-be new employer may write to your sponsor for a reference, so it's important to leave your sponsoring company on good terms.

Should I try the armed forces?

The three armed forces offer very generous sponsorships, which can cover fees and full living costs. But their Cadetship and Bursary schemes are not open ended. There is a service commitment involved and those taking them up should think very carefully about what they are getting involved in. Full details are available from:

▶ Army Officer Entry, Freepost LON15 445, Bristol BS38 7UE. Tel: 08457 300111. Websites: www.army.mod.uk/ (for students looking for an army career); www. armyjobs.mod.uk/.

▶ Royal Air Force, Officer Careers, Freepost 4335, Bristol BS1 3YX. Tel: 0845 605 5555; website: www.raf.mod.uk/careers.

▶ Royal Navy and Royal Marines Careers Service, Dept BR211, FREEPOST GL672, Cirencester GL7 1BR. Tel: 0845 607 5555; website: www.royalnavy.mod.uk.

Will I pay tax on my bursary?

You do not have to pay tax on a bursary. But if your annual earned income is above the tax threshold – currently £6,475 (2009–2010) – you would have to pay tax. So in theory a year's placement would not be tax-free. However, since your year's work probably falls into two tax years you may find you pay very little or none at all.

Can I get sponsorship once I've started my degree?

Yes. As we said in the 'When should I apply for sponsorship?' section, more and more companies are giving sponsorship just for the final year or from the second year of a course. These sponsorships often develop from a successful period of work experience during the summer vacations, or through an industrial placement during a sandwich course.

Should sponsorship determine which course I choose?

In theory, no. First you should decide on the course that best suits you. You're going to spend at least three solid years – and possibly more – studying, so make sure you're going to enjoy it, otherwise the results could be at best disappointing and at worst disastrous.

advice note *i*

Were you unlucky in securing sponsorship? Try the back-door entry. When you're looking for a summer vacation job, seek out companies that you feel could be interested in sponsoring your particular skills. You may be lucky, and there's no harm in asking.

I'm a sponsored student, but find I don't like the course I'm studying: what can I do?

This happens. You choose a course in something that you may never have studied before, and after a term or so you discover that you and the subject just don't get along together. A sponsorship is not a life sentence, and neither is a degree course. Talk first to your college tutor. It may be just one aspect of the course you don't like. Then talk to your sponsor. You will probably be able to change your degree course, but it may be more difficult – or impossible – for your sponsor to put you on an appropriate sponsorship scheme. Don't despair. Whatever you do, be frank about your change of heart – and the sooner the better, before too much time and money are wasted.

To sum up

What do I gain from being sponsored?

► Money – probably an annual bursary plus good rates of pay when working.
► Training – most sponsorships will involve some form of training.
► Meaningful work experience.
► Guaranteed employment for the summer in an area that will assist you with your studies.
► Chance of future employment – but no guarantee.
► Help with final-year project work – possibly.
► Opportunity to gain first-hand knowledge of the working environment where you might possibly start your career.
► Understanding of what it means to work in industry.
► Chance to gain new skills.
► Plus-point to put in your CV.

What do I lose?

► Your holiday time is not your own. So, for example, you would not be able to spend the whole summer abroad going InterRailing.
► You have the chance to see only one industry/company during work experience.
► You make a career choice at 18 that may not be what you want at 21.
► You may be obliged to work for a company whether you want to or not, because of a payback clause.
► You may be asked to work in locations that are not very appealing and possibly a long way from home.

Further information

Who to contact

▶ The Year in Industry (see page 151).

▶ Local employers that interest you – many employers prefer to sponsor local students.

▶ Don't forget the smaller companies. Some may never have thought of offering work experience before, so it can be a matter of making yourself sound a good bet.

▶ Your course director.

▶ Your university or college may well have a list of sponsors who are interested in sponsoring students on your particular course. Some universities advertise in the books listed below.

▶ Black and Asian high-flyers can also try the Windsor Fellowship Undergraduate personal and professional development programmes, which include summer work placements and community work. Application forms and further information can be downloaded from www.windsorfellowship.org/leadership.

What to read

▶ *Everything You Wanted to Know about Sponsorship, Placements and Graduate Opportunities*, regularly updated and published by Amoeba Publications. Available from Trotman, tel: 0870 900 2665, or visit www.trotman.co.uk/bookshop.

▶ *Engineering Opportunities for School Leavers, Students and Graduates*, published by the Institution of Mechanical Engineers on behalf of the engineering profession. It lists sponsors and universities with sponsored courses, and companies offering industrial placements and internships. Available free from IMechE c/o Marketing & Communications Department, 1 Birdcage Walk, London SW1H 9JJ, email: education@imeche.org.uk.

▶ *University Scholarships, Awards and Bursaries*, published by Trotman. To order, tel: 0870 900 2665 or visit www. trotman.co.uk/bookshop.

CHAPTER 8

Other sources to tap

In this chapter we investigate all the other legitimate sources of finance you could tap to raise extra cash, and how to set about approaching them. They include trusts, charitable awards, scholarships, grants, bursaries (from sources other than Student Finance England
your local authority or university) and competitions.

The topics covered in this chapter are:

Other sources of finance: a reality or a vain hope?

You'd be right to be a little sceptical. If there were a prodigious number of organisations all eager to hand out money to students, you wouldn't have seen so many student demonstrations called to highlight their financial plight or stories in the press about the difficulties students face. But there are a surprising number of educational charities, trust funds and foundations, professional bodies, and benevolent funds in this country that offer financial help to students. This may take the form of a scholarship or charitable award. One directory of grant-making trusts we consulted listed over 1,500 organisations under the broad heading of Education. But before you get too excited and think you've found the route to a crock of gold, be aware that when you start sifting through the many restrictions which trusts generally have to abide by, you soon realise there are relatively few – if any – that could meet your exact needs.

What is a scholarship?

Scholarships differ from sponsorships in that they provide money while you study, but without the industrial training. They can, of course, be for a specific purpose, such as travel, to fund some special area of research or possibly to study abroad. They are usually, though not always, given by an institution – this could be your university, a professional institute or a charitable trust – rather than by individual companies.

It's a Fact

Who gives bursaries and scholarships?
Charitable trusts, universities and colleges, professional bodies and institutions.

How much?
From £12 to £4,000 and everything in between.

What is the success rate?
Low.

Competition is keen. Awards can be made on grounds of academic achievement or need. Whatever the criteria, they are not going to come your way without considerable effort and often disappointment, so be prepared. Nobody gives money away easily.

How does a scholarship differ from a bursary?

It doesn't, really. Look up 'scholarship' in the dictionary and you'll find the definition is: 'award of money towards education'. Look up 'bursary' and it says, 'scholarship or grant awarded to students'. Sometimes a bursary is awarded if you meet certain criteria – for example, bursaries are given to low-income students under the funding arrangements – for English students see Chapter 2, for all other students, including nurses/midwives, for whom the bursary isn't means tested, see Chapter 4. To win a scholarship there is more likely to be an element of achievement (for example academic, musical or sporting).

What is a charitable award?

The difference between a scholarship and a charitable award is, again, very indistinct, and you could say there is no difference at all, as charitable awards can often be scholarships. Charitable awards are always paid out by a charitable organisation, which must abide by the terms and conditions of the original endowment. So, however good and reasonable your case may be, if the money has to be paid out to a student from Gloucester studying chemistry, it is no good being an arts student from Leeds, or even Gloucester. To claim an award, both you and your financial predicament must fit the charity's help profile.

What kind of awards are available?

Often the payments are small – to buy books or equipment – but they can be quite substantial and cover fees or maintenance. So the amount of money available could range from a few hundred pounds to a few thousand. They can be one-off payments, or given each year for the duration of your course.

Who gives scholarships and charitable awards?

Universities, schools, trust funds, professional institutions.

Finding out about scholarships and charitable awards

Can my school help me?

Yes. Most schools will have a list of local charities that offer help to students. The fact that you have been to the school could be a condition of receiving a grant. Also try your primary school. It is a good idea to find out if such scholarships, grants and charitable awards are available before you send off your

UCAS application, as these sometimes stipulate a certain higher education establishment.

Can my local authority help?

Your local authority should have details of any local charities offering help to students in higher education. Also try the following.

▶ The Welsh Assembly, which offers bursaries to Welsh-born students attending Welsh universities.

▶ The Carnegie Trust for the Universities of Scotland, which provides financial assistance to students of Scottish birth or who have at least one parent born in Scotland or who have completed at least three years' secondary education in Scotland, and who want to attend a Scottish university to study for a first degree. They also offer vacation scholarships to enable undergraduates at Scottish universities to undertake a research project during the long vacation. Scholarships are also given to graduates from Scottish universities with a first-class honours degree for three years' postgraduate research at a university in the UK, usually in Scotland. Contact Carnegie Trust for the Universities of Scotland, Andrew Carnegie House, Pittencrief Street, Dunfermline, Fife KY12 8AW. Tel: 01383 724990. Fax: 01383 749799. Email: jgray@carnegie-trust.org. Website: www.carnegie-trust.org.

▶ The Student Awards Agency for Scotland, which maintains a Register of Educational Endowments on Scottish trusts, many of which are local and open only to Scottish-born students who want to attend Scottish universities and colleges. The agency will search the register on behalf of any student who submits an enquiry form. Forms are available from the Student Awards Agency for Scotland, Gyleview House, 3 Redheughs Rigg, Edinburgh EH12 9HH. Tel: 0845 111 1711. Email: www.saas.gov.uk/contact.htm.

▶ See also 'What to read', page 215, for directories and registers on trusts.

Check out your parents' employers!

Or at least get your parents to. A surprising number of companies and large employers have special trusts set up to help with the education of their employees' or past employees' children. Typical examples are:

▶ the National Police Fund, which helps the children of people who are serving in or have served in the police force

▶ the Royal Medical Benevolent Fund, which helps the children of medical graduates, and the Dain Fund Charities Committee (contact the BMA), which helps the children of registered members of the medical profession

▶ the Royal Pinner School Foundation, which helps the children of sales representatives.

Do universities and colleges give scholarships?

Some higher education institutions are endowed by generous benefactors and can award scholarships and bursaries to selected students who meet the required criteria. Usually an institution will have a very mixed bag of awards, which bears very little relation to its academic strengths and interests. Most establishments don't give many awards, and competition in the past has been keen. But with the advent of top-up fees, universities are having to provide bursaries for students to offset the high cost of university education (see page 49). Many of the university scholarships on offer have a subject or location condition attached, which does considerably limit those eligible to apply.

University Scholarships, Awards and Bursaries (published by Trotman) supplies full information on the bursaries universities give, especially to students from low-income families, and lists over 100 institutions offering scholarships or awards. These are largely for people studying specific subjects, or are travel awards. Subjects range from the more usual (engineering, history, geography, languages, law, the sciences) to the distinctly unusual, such as cultural criticism studies, paper science, rural studies, retail studies, leisure, town planning, textiles – and a whole lot in between.

Sports scholarships and bursaries are increasingly commonly available. These cover areas such as rugby, cricket, netball and even golf. A sports scholarship is a boon for any student who plays in a national team and needs to take time out and coaching to train for an international/world cup series. You can be studying any subject to get a sports scholarship.

A number of universities and colleges give music or choral awards. Many of these are old foundations, and the award may include a commitment to take part in services in the college chapel or local church or cathedral. Then there are awards with geographical restrictions. For example, students at Bangor University might get an award of £300 if they live in Criccieth or, better still, £1,500 if they were born in one of the counties of Anglesey, Conwy or Gwynedd; and Exeter University students whose parents have resided in Devon for at least three years could be in line for a scholarship ranging from £12 to £80 p.a.

Your university may also give travel awards to undertake special projects during the vacation, for certain subjects. Ask your university for details of possible awards, and check their prospectus/website (see also *University Scholarships, Awards and Bursaries*, published by Trotman). For English universities try http://bursarymap.direct.gov.uk.

Are there awards for foreign students?

Yes. Overseas students are eligible to apply for many of the awards offered by universities. In some universities there are awards specifically for foreign students. For example, engineering and applied science at Aston (£1,500–£3,000), law at City University (£1,500 approx.) and a number of scholarships for students from Japan, Malaysia, Singapore, Thailand and the USA at Edinburgh. For further information contact the British Council or British Embassy in your own country, the British Council in the UK (www.britishcouncil.org) or the university where you will be studying.

How much would a college scholarship be worth?

Awards vary tremendously: some are given annually for the length of the course, others are a one-off payment. The highest award we found for undergraduates was £5,000, while the lowest we found, at Exeter, was £12 – this is because the foundation was made in the nineteenth century, when £12 was a lot of money, and its status cannot be changed.

Thrift Tips

'Student tutoring for GCSEs and A levels pays extremely well.'
3rd year Medicine student, Oxford

'Borrow from your parents: they are interest-free loans.'
3rd year Applied Psychology student, Liverpool John Moores

'Get the free overdraft and put it in a high-interest account, bond or ISA.'
Business Studies student, Staffordshire

How would I go about getting a college scholarship?

Scholarship distribution methods differ from institution to institution and, of course, according to the terms of the foundation. Aberystwyth, for example, holds formal examinations during February, which can be taken at the student's own school or college. It gives some 300 Entrance Scholarships and Merit Awards annually worth between £1,000 and £1,200 a year. Music bursaries (£400) are also available to experienced players of orchestral instruments who can make an active contribution to the university's wide range of orchestras and bands. Closing date for applications for these is mid-April.

The ancient Scottish universities all offer a range of bursaries. Those at Glasgow are awarded once students have begun their courses. However, at Aberdeen, Edinburgh and St Andrews, bursaries are available to entrants. Traditionally, awards were made on the basis of exam performance, but at Aberdeen and Edinburgh, in particular, the bursary schemes have developed to include a significant number of awards which take into account applicants' financial and personal circumstances. Application forms are available from the universities concerned; increasingly, bursary information and application forms can be found on university websites. Most of these scholarships are worth £1,000 for each year of degree study (in total, £4,000 for a Scottish Honours degree or £5,000 for a degree in clinical medicine).

First look at the college prospectus or its website – it should either list the awards available, or give you an address to write to for details. This should be done early in the autumn term of your final school year and before or about the time you are filling in your UCAS form. Obviously at this stage you do not know which university you are likely to go to, and any exam can be held early in the academic year, before you have made your final decision.

it's a fact

Remember, scholarships and bursaries are not necessarily for students from low-income families and are totally different from those offered by universities now that top-up fees have been introduced.

Professional institutions

Do professional institutions give scholarships?

Some do, some don't. The engineering institutions are among the most generous. Awards are made to students studying accredited degree courses.

Institution of Engineering and Technology (IET)

Michael Faraday House, Six Hills Way, Stevenage, Hertfordshire SG1 2AY. Email: awards@theiet.org. Through its scholarships and awards the IET promotes engineering as a career, rewards achievement and assists with postgraduate research. In 2009, the IET will award a number of scholarships of £1,000 per annum for the duration of an IET-accredited MEng degree course. There are also grants of £1,000 (one year only) available for final-year undergraduate students. For postgraduates there are scholarships ranging from £1,250 to £10,000. To find out more, go to www.theiet.org/ambition. See also information on sponsorship through the Power Academy, page 180.

Institution of Civil Engineers (ICE)

One Great George Street, Westminster, London SW1P 3AA. Tel: 020 7665 2193; email: quest.awards@ice.org.uk; website: www.ice.org.uk/quest. The Queen's Jubilee Scholarship Trust (QUEST) aims to award around 100 scholarships each year to students intending to achieve Chartered, Incorporated or Technician Membership of ICE by embarking on a JBM-accredited course at university. The awards are up to the value of £3,000 per year for the duration of the course, to a maximum total value of £12,000 for one undergraduate course of study. Most QUEST awards are now provided in partnership with top engineering and construction companies that provide summer work placements and possible graduate employment. Students are also provided with mentors, who can give them a head start on the path to becoming professionally qualified.

Institution of Mechanical Engineers (IMechE)

Prizes and Awards Department, ASK House, Northgate Avenue, Bury St Edmunds, Suffolk IP32 6BB. Tel: 01284 717887 or 717882. The institution gives 30 undergraduate scholarship awards of £1,000 p.a. for a maximum of four years (students must be or become an affiliate member of the Institution and have a place on an IMechE-accredited degree course); two Postgraduate Research Scholarships valued at £6,500 p.a., two Postgraduate Master's Scholarships valued at £6,500; 20 awards of up to £750 for students studying or taking a work placement overseas; three awards of up to £1,000 for overseas voluntary or project work; 10 hardship awards of up to £1,000 for students on IMechE-accredited degree courses; around 20 postgraduate awards of up to £1,000 for advanced study, research programmes, hardship or overseas projects; and additional funds available for original research in the science or practice of mechanical engineering. They also handle the awarding of up to 10 Whitworth Scholarships for undergraduate degree-level courses (including MEng and MSc) valued at £4,500 p.a. (full-time study) and £3,000 p.a. (part-time study). These scholarships are for outstanding engineers who have served at least a two-year 'hands-on' engineering apprenticeship before commencing their undergraduate studies. (See 'How I got a Whitworth Scholarship', on the next page.) Whitworth Senior Scholarships of £7,500 are also awarded to postgraduate students who go on to study for a PhD or EngD. Whitworth Scholarships are open to engineers of any discipline, not just mechanical engineers. Applicants must be British, Commonwealth or European Union citizens normally resident in the UK for at least three years prior to commencing their degree-level course.

Institute of Marine Engineering, Science and Technology (IMarEST)

80 Coleman Street, London EC2R 5BJ. Tel: 020 7382 2600. Up to seven scholarships of £1,000 are awarded each year to undergraduate students attending approved accredited courses leading to registration for Chartered

status – Chartered Engineer (CEng), Chartered Marine Scientist (CMarSci) or Chartered Marine Technologist (CMarTech) – who demonstrate a commitment to maritime engineering, marine science or marine technology by spending at least two years in the industry or in study. The institute also offers awards to postgraduates through the Stanley Gray Fellowship scheme and prizes to students through various industry schemes. More information at www.imarest.org.

How Paul got a Whitworth Scholarship

Paul Tuohy left school at 16 with a clutch of 11 GCSEs and then started to study for his A levels. But illness meant that he would have to repeat a year and he decided to begin a Modern Apprenticeship instead. Having scored excellent marks in a BTEC ONC and HNC through day release, he wanted to continue studying. This is his story.

'I liked to learn something new, I had the study bug; so when the personnel officer at the company where I was working said the firm would sponsor me if I wanted to take a degree part time, I jumped at the chance. However, there was one proviso: I needed the permission of my boss, the chief engineer. It seemed like just a formality, but to my horror he said categorically "No!" I could not believe it. Nor could anyone else. A few months later I left the company.

'To be honest, he probably did me a favour. I decided to study for a degree anyway, but to do it full time. It was to be a BEng (Hons) in Mechatronics with Industrial Experience. Fortunately I lived in Manchester and the course being offered at Manchester University was much better than the part-time course I had considered. Even though I had no A levels, the university said they would give me a chance. "You may struggle with the maths," they said, and they were right, but other topics came more easily and I was prepared to work hard.

'I was used to having plenty of money to spend – I'd been on a salary of over £20,000 – and wondered how I would cope as a student. I had some money saved. I took out a student loan. My parents said I could live at home free while I studied and I bought a bicycle to save on travel fares.

'In my first semester my results averaged 76%. In my second semester I did even better, and with an average of 81% was awarded the Mechatronic Student of the Year Prize. It was then that our Industrial Liaison Manager, Eddie Welch, suggested I should apply for a Sir Joseph Whitworth Scholarship given by the Institution of Mechanical Engineers (IMechE).

'There were around 40 applicants that year and only 10 scholarships to be awarded. Having filled in an application form, I attended an interview with a panel of some five lecturers and engineers down at the IMechE in London. It was tough. Two days later they phoned to say I had been awarded a scholarship valued at £3,000 a year. That certainly helped with my finances.

'The next year I spent in industry, at Rolls-Royce. When I returned to uni for my final year I received another award under the Whitworth Scholarship scheme – this time £4,000.'

Paul graduated with a first class honours degree in mechatronic engineering. As a Whitworth Scholar he can put the prestigious letters BEng WhSch after his name. He is now doing a PhD at Manchester, in the development of a new type of marine propulsion engine, in collaboration with Rolls-Royce, and receives a £12,940 stipend to live on. In addition he has been awarded a Whitworth Senior Scholarship which this year amounts to £7,500.

Charities and trusts

Which charities and trusts give help to students?

You may be surprised to learn that it would take a book several times the size of this one to list them all. For example, the *Educational Grants Directory* (see the book list at the end of this chapter) lists more than 1,600 charities that between them give away more than £60 million a year – and this is by no means an exhaustive list.

But before you get too excited, most charities have restrictions on how much they can give away, to whom and for what reasons. Also, most charities and trusts will only consider you after you have exhausted all the more conventional avenues such as loans and Access funds.

Trusts and charities fall largely into four major groups.

▶ Need – e.g. charities for people with disabilities. Well-known organisations such as the RNIB (Royal National Institute of Blind People) and the RNID (Royal National Institute for Deaf People) fall into this category, along with less familiar organisations such as the Shaftesbury Society and Scope.

▶ Subject – charities that will give help to students studying certain subjects. For example, the Company of Actuaries Charitable Trust Fund helps those studying to be actuaries; the Chartered Surveyors Company Charitable Trust and Mr Sidney A. Smith's Fund help those studying surveying; the Honourable Society of Gray's Inn is just one of a number of charities helping would-be lawyers; and there are quite a few charitable organisations set up to help those studying medicine, for example the Charity of Miss Alice Gertrude Hewitt, which helps some 40 students aged under 25.

▶ Parents' occupation – this can be a great source of additional income. If one of your parents is an airline pilot, artist, banker, barrister, in the clergy, coalminer, gardener, in the precious metals industry – you name it, there could be some help. Some trusts stipulate that your parent should be dead, but fortunately not all.

▶ Geographical location – where you study and also where you live can really make a difference. Take, for example, the lucky students living in the parishes of Patrington and Rimswell in East Yorkshire, in Oadby in the Midlands or in Yeovil in Somerset – they could be in line for help towards books, fees, living expenses or travel abroad. There are literally hundreds of these trusts covering many areas of the country. It has to be said that pay-outs can be small – under £100 – but they can be substantially more – say £1,000.

'My income was extremely low, so I applied for as many bursaries (in and outside college) as possible. The effort paid off: I got a bursary from college for around £2,000 and another from a company trust of £1,000.'

1st year Law student, Cambridge

What sort of help do trusts give?

Help with fees, maintenance, books, equipment, travel either to and from your college or abroad, special sports activities, child-minding and special projects. They all vary in what they will offer, and to whom.

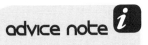

Is there anybody who could advise me on applying to charitable trusts?

advice note

Before making an application to a charity, it is important to be clear in your own mind exactly what kind of student they are likely to help, and what kind of financial assistance you are after, otherwise you could be wasting both your time and theirs.

EGAS (the Education Grants Advisory Service), which is part of Family Action, is an independent organisation that offers a range of services providing information on funding for those in post-16 education in England. EGAS specialises in funding from charitable trusts and maintains a database of trusts and charities that assist students. You will need to insert your information into their online database, which will then match you to the charities and trusts that are most likely to help you. The criteria for eligibility are set by the individual trusts and charities or by the people who bequeathed the legacy, not EGAS, and these are extremely diverse. Trusts can seldom help in an immediate financial crisis. The more time you have to raise the funds, the more likely you are to succeed.

To find out more and carry out your own search of trusts, the quickest route is to visit Family Action's website: www.family-action.org.uk. Alternatively, you can request that a search is carried out for you by downloading a questionnaire from Family Action's website or sending a large stamped addressed envelope to EGAS, 501–505 Kingsland Road, London E8 4AU, requesting a questionnaire. Please note, however, that it can take up to six weeks to receive an initial response, so wherever possible, students are encouraged to carry out their own search online.

For further assistance you can phone the EGAS helpline on 020 7241 7459, open Tuesday, Wednesday and Thursday 2–4p.m.

Can EGAS help overseas students and those wanting to study abroad?

It is very difficult to find trusts willing to fund overseas students who are already studying in the UK, and EGAS cannot assist students wishing to study outside the UK. However, there are trusts that give funding for travel, and these should be contacted directly. See the booklist at the end of this chapter for help if you would like to winkle them out.

What are my chances of hitting the jackpot?

Your chances are slim, though the odds are certainly better than the likelihood of winning the national lottery. Competition is fierce. Last year EGAS received around 4,650 written applications, and its website expects to receive over 148,000 visitors with some 27,000 people completing a search.

Family Action administers over 30 educational trusts, providing small grants principally to families and individuals on low incomes, particularly those living on benefits. Applicants must be studying at a college or university affiliated to EGAS, unless they are a serving prisoner. Funds are not available for: items already covered by statutory funding; private school fees; and repayment of loans.

Last year Family Action gave some 1,700 grants totalling around £318,000 to HE and FE students. However, any funding it does offer is usually small, around £150, for something specific like books, equipment or travel. It handles about 350 grant applications a month and most grants are given to help students in their final year. Typical examples of why money might be given are:

► for books or equipment
► if a parent is suddenly made redundant and can't continue to finance your college course fees
► to a student who has been paying their way through part-time work but feels they need to give up their job to concentrate on that final two-month push.

Additionally, Family Action delivers the Horizons Education Fund. Funded by Barclaycard, this fund aims to support lone parents who have the motivation, determination and ability to improve their employment prospects. The fund operates until summer 2011. Further details can be found at www.family-action.org.uk.

The EGAS website also includes a 'Guide to Student Funding', which has information on HE and FE funding throughout the UK, and the implications of student funding on benefits.

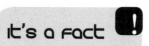

it's a fact

The last word: be realistic when contacting EGAS. Don't expect miracles – they can rarely be worked.

Is there any other way to find out about charities and trusts?

Search the net. The web has a fund of information on sources for finding charities and trusts. Type 'educational grants charities and trusts' into your favourite search engine and follow the leads. Sites such as www.hero.ac.uk and www.londonmet.ac.uk should come up for a start. Refugees could strike lucky if they log onto www.lasa.org.uk. careersadvice.direct.gov.uk is another helpful site.

One really excellent site is Hotcourses. Go to www.scholarship-search.org.uk, where you'll find an extensive database so you can find out just what's available and, more important, whether you are eligible for an award.

When should I contact a trust?

Most trusts have an application deadline. This is usually given along with the general information in the trusts and grants directories. Check out each entry carefully; they are all different. Trusts are not the answer for a fast financial fix. Like all bodies, they tend to move exceedingly slowly. Your case will be scrutinised along with many others, so it could be months before you get an answer.

Could I get through higher education funded only by a charitable trust?

It could be done, but don't depend on it. Many charities won't consider you until you have tried all the usual channels available to students, and they do tend to give help towards the end of a course, rather than at the beginning.

If I get help from a charity, will it affect my loan and fees?

It shouldn't. Charitable awards, scholarships and sponsorships are not generally taken into consideration when calculating your grant and loan package.

Can I apply to more than one charity?

Yes, but blanket application is not advisable. Limit your applications to organisations that are really likely to give you funds.

How do I go about applying to a charity?

There are no set rules. What one charitable trust wants, another doesn't. Here is the usual procedure.

- ▶ Put together a list of suitable charities by consulting either EGAS or the directories in the library.
- ▶ Find out exactly what each charity is offering and whether you meet their criteria. Check if there is a final entry date for applications.

▶ Write a brief note to selected charities, explaining your need and asking for an application form.

▶ Fill in the application form. Make sure answers are clear, concise and truthful. You may be questioned on them later. Bear the trust's criteria in mind.

▶ Photocopy the completed form before you send it back.

▶ Wait patiently. These things can take many weeks to process.

Do students actually get help?

'As an engineering student I needed a computer, but couldn't afford one. Were there any charities that could help? I searched around, and discovered the Earl's Colne Educational Trust, which assisted students living within 10 miles of Earl's Colne in Essex. I lived in Halstead, just within the limits – it was worth a try. I wrote to them explaining my needs; they sent me a form; I filled it in; I waited; I went for an interview. The result: £500 – easy money. It cost just two sides of A4!'
Jonathan, when studying Electronic Engineering at Loughborough University

Are the 'givers' cutting back because of the credit crunch?

Two of the professional institutions featured in this chapter certainly had to trim their offer to students, by reducing the number of scholarships/bursaries given, and in some cases the amount they can give. The reason given, certainly by the IET, was the reduction in income from investments because of the economic downturn. The chief executive of Family Action (of which EGAS is a part) also said that the number of educational grants that they can make was being affected by the low income from their investments. While we haven't checked with the many hundreds of charities and trusts that offer educational help to students, it is fair to assume their income and therefore their ability to help has been hit. So it's not so much that the 'givers' are cutting back; more that they don't have the money to give – and just when students need it most.

Competitions

Are they worth it?

The world is full of competition addicts. There are magazines devoted solely to the topic, steering readers to the next give-away bonanza. Whole families eat crazy diets just to get the labels off the right tins and jars. People do win

– holidays in exotic places, new cars, toasters, DVD players, washing machines and cuddly toys. It's always worth having a go, if it only means the cost of a stamp and perhaps writing a catchy slogan. However, competitions cannot be seen as a serious means of raising finance.

If it's a competition set by your university with prizes for excellence, in a subject area you know well, you're in with a real chance, and winning could be a useful addition to your CV.

A little icing on the cake is the best you can hope for, and even that is a long shot. But don't dismiss competitions altogether. If it's a competition aimed specifically at students, it very often involves writing an essay. Students, being the overworked (or lazy?) lot they are, tend to give them a miss, so the number of entries can be low. All the more reason to give it a try. How does this grab you?

Win £700

All you have to do is write a 900-word essay about your industrial placement and you could win £700. The winner this year is Tim Chapman from University of Kent who wrote about his placement at BAE Systems in Rochester. Two commendations and special runner-up prizes of £100 went to Alyzandra Milne from Liverpool John Moores University, who worked at Chester Zoo, and Stephanie Rostron from Leeds Metropolitan University, who spent her placement at Dorint GmbH, a German hotel chain. Next time it could be you. The competition is run by ASET, the Association for Sandwich Education and Training. Entries should be in by the beginning of December, and the results are announced in February.

On the other hand, you might find it more fun, though not as lucrative, to enter ASET's bloggers competition, called Student Stars. For this you have to produce a blog at various stages during your placement year. Successful blogs will be put on the ASET website and could win you £200. To find out more about both competitions, log onto the ASET website: www.asetonline.org/comps, email aset@asetonline or phone 0114 221 2902. Best of luck!

Who won the *Guide to Student Money* £100?

Any student who filled in the *Guide to Student Money* questionnaire this year was automatically included in our £100 prize draw. This year's winner was Hannes Rohtsalu, a first-year chemistry student at the University of St Andrews, and a very deserving candidate he turned out to be. Hannes is from Estonia, and is struggling to pay his way through university.

'When I first received the email saying I had won I was really surprised, and wasn't sure it was real,' says Hannes. 'When I found it was genuine, I was very pleased. I shall use the money to buy books for my course. Until now I have had to use the library, I just couldn't afford the books I needed.'

As an EU student studying in Scotland, Hannes doesn't have to pay fees, something that helped him decide where in the UK to study, but he can't get a student loan. He receives £1,200 help from the Estonian government, and his parents send a little when they can afford it (no more than £200 a term). The rest he has to find himself, by working in the vacations. He lives in halls, but chose self-catering because it is cheaper.

Three £1,000 Green Cheese Scholarships to be won

Every year, BUNAC awards three scholarships of up to £1,000 each to help applicants cover the costs of taking part in a BUNAC work-abroad programme to the USA or Canada. To enter the Green Cheese Scholarships, all you need to do is submit a humorous piece of original creative writing based on a travel-related topic. You're free to write about anything at all – whether it's a trip to the other side of the world or a journey you made closer to home. Entries should be no more than 1,500 words. Contact your university/college or BUNAC, 16 Bowling Green Lane, London EC1R 0QH. Tel: 020 7251 3472. Fax: 020 7251 0215. Email: enquiries@bunac.org.uk. Website: www.bunac.org.

Lotteries

Then, of course, there's the lottery. Not strictly a competition, but an option. This book is not in the business of advocating gambling, and at £1 a go, or at least £104 a year, depending on how addictive it becomes, is it worth it? The odds on winning the jackpot are 14 million to one, and if you did win, what would happen to your studies?

The web

Finally, students have been writing in with news of competitions on the web and in the media. Here are a couple of their stories:

advice note

The litmus test with any competition has to be: 'Is it worth it?' Look at the hassle involved, the cost, the time factor, the number of cans of baked beans or cat food you have got to get through and, above all, the odds – and then make your decision. The drawback with any competition is that the winner takes all, and the also-rans get nothing. Still, it doesn't hurt to keep your eyes open.

Try www. prizefinder.com, ukcompetitions. com, or even www.studentstuff.com or type 'competitions' into your search engine. This will give you information on all the competitions that are available on the web at the moment – best of luck!

'Enter internet competitions using uni computers, since the web is free. I did and won a round-the-world trip, a TV, a video, a computer and £1,000 in cash.'

3rd year Economics student at York University

'Whatever the prize, have a go. You can always sell it. I won a scooter worth £1,000 in a radio competition. It was a life-saver. I sold it immediately, and was able to solve my financial problems, which were dire. I still have a student loan, of course, but no overdraft.'

2nd year student, Lancaster

Further information

Where to look

- ▶ On your college noticeboard.
- ▶ In the careers office.
- ▶ National newspapers.
- ▶ Student newspapers.
- ▶ The web.

Who to contact

- ▶ EGAS helpline: tel: 020 7254 6251; website: www.egas-online.org.uk/fwa/trustsearch.htm.
- ▶ Scholarship Search UK: www.scholarship-search.org.uk.

What to read

- ▶ *The Grants Register* lists over 3,500 awards. Published by Macmillan. Tel: 01256 329242. Email: macdir@macmillan.co.uk. Very expensive (£185 for the new 2008 edition) – try your local library.

▶ *Directory of Grant-Making Trusts*, published by the Charities Aid Foundation. Available from Trotman, tel: 0870 900 2665, or visit www.trotman.co.uk/bookshop. See also grantsonline.org.uk.

▶ *University Scholarships, Awards and Bursaries*, published by Trotman. To order, tel: 0870 900 2665 or visit www.trotman.co.uk/bookshop.

▶ *Educational Grants Directory* available from Trotman. To order, tel: 0870 900 2665.

Most voluble students

	Weekly spend on telephone
London	£11.76
Leicester	£11.68
Cardiff	£11.45
Swansea	£11.39
Portsmouth	£10.98
Belfast	£10.94
Nottingham	£10.81
Bristol	£10.65
Exeter	£10.48
Brighton	£10.30

Source: *NatWest Student Living Index*

CHAPTER 9

Postgraduate study: where to find funding

The number of postgraduate students in the UK keeps increasing. In the last 10 years the number of students on postgraduate courses has almost doubled. How are they managing to pay for their studies? Has funding kept pace with the demand? In this chapter we look at the main sources of finance for postgraduates.

The main topics covered in this chapter are:

The *Berlin School of Mind and Brain* is an international research school, located in the vibrant heart of Berlin. Founded in 2006 as part of Germany's *Excellence Initiative*, it offers a unique three-year interdisciplinary doctoral programme in English in the mind/brain sciences.

Research within the School focuses on the interface between the humanities and the neurosciences. Of particular interest are research areas that fall on the borders between the mind sciences (e.g., philosophy, linguistics, behavioral and cognitive science, economics), and the brain sciences (e.g., neurophysiology, computational neuroscience, neurology, and neurobiology). Major topics of research within the programme include: 'conscious and unconscious perception', 'mental disorders and brain dysfunction', 'decision-making', 'language', 'brain plasticity and lifespan ontogeny', and the 'philosophy of mind'. However, research is not limited to these areas, and students are strongly encouraged to develop and work at their own initiative on any projects that are relevant to interdisciplinary questions relating to mind and brain.

The School is situated in the centre of Berlin, on the grounds of the Charité, the largest medical campus in Europe.

The city itself is a major centre for culture, politics, media, and science; and is globally recognized for its rich art-scene, museums, internationally renowned festivals, and a pleasant and highly affordable standard of living.

Each year the School accepts ten to fifteen doctoral candidates into its programme. Here are some excellent reasons why students might wish to be considered for one of these highly sought after positions at the *Berlin School of Mind and Brain*:

Excellence in Training and Research

• The School has a faculty **comprised of 60 distinguished researchers**, including **four Max Planck directors**, which cover the gamut of research in the mind and brain sciences.

• **Research within the School is strongly embedded in the basic and clinical research conducted within the region** allowing for strong synergistic research initiatives and opportunities. Hosted by the Humboldt University, the School's research programme includes scientists from the Free University, the Technical University, the Bernstein Centre for Computational Neuroscience, the Max Planck Institute for Human Development (Berlin), the Max Planck Institute for

Human Cognitive and Brain Sciences (Leipzig), and the nearby universities of Potsdam and Magdeburg.

· **Students acquire a strong foundation for interdisciplinary work** by attending ten one-week classes during the first half of their doctoral programme, which cover all fields relevant for mind/brain-related research, and allow students to explore research methods and topics that they have not been previously exposed to. Each doctoral candidate is assigned two professorial advisors – one from the brain sciences, one from the mind sciences – in order to maximize the interdisciplinary impact of their work.

· Students **meet with leading international researchers** via the School's Distinguished Lecture Series, interactions with its senior visiting faculty, as well as by attending international workshops and meetings. As part of the School's commitment to maximizing students' research opportunities, the School also encourages and provides **assistance for students to spend time studying and conducting research abroad** during the course of their doctoral candidacy.

· **Extensive practical services for international doctoral candidates** are available, including assistance with visa applications, matriculation, health insurance, local authorities, scientific soft skill courses, and language classes.

Finally, there are good financial reasons for studying at the Berlin School of Mind and Brain:

· There are **no tuition fees** associated with the programme.

· **Administrative fees are very low.** Administrative fees for attending the Humboldt University come to only approximately 250 euros per semester.

· The School offers **generous scholarships to the best applicants**. Students who were not successful in winning one of the School's own scholarships will receive support in obtaining alternative sources of funding (e.g. a research post within a university department or with one of the School's research groups, or help in finding alternative funding sources for a scholarship).

Recent progress in the neurosciences has opened up new and exciting avenues for research that raise challenging conceptual and ethical questions calling for an interdisciplinary approach. The *Berlin School of Mind and Brain* offers a unique research and training environment for doctoral candidates to work at this exciting interface between the sciences and the humanities.

For further information please contact: funding2010@mind-and-brain.de
www.mind-and-brain.de

Is it worth obtaining a postgraduate qualification?

It's a Fact

The online postgraduate applications system enables postgraduate students in the UK and overseas to apply electronically to HE institutions. Access is via www.prospects.ac.uk, which hosts the national postgraduate database, or through a participating institution's website.

If you are going to enter a career in which you will need extra qualifications, such as the legal profession, or if you are seeking a post in academia or the teaching profession then of course further study is worth every penny. But otherwise, will it actually earn you extra cash? Employers don't always agree on this one. Some value additional qualifications, others ignore them. However . . .

A report published by Universities UK in 2007 suggested that holders of postgraduate degrees earn more than their graduate counterparts – on average £70,000–£80,000 over a lifetime; less if you hold a postgraduate certificate: average £30,000–£40,000 over a lifetime.

More up-to-date information from the *AGR Winter Graduate Recruitment Review 2009* suggests that further qualifications are worth a premium of £3,500 for a PhD (median figure) and £2,000 for a postgraduate qualifications (median figure.) But only 18% of AGR's members gave information and these figures are down by about 40% on last year. We have no data as to whether this differential is still the same. An MBA can attract very high rewards, according to the AGR review, with a median figure of £21,000. However, actual premium for an MBA is greatly influenced by individual organisations.

How much will it cost?

Tuition fees

UK residents and EU nationals:

- ▶ fees: £3,390 plus (research councils' fee level) – average figure. Certain courses may cost more. Part-time students: about half the full-time rate
- ▶ law: Graduate Diploma in Law/CPE course £2,500–£7,000. LPC course £5,200–£12,500 and possibly more
- ▶ MBA general range: £10,000–£16,000 (£12,000 median, but could be more than double that at top schools).

Students from abroad: average for 2008–2009

	Taught	Research
Classroom	£9,300	£9,300
Laboratory/workshops	£11,000	£11,300
Clinical (Medicine)	£22,700	£22,700

Maintenance

The results of research given in Chapter 1 will give you some idea of how much it is going to cost you to live. Just for basic costs that's around £255 a week. The NUS reckon it would be much higher – £12,624 would be needed if living in London and £10,481 everywhere else, but that is just for a 39-week academic year and was based on NUS figures for 2008–2009. And remember, none of these figures includes fees.

> **cash crisis**
>
> London is a lot more expensive than you think: just a two-zone day pass on the Tube is over a fiver; and landlords can ask for up to two months' rent as a deposit.

Sources of funding

Will I get funding?

Don't bank on it. Competition for funding for postgraduates is phenomenal. There is no all-embracing funding system as for first degrees, and students generally have to search around to get help. It is much easier to get a place on a course than it is to get the money to pay for it. Many postgraduates have to finance themselves with loans, etc., which is probably why part-time study for postgraduates is increasing in popularity. If you are offered funding, make sure it covers both tuition fees and maintenance.

> **It's a Fact**
>
> The latest figures show that 333,655 postgraduate students are enrolled on postgraduate courses in the UK – 115,335 full time, and 218,320 part-time. (HESA figures 2007–2008)

What are the possible sources of funding?

1. Government funding from research councils – these are by far the largest sources of funding in the UK. Some 7,000 new awards are made each year. Each 'awarding body' funds different courses and there is little overlap, so it is important to

identify the appropriate body for your needs (see page 223; for Scotland and Northern Ireland see also pages 236 and 237).

2. Erasmus (often known as Socrates–Erasmus) is a programme developed by the European Commission to provide funds for the mobility of students and staff in universities throughout the EU member states and the countries of the European Free Trade Association (EFTA). See page 114 for full details and information on Erasmus and other similar programmes, such as the Leonardo da Vinci scheme.

3. Employers will occasionally sponsor employees through courses, especially MBAs.

4. Companies may sponsor students on a research project. This could be as the result of a work experience association during a first degree, or in co-operation with one of the research councils.

5. Trusts and charities are more likely to award small amounts of money than full financial support, but they are certainly worth considering (see Chapter 8). Your local authority awards officer would have details of any local charities. Otherwise contact EGAS (see page 208 for details) or look in the published charities and grant-making trusts' directories and registers. Apply early: processing can be inordinately slow.

6. Local authorities. Except in the case of teacher training, local authorities are not required by law to fund postgraduates. Funding is discretionary, is given mainly for vocational courses that lead to certificates or diplomas, is means tested and is subject to different criteria according to the local authority. Likely subjects are accountancy, journalism, law, music, secretarial work, youth work and computing. If you are tapping your local authority it is essential to apply early as their funds are limited, and you'll need to present a good case for yourself. But because there are no set rules for funding, it is always worth a try.

7. Universities' own postgraduate studentship awards. Many institutions have a small number of studentships available for specific courses. Aberystwyth, for example, gives around 12 awards each year to UK/EU students for research degrees. Awards generally cover fees and maintenance. Closing dates vary. For the Aberystwyth competition it's 1 March. Check your university of choice for details.

8. University departments. They may have nothing, and probably won't advertise. But if they particularly want you, or there's something they are interested in doing, they may have sources they can tap. You could find that they stipulate you have to take on some tutorial work or assist the department.

9. Research assistantships are salaried posts in academic departments, which provide the opportunity to study for a higher degree. Salaries vary and opportunities can become available throughout the year. Watch the relevant press for adverts – the *Guardian*, *The Times*, *New Scientist*, *Nature*, *Prospects* – and the web, etc.

10. Loans from banks – see later in this chapter, page 253.

Thrift Tips

Tip from Aberystwyth: 'We say to graduates it's always worth a try; all it needs is the right phone call just at the right time.'

Can I get a student loan?

Only if you are taking a Postgraduate Certificate in Education (PGCE). Even though it's generally only a one-year course, you will be classed as a first- rather than a final-year student, so you can take out the maximum loan offered. You can also take out a loan to cover fees. (See page 241 for full details of special funding arrangements for PGCE.) Or you could try a bank loan (see page 252).

Funding from research councils

These are the main sources of government funding for postgraduates. There are eight major award-making bodies in the UK. Each one operates independently and the awards they offer are all slightly different, as are their regulations. The information given here should therefore be seen as a general guide to what you could expect to get. All the award-making bodies issue information about their own awards, which you can get by writing to them or phoning them (addresses are given later in this chapter) or by looking on the internet. The areas of study covered by individual research councils can change, so make sure any information you get is up to date.

> **cash crisis**
>
> From a student who knows: *'You always need double the money you think you need when you are moving to a new location to study. There are always hidden costs.'*

What kind of award could I get?

There are essentially four kinds of awards for postgraduate students.

► Research Studentships, which are generally a three-year award leading to a doctorate (PhD or DPhil).

► Collaborative Research Studentships, when the research project is part funded by an external industrial organisation and may well give the student some experience outside the academic environment. The collaborating company generally gives the student extra cash on top of the studentship award. The awarding body may also give an additional award on top of the basic studentship. This is certainly so with CASE awards (Co-operative Awards in Science and Engineering).

► Advanced Course Studentships, given for taught courses which must be of at least six months' duration, but are generally for one or possibly two years, often leading to a Master's degree (MSc, MA) or other qualification.

► Bursaries, which are allocated by the Central Social Care Council for courses in social work; the amounts offered are much lower.

Not all awarding bodies give all types of award. And some give additional awards and fellowships.

Is the award means tested?

Only maintenance grants for training in social work are means tested.

What could an award cover?

► Payment of approved fees to the institution.

► Maintenance allowance.

► Dependants' and other allowances.

► Assistance with additional travel and subsistence expenses for something like fieldwork.

Do I have to get a 2:1 to take a postgraduate course?

Each course will set its own requirements. If you are thinking of specialising in your degree subject, a first or 2:1 is probably what you will need. For a vocational course, you'll need to show real commitment and interest in the subject. If, however, you are seeking funding from a government funding council, they will generally demand:

► a first or upper second-class honours degree, or a lower second with a further qualification such as an MA for a Research Studentship

► at least a lower second-class honours degree for a taught/one-year course. (This does not apply to social work courses.)

How do I go about getting funding?

Start with the university careers office where you want to study. Most are clued up when it comes to tapping the scarce resources available to postgraduates. They may even publish a special leaflet on sources of funding for postgraduate study. Many of the publications listed at the end of this chapter, which we suggest you consult, should also be in the university careers library. Talk to the tutors in your department, especially if you want to undertake a research degree, as they will know what projects are likely to gain funding. Consult university prospectuses.

When should I approach the award-making bodies?

If you want general information on their award scheme – any time. It is important to read thoroughly the individual information produced by the different award-making bodies, as closing dates, methods of application and what is on offer will vary. In most cases, application for awards is done through the institution you hope to join. Check information for procedure.

How do I apply for funding?

In the case of most research councils (Biotechnology and Biological Sciences Research Council (BBSRC), Engineering and Physical Sciences Research Council (EPSRC), Economic and Social Research Council (ESRC), Medical Research Council (MRC), Natural Environment Research Council (NERC), Science and Technology Facilities Council (STFC)), funding to students is funnelled through university departments and courses. They select the students for their courses/projects and submit their names to the awarding body. Application forms are obtained from the department for your intended studies, and must be returned well in advance of the end of July, when the department will submit them to the appropriate awarding council.

The Arts and Humanities Research Council (AHRC) has changed their funding allocation mechanism this year so that there are two ways you can be asked to apply. There is the block grant which is awarded to an institution and then the institution will nominate students to each place where funding is awarded. Alternatively, there is the Studentship competition where the student applies to the institution and their application is forwarded to the AHRC with attachments from referees and the institution. Either way, your first port of call is the institution where you want to study.

"Human Development in Landscapes"
– a new Graduate School at Kiel University

To gain an understanding of human development, one needs to detail the interactions between mankind and both, its physical and perceived environment. Intensified cross-linkages between academic disciplines, graduate researchers' growing needs for analytical equipment and an efficient infrastructure, as well as an increasingly internationalized research environment, have encouraged the set up of a multidisciplinary Graduate School (GS). This school makes available new research and communication structures to our graduate students, enabling them to do innovative research. The new training programmes, communication networks, and interdisciplinary research foci will strengthen and enhance the existing CAU infrastructure and establish the GS as an international research and educational centre. We build on existing research networks that emphasize interdisciplinary research to further a holistic approach to the study of human societies´ development in changing landscapes.

We define landscape as a dynamic space of social, cultural, and ecological significance, which develops interactively with the human societies occupying it. Accordingly, our concept merges information from molecular biology and archaeology, geoinformatics and art history, geophysics and isotope research, ancient languages and paleo-ecology, written/oral traditions and paleo-climate to study and understand this interactive development. The dynamics of human development – and thus of landscape and living space - are captured by a complex interplay of diverse factors (biological traits of social groups, conditions of the natural environment, social constants and their material representations) covered by the joint research of our disciplines. The results of the research could give new impulses for present landscape and cultural management.

The education and research at the school is organised in three clusters and supported by three research platforms. The students will receive necessary skills during a three-year study programme. Adjustments to the study regulations will further interdisciplinary international graduate research. Within the framework of a GS, we are able to provide individual tutoring of graduate students, interdisciplinary graduate clusters as well as the technological means and expertise to collect, process, visualise, and analyse spatial and temporal data from multidisciplinary sources. New research tools, developed to obtain and process scientific and cultural data, will promote international excellence in graduate training and research, attracting a national and international graduate student population to Kiel. The GS builds on a combination of academic structures, which is unique to Kiel: technological resources for scientific analyses including genetic and isotope analysis and an almost complete range of material analysis combined with a strong arts and humanities programme. The GS also benefits from a long-standing expertise in graduate education in different fields of the arts and humanities especially in analysing concepts of spatial organisation of regions and landscapes. This integration of inter-disciplinary supervision distinguishes Kiel as an optimal location for studies in 'Human Development in Landscapes'.

The GS "Human Development in Land-scapes" is focussed on the research concept of the natural and cultural space. This implies that it does not just concern the interdisciplinary cooperation of the many scientific disciplines of the natural and social sciences and arts and humanities participating in the GS and its research focus. Instead, it daringly undertakes to use the study of 'reality' as a mean to realise the universal attempt to consider in principle human behaviour, with the whole of human activities, expe-riences, and understanding, within their spatial surroundings and their culturally modified, space-related living conditions. The research concept intends to uncover the layers of our knowledge regarding the development of humans in their spatial environments one by one, by elucidate the initial and boundary spatial conditions of this development and their social conse-quences. This research will also provide tools to master the present. The concept points toward the total complex of the natural, social, and cultural phenomena and processes in the comprehensive sense, at climatic and vegetation changes, at technical innovations, sustenance bases and settlement development, and at their social limitations and consequences, at the development of mentalities, commu-nication, and social interaction. Therefore, society and its environment cannot be separated. An integrating synopsis with simultaneous analytical separation can only be realized by an extensive teaching and research group with a large number of coordinated discrete steps of data reduction and analysis. The research areas of such a synopsis are mainly found in the integrated studies of paleo-ecology, paleo-climatology, archaeozoology, ar-chaeology and cultural history. The inte-gration of research areas of many science related subjects (physics, mathematics, geo- and archaeoinformatics, materials science) and cultural anthropology is necessary to form platforms for the elabo-ration of research areas. Hence, human development in landscapes provides an interdisciplinary research theme of broad interest to society which requires this universal approach bridging the traditional boundaries between individual disciplines and faculties. The scientific concept of the GS builds on proved excellence and well-established networks of participating institutes and non-university institutions, including international partners and networks and integrates further disciplines into a wide-ranging and forward-looking theme.

For further information, please contact:
Prof. Dr. Johannes Müller (johannes.mueller@ufg.uni-kiel.de)
Dr. Mara Weinelt (mweinelt@gshdl.uni-kiel.de)
Postal address: Graduate School "Human Development in Landscapes", Olshausenstraße 40, CAU zu Kiel D-24098 Kiel (Germany)

www.uni-kiel.de/landscapes

A Fresh Approach to Flexible Work

Need to earn while you study? FreshMinds could be the answer. FreshMinds is an award-winning research and recruitment consultancy that allows some of the brightest brains in the UK to flex their intellectual muscles while working at big-name clients in every sector from banking to government. Among the pool of Minds are top graduates, postgraduates and business analysts drawn from the world's leading universities, business schools and companies. If you're in between periods of study or looking for a job, FreshMinds can help you find the perfect way to while away the time and bring home some much-needed money.

Research ranges from information and data gathering to more complex analysis, including market research, company profiling and competitor benchmarking. Depending on where the wind takes you, you could be working in the heart of FreshMinds' Holborn office or on placements with clients for anything from three days to six months. FreshMinds only works with the best – graduates who not only have a 2:1 degree or better from a top university, but who have revelled in excelling among their peers. If you are a glowing example of a fresh, young Mind take a look at www.freshminds.co.uk or give them a ring on 020 7692 4300 to find out more.

Will it make a difference where I choose to study?

Yes. Not all courses or departments attract funding. It is important to find out the situation when you apply. And just because a course is eligible for studentships, and you have a place on that course, it still doesn't mean you will necessarily get one. It is very competitive. And remember, if you don't get funding it could mean you have to pay not only your own maintenance but also your course fees. In that case, a university close to your own home might be the answer, or studying part time (day release, evening courses or distance learning).

When and how can I find out what projects have funding?

From April onwards your university should have a list of university departments that have been given funding by the awarding bodies. Under the scheme, universities are committed to attracting the very best students for the awards, so they must advertise for candidates outside as well as within their own university. Typical media: *New Scientist*, *Nature*, the *Guardian* or university magazines, depending on the topic.

If you want a list of which courses and projects throughout the country have received funding, contact the appropriate awarding body after 1 April. Information may also be on their websites.

Can I approach more than one awarding body?

No. There is generally no overlap between the awarding research councils: they each have their own designated areas. So it is important to identify which body to apply to, as you can only apply to one. In the case of the Arts and Humanities Research Council there does appear to be some overlap between its three different arms. However, a course that attracts bursaries from one will not generally gain funding from other state sources.

Quick check

Awards		In London	Elsewhere	Any location
BBSRC		£15,290	£13,290	Vet £20,510
ESRC		£15,290	£13,290	
MRC		£15,510	£13,290	
STFC		£15,290	£13,290	
AHRC	Research Master's	£11,280	£9,280	
AHRC	Professional Master's	£10,650	£8,650	
AHRC	Doctoral Award	£15,290	£13,290	
EPSRC	PhD studies			£13,290
NERC	PhD studies			£13,290
NERC	Advanced course	£10,500	£8,500	
GSCC				Not supplied

The award-making bodies

Subjects given for each body have been selected to give a broad view of topics covered, and are by no means exhaustive. Candidates should check with the appropriate organisation, or on the appropriate website.

Arts and Humanities Research Council (AHRC)

Awards are available for Master's degree courses and doctoral study across a number of subject panels and these are continually evolving. Typical subjects are:

- classics, ancient history and archaeology
- English language and literature
- medieval and modern history
- modern languages and linguistics
- librarianship, information and museum studies
- music and performing arts
- philosophy, religious studies and law.

The AHRC offers studentships through four different competitions:

- Block Grant Partnerships (BGP)
- Studentship Competition (SC)
- Collaborative Doctoral Awards (CDA)
- Research grants with Project Studentships (PS) attached.

Within these competitions the AHRC operates three separate schemes:

- Doctoral Awards (DA)
- Research Preparation Master's (RPM)
- Professional Preparation Master's (PPM).

For more details see AHRC's website.

Research Preparation Master's Scheme
Type of award:
Support for students undertaking Master's degree courses that focus on advanced study and research training which provides a foundation for further research at doctoral level. Awards will normally be for one year's full-time study or two years' part-time study

Amount:
Studying in London: £11,280.
Elsewhere: £9,280.
Part-time study: £4,640 (London £5,640).
Tuition fees: £3,390 full-time/£1,695 part-time.

Professional Preparation Master's Scheme
Type of award:
Support for Master's degrees or postgraduate diploma courses that focus on developing high-level skills and competencies for professional practice. Awards will normally be for one year's full-time study and two years' part-time study.

Amount:
Studying in London: £10,650.
Elsewhere: £8,650.
Part-time study: £4,330 (London £5,330).
Tuition fees: £3,390 full-time/£1,695 part-time.

Doctoral Scheme
Type of award:
Support for up to three years of full-time study or up to five years' part-time study leading to a doctoral degree.

Amount:
Studying in London: £15,290.
Elsewhere: £13,290.
Part-time study: £7,970 (London: £9,170).
Tuition fees: £3,390 full-time/£1,695 part-time.

Address:
Programmes Division
Arts and Humanities Research Council
Whitefriars
Lewins Mead
Bristol BS1 2AE
Tel: 0117 987 6543
Fax: 0117 987 6544
Email: pgenquiries@ahrc.ac.uk
Website: www.ahrc.ac.uk

Biotechnology and Biological Sciences Research Council (BBSRC)

Subject areas:
Biological sciences and associated technologies (agriculture and food sciences, animal sciences, biochemistry and cell biology, biomolecular sciences, engineering and biological systems, genes and development biology, plant and microbial sciences).

Type of award:
► Research Studentship
► Master's Studentship.

Amount:
Study in London: £15,290.
Elsewhere: £13,290.
(Doctoral Training Account minimum stipend can be higher.) For students with a recognised veterinary degree: £20,510. Students holding a first degree who wish to intercalate a PhD during their veterinary training receive an annual

supplement of £2,000 p.a. from BBSRC. CASE awards (Co-operative Awards in Science and Engineering) – additional minimum £2,500 by collaborator.

Address:
Biotechnology and Biological Sciences Research Council
Polaris House
North Star Avenue
Swindon SN2 1UH
Tel: 01793 413200
Email: postgrad.studentships@bbsrc.ac.uk
Website: www.bbsrc.ac.uk

Economic and Social Research Council (ESRC)

Subject areas:
Area studies, economics, economic and social history, education, human geography, linguistics, management and business studies (accounting, finance, industrial relations and other specialist management courses), planning, politics and international relations, science technology and innovation studies, psychology, social anthropology, social policy, socio-legal studies, sociology, sports, statistics, research methods and computing as applied to the social sciences.

Type of award:

- ▶ Annual Studentship Competition (1+3 & +3)
- ▶ 113 Quota awards.
- ▶ Joint ESRC/NERC Studentships
- ▶ Joint ESRC/MRC Studentships
- ▶ Joint ESRC/Department for Transport Studentships
- ▶ Joint ESRC/Scottish Executive Studentships
- ▶ Joint ESRC/Department for National Statistics Studentships
- ▶ GLC Grants Research Studentships
- ▶ GLC Grants, one-year Master's
- ▶ Welsh Assembly Research Studentships
- ▶ CASE Studentships
- ▶ Centre Linked Studentships
- ▶ Language Based Area Studies
- ▶ Project Linked Studentships
- ▶ Capacity Building Cluster (CBC) Case Studentships.

Amount:
Studying in London: £15,290
Elsewhere: £13,290.
(Enhanced stipends given by the Welsh Assembly and Scottish Executive of £2,000, if studying Economics or Quantitative Methods an additional £3,000.)

Address:
Economic and Social Research Council
Research, Training & Development Directorate

Polaris House
North Star Avenue
Swindon SN2 1UJ
Tel: 01793 413150
Email: ptd@esrc.ac.uk
Website: www.esrc.ac.uk

Engineering and Physical Sciences Research Council (EPSRC)

Subject areas:
Engineering, chemistry, mathematics, physics, information and computer technologies, materials science and the life sciences interface.

Types of support:
EPSRC supports all of its postgraduate training through packages of funding provided to the universities. It is the responsibility of the university to assess student eligibility for and select students to receive funding. Prospective students should contact universities or departments direct.

Funding is provided for:
► Standard Research Studentships
► Industrial CAS Studentships
► CASE for New Academic Appointees
► engineering doctorate (EngD)
► Master's degrees (MSc and MRes).

Amount:
Amounts may vary, depending on university, but EPSRC requires that PhD students receive a stipend of at least the national minimum rate.
PhD students: £13,290.
Research engineers at engineering doctorate centres: £14,400 (2008–2009 figure).

Address:
Engineering and Physical Sciences Research Council
Polaris House
North Star Avenue
Swindon SN2 1ET
Tel: 01793 444000
Website: www.epsrc.ac.uk

General Social Care Council (GSCC)

Subject area:
Social work.

Type of award:
The social work bursary for students on full-time postgraduate courses is available to students normally resident in England studying on an approved full-time postgraduate course. Students must also meet certain other eligibility criteria. The bursary consists of a non–income-assessed basic grant including a fixed contribution towards practice learning, opportunity-related expenses and tuition fee support. It also includes an income-assessed maintenance grant and income-assessed allowances to assist with certain costs of living, as recipients of the postgraduate bursary will not ordinarily be entitled to local authority funding. Financial awards are dependent on individual circumstances

Address:
Social Work Bursary
NHS Business Services Authority
Sandyford House
Archbold Terrace
Newcastle Upon Tyne NE2 1DB
Tel: 0845 6101122
Email: swb@ppa.nhs.uk
Website: www.ppa.org.uk/swb

Medical Research Council (MRC)

Subject areas:
Medicine (including tropical medicine); areas of biology including cancer, clinical neurosciences and mental health, clinical psychology, cognitive science, epidemiology, health services research, imaging, infections and immunity (including HIV and Aids), inheritance, medical statistics, molecules and cells, neurobiology, quantitative biology, reproduction and child health.

Types of support:
MRC supports much of its postgraduate training through packages of funding provided to the universities as Doctoral Training Accounts. Prospective students should contact universities or heads of departments direct to see if there is funding available.

Funding is provided for:
► research PhDs
► research Master's (MRes)
► collaborative PhDs
► Advanced Course Master's Studentships
► Capacity Building Area (Priority Area) Studentships
► Industrial Collaborative Studentships
► MRC/ESRC Interdisciplinary Studentships.

Amount:
May vary, depending on university, but a PhD student should receive a
minimum stipend of:
Studying in London: £15,510
Elsewhere: £13,290.

Address:
Barry Wynne
Medical Research Council
20 Park Crescent
London W1N 4AL
Tel: 020 7670 5408
Email: students@headoffice.mrc.ac.uk
Website: www.mrc.ac.uk

Natural Environment Research Council (NERC)

Subject areas:
Atmospheric chemistry, earth observation and associated science, freshwater
ecology, geology, geophysics, hydrology, marine ecology, organic pollution,
physical oceanography, science-based archaeology, soil sciences, terrestrial ecology.

Type of award:
PhD (3-year Research Studentship): can be a straight research award, a CASE
award or an OPEN CASE Award (these studentships are awarded to the
universities in competition – approx. 25 a year)
MSc and MRes (one-year Advanced Course Studentships).

Amount:
PhD stipend: £13,290 p.a.
Advanced Course stipend: £8,500 (£10,500 in London)
Extra PhD allowances: conference allowance, £450
Research support
Training Grant (RTSG): £3,000 (CASE awards – minimum of £1,000 p.a. by
   collaborator)
London weighting: £2,000 for PhD, MSc and MRes students.

Address:
Natural Environment Research Council
Polaris House
North Star Avenue
Swindon SN2 1EU
Tel: 01793 411500
Website: www.nerc.ac.uk

Science and Technology Facilities Council (STFC)

(Formerly Particle Physics and Astronomy Research Council (PPARC).)

Subject areas:
Astronomy, astrophysics, nuclear physics, particle physics, solar system science.

Type of award:
► Research Studentship – 251 allocated
► CASE – 10 allocated.

Amount:
Studying in London: £15,290 p.a.
Elsewhere: £13,290 p.a.
(CASE award – additional £615 p.a. given plus minimum of £2,760 p.a. by
   collaborating company.)

Address:
Science and Technology Facilities Council
Polaris House
North Star Avenue
Swindon SN2 1ET
Tel: 01793 442000
Email: studentships@stfc.ac.uk
Website: http://www.stfc.ac.uk/

See table on page 229 for a quick reference guide to postgraduate awards.
Those taking postgraduate teaching courses should turn to page 241.

Wales

Graduates are eligible for funding from the research councils listed above. Those
taking a postgraduate teaching courses should turn to page 241.

Scotland

Graduates seeking funding for science-based subjects are eligible for
studentship awards from most of the research councils mentioned here. Funding
for postgraduate vocational courses mostly at diploma level (usually for one
year) may be available through the Postgraduate Student Allowance Scheme
(PSAS). Not all postgraduate courses are supported. Students taking PGCE or
PGDipCE will be funded in the same way as undergraduates. Tuition fees up to
a maximum of £3,315 will be paid for eligible students. All funding is means
tested. Contact SAAS on 0845 111 1711 for general enquiries.

PSAS rates for 2008–2009

Location	Grant
London	£4,780
Elsewhere	£3,770
Parents' home	£2,850

Northern Ireland

▶ Postgraduate students can compete for funding from the award-making bodies already listed.

▶ The Department for Employment and Learning (DEL) offers two types of award: for research (MPhil, DPhil, PhD) and for approved courses of advanced study (Master's degrees) in fields of humanities, science and technology and the social sciences. Awards are not means tested.

▶ For studentships to pursue postgraduate study in Northern Ireland (at either Queen's University Belfast or the University of Ulster), apply to the university for an application form. The offer of a place does not mean that funding will be provided.

▶ The Northern Ireland Department of Agriculture and Rural Development provides funds for study (in Northern Ireland) in agriculture including horticulture, and

related sciences such as agricultural economics, engineering science and food science (closing date: last Friday in February).

▶ Medicine – see the Medical Research Council details, above.

▶ The basic rate of maintenance grant for 2009–2010 is £13,290. Additional allowances may also be paid for dependants and students with special needs.

▶ CAST awards (Co-operative Awards in Science and Technology) support research projects at Northern Ireland universities for one year or three years in collaboration with industry. Maintenance grant of £13,290 p.a., and should be supplemented by a payment from the collaborating body.

▶ Johns Hopkins Fellowship Award – a one-year Fellowship Award covering fees only for the Johns Hopkins University's School of Advanced International Studies in Bologna.

▶ One student is funded by DEL to take a one-year course in Administration, Economics and Law at the College of Europe, Bruges.

For further information tel: 028 9025 7699, email: studentfinance@delni.gov. uk or check the web: www.delni.gov.uk/studentfinance.

Channel Islands/Isle of Man

Apply direct to the appropriate education department. For idea of fees go to www.universitiesuk.ac.uk/PolicyAndResearch/Statistics/Island-Fees.

David's story

How I got £25,600 tax free to study for an EngD

'I was in my final year at Manchester and thinking of going on to take a PhD when an advert came through for an engineering research doctorate working in collaboration with the engineering firm NIS Ltd. The project involved RF imaging for industrial processes, just up my street.

'It was actually for an EngD, which I preferred since it included a management element, and was sponsored by EPSRC, who would pay my fees and provide a stipend of £13,800 p.a. What's more, by working with a company, I not only received another £3,500 p.a., but would gain valuable work experience. Everything was falling into place.

'Then, for the first time, the Whitworth organisation decided to give Whitworth Senior Scholarships to postgraduate engineers doing a PhD or EngD – £7,000 a year for the length of your course – so I applied.

'To be eligible for a Whitworth scholarship you have to be an "outstanding student" – their words, not mine – who has done a "hands-on" engineering apprenticeship before taking your degree – which I had.

'Whitworth scholarships are open to engineers from any discipline, but as they are awarded through the Institution of Mechanical Engineers, I had no idea that an electrical engineer, like me, was eligible. If I had, I would have applied during my first degree – now that would certainly have helped the finances and debt.'

What David receives:

	1st year	2nd year	3rd year
Stipend from EPSRC	£13,800	£14,100	£14,400
Allowance from sponsoring company	£4,000	£4,000	£4,000
Senior Whitworth Scholarship	£7,000	£7,500	£7,500
Fees paid by EPSRC			
Total	£24,800	£25,600	£25,900

And all tax free.

I want to study abroad: can I get funding?

There are a number of routes you can take.

If you are thinking of undertaking postgraduate studies at the European Union Institute (EUI) in Florence, the College of Europe in Bruges or Warsaw, or the Bologna Centre in Bologna you may be eligible for an award from the Department of Innovation, Universities and Skills in England, the Student Awards Agency for Scotland or the Department of Education and Learning in Northern Ireland.

Hot Tips on Funding from an Edinburgh Postgraduate

▶ Many departments provide opportunities for undergraduate teaching and demonstrating. Pay varies – it may only be a few pounds a term (e.g. £500 a year) or could amount to several thousand.

▶ Work as a research assistant. Many staff secure a funding award that they must spend on their project, which includes assistants.

▶ Don't aim to fund tuition and living costs by taking a job. It is possible for Master's students to maintain a part-time job – and many do. But it is rare for a full-time PhD student to do so: a PhD is a job in itself. A few hours' work a week can ease the financial burden and provide useful respite from academic work – but only that.

▶ Try raising funding for individual experiments. Start with your department and funding sources for your individual subject. Success is more likely with experimental degrees than bog standards like French literature.

▶ Don't underestimate the time your PhD will take. Practically all PhDs overrun. It can easily take four or more years to complete. Research Council funding lasts for three years only and they won't pick you for the fourth year. Budget for this. There is a good chance there'll be good money coming in once you qualify. In the meantime have a contingency plan – it would be dreadful to give up on the last lap.

▶ Money, or perhaps one should say lack of it, is a major stress factor for many postgraduates. Excellent students quit because they can't afford to be a student any longer. Unrealistic budgeting undoes many: whilst rent and food are generally factored in, things such as holidays, contents insurance, etc. are not. These all add up.

Socrates–Erasmus, generally known as Erasmus (the European Community Action Scheme for the Mobility of University Students), and Leonardo da Vinci, which covers vocational training (see page 116).

The UNESCO publication *Study Abroad* has over 2,570 entries and provides information on courses, international scholarships and financial assistance available in countries and territories worldwide. It should be available at your local library or careers office or can be purchased from the Stationery Office. (See booklist at the end of Chapter 4, page 122.)

What help can I get if I want to train as a teacher?

England

Up to £9,000 just to train. This is the package of incentives available for students beginning a postgraduate course of initial teacher training (ITT) in England.

- ▶ Training bursary of £9,000 (non-repayable) for students training to teach the following secondary shortage subjects: design and technology, information and communications technology, maths, modern languages, music, RE, science.
- ▶ Training bursary of £6,000 (non-repayable) for students training to teach all other secondary-phase subjects not listed above.
- ▶ Training bursary of £4,000 (non-repayable) for trainee primary phase postgraduate students.
- ▶ A non-means-tested loan to cover the cost of fees – up to £3,225.*
- ▶ A non-means-tested non-repayable grant of £1,260 may be given to all students.
- ▶ An additional means-tested grant of £1,580, which is non-repayable.*
- ▶ Student loan based on the full-year allowance for students (up to £6,928 in London and £4,950 elsewhere or £3,838 in parents' home), 28% of which is means-tested (see Chapter 2).
- ▶ Postgraduate students taking a subject enhancement course prior to an ITT course leading to qualified teacher status will receive £200 per week and fees will be paid.
- ▶ 'Golden hello' paid to secondary-shortage-subject teachers on completion of their induction year: £5,000 to those teaching maths, science and applied science; £2,500, to those teaching applied ICT, modern languages, music, RE.

The training bursary will be given in nine monthly instalments (18 monthly instalments if you are studying part-time). It is not means tested and is not a loan. Tax and National Insurance will have to be paid on any golden hello. For more details see www.tda.gov.uk.

Wales

The package of incentives on offer in Wales for 2009–2010 ensures that Welsh-domiciled students receive a level of support comparable with their

---

*Note: maintenance loan and tuition fee loan to be repaid in line with income after students have left their courses and are earning over £15,000 per annum.

English counterparts. The level of training incentive grant offered in Wales takes account of the fact that Welsh-domiciled PGCE students studying in Wales will be entitled to a tuition fee grant of up to £1,940 (depending on the level of course fees), which is not available in England.

Domiciled and training in Wales

▶ Training grant of £7,200 (non-repayable) for postgraduate students training to teach secondary priority subjects. (Priority subjects include: design and technology, information and communication technology, maths, modern languages, music, RE, science and Welsh.)

▶ Training grant of £4,200 (non-repayable) for students on all other secondary postgraduate initial teacher training courses.

▶ Training grant of £2,200 (non-repayable) for students on primary postgraduate ITT courses.

▶ Fee grant of up to £1,940 (non-means-tested and paid direct to place of study).

▶ Fee loan available for balance of fees up to £1,285.

▶ A means-tested Assembly Learning Grant (ALG) of up to £2,906. The first £1,288 (if studying for 10 weeks or more; the first £644 if studying for 6–10 weeks) for PGCE students is non-means-tested.

▶ A means-tested student loan for maintenance (see page 53).*

▶ A teaching grant for eligible trainees who go on to complete at least four months as a qualified teacher in a maintained school in a secondary priority subject, following completion of their induction period : £5,000 for those teaching mathematics and science; £2,500 to those teaching other secondary priority subjects.

▶ There is also the Welsh Medium Incentive Supplement Scheme for students who wish to undertake a secondary postgraduate course through the medium of Welsh. This scheme is aimed at students on eligible courses who need additional support to raise confidence in their ability to teach effectively through the medium of Welsh. A bursary of £1,800 is available to those on mathematics and science secondary postgraduate courses and £1,500 for those on other secondary postgraduate courses. Enquiries about this scheme should be directed to the ITT provider with which you wish to study.

▶ Finally, the Financial Contingency Fund is available to institutions to pay discretionary grants to support students who are experiencing financial difficulties, in particular to help them access and remain in higher education. The student must make application to the ITT Provider.

To find out more about teacher training in Wales, phone 0845 600 0991 (or 0845 600 0992 for a Welsh-speaking consultant) or visit www.tda.gov.uk/ Recruit.aspx.

Welsh-domiciled but studying in another part of the UK

If you are domiciled in Wales but choose to study in another part of the UK, i.e. England, Scotland or Northern Ireland, you should contact Student Finance Wales (website: www.studentfinancewales.co.uk) for information on the full range of available student support. Also check your entitlement to any other grants with the ITT provider with which you are hoping to study – you may be in for a surprise.

Teaching in Scotland

There is no training bursary or secondary-shortage-subject scheme in Scotland. Scotland does not suffer from the same shortage of teachers as some parts of England. In Scotland teachers are employed by local authorities (LAs), and there are 32 LAs in Scotland. Some of the more rural LAs find it hard to attract the number of teachers they would like. A pilot scheme was introduced for teachers trained in Scotland who are eligible for the teacher induction scheme. If you tick the box to say you will teach anywhere in Scotland during your induction year, you will be given what's called a 'preference waiver' payment of £8,000 for secondary school teaching and £6,000 for primary teaching. This is given in three instalments. If you are allocated to a Scottish island you may also qualify for the Distant Islands Allowance, which would give you an additional £1,728 p.a. The success of the 'preference waiver' scheme is assessed each year. To find out more, phone 0845 345 4745, or visit www.scotland.gov.uk/education/teaching, or www.infoscotland.com/teaching. The preference waiver payment is only available for teachers trained in Scotland. If you have trained as a teacher in another part of the UK you will not receive the funding offered.

Teaching in Northern Ireland

While students will receive the same general funding as undergraduates in Northern Ireland (see Chapter 4), no additional incentives are available. However, if you train in England you will receive the incentive package offered to students there. So those training to teach secondary priority subjects (design and technology, information and communications technology, maths, modern foreign languages, music, religious education and science) may be eligible for a £9,000 bursary; those training to teach other subjects in secondary schools for a £6,000 bursary; and those training to teach in primary schools for a £4,000 bursary. See page 241.

What do Graduates Do?

A HECSU (Higher Education Careers Services Unit) survey looked at what graduates who qualified in 2007 were doing six months later at the start of 2008. It has to be stressed that this snapshot was taken at a time when the credit crunch still hadn't really surfaced. The picture now might look very different. Of the 209,120 (80%) of graduate qualifiers who responded to the survey:

▶ 13.9% went on to do further study

▶ 9.1% were combining work with study

▶ 5.5% were unemployed, but that's down on the previous year's figures of 6% – and the lowest since the year 2000

▶ 63.3% had entered employment

▶ the most popular destination was the health profession and associate professions (13.5%)

▶ also popular was commercial, industrial and public sector

management at 9.2%, though the number of graduates entering this career area fell

▶ three-quarters (73.7%) of marketing graduates were employed six months after graduation

▶ the number of civil engineering graduates rose by a fifth (18.8%) and the number of architectural and building graduates rose by 8.6%, while unemployment in that sector fell from 3.4% to 2.9%. (One wonders what the future holds now!)

▶ IT graduates are still in decline, but not enough as unemployment in this sector is high at 9.5%

▶ the number of graduates going into business and financial professions rose by 8.8% compared with the previous year. However . . .

▶ the number actually going into the financial *industry*, as opposed to working in financial-type jobs, dropped by 2.7%.

(*What Graduates Do, 2009*: Higher Education Careers Services Unit (HECSU) survey based on 2007 graduating cohort six months after leaving university)

Further information for trainee teachers

▶ In England – Teaching Information Line: 0845 6000 991; website: www.tda.gov.uk.

▶ In Wales – Teaching Information Line: 0845 600 0991 (English); 0845 600 0992 (Welsh language); websites: www.tda.gov.uk/Recruit.aspx (available in English and Welsh).

▶ In Scotland – tel: 0845 345 4745; website: www.teachinginscotland.com, www.saas.gov.uk.

▶ In Northern Ireland: contact the Department of Education (DENI): tel. 02891 279100; email: mail@frni.hob.uk; website: www.deni.gov.uk/index/teacher-pg.

Is there any help if I want to study medicine?

There is a special deal for graduates domiciled in England and Wales who are on the four-year fast-track medical programme.

Year one: you can apply for same support as undergraduates – student loans for fees and maintenance.

From year two onwards:

▶ help with tuition fees

▶ you are eligible for a means-tested NHS bursary

▶ 50% of student loan.

I want to study law: what help is there?

With full-time course fees for the Graduate Diploma in Law (GDL)/Common Professional Examination (CPE) about £2,500–£7,000, and the Legal Practice Course (LPC) running at an average of £5,200–£12,500 plus, most students are going to need some help.

▶ Training contract. This is the best route financially. A firm providing a training contract will generally give a sponsorship for one or two years while you are at law school, which could involve paying your fees and providing a maintenance allowance. But sponsorship is competitive and even the best students can find it difficult to get. There is an increasing number of good people around to choose from. Those who do secure sponsorship would normally expect to complete their training contract with that firm. Occasionally a longer commitment to employment is demanded.

   Clifford Chance, a leading international law firm, recruits 130 trainee lawyers each year. The firm will cover the cost of tuition fees for its future trainees on the GDL and LPC and will provide a maintenance grant during this period. This is also a valuable time in which you can build networks before commencing your actual training contract.

   For sponsorship information see the Careers Service Unit (CSU) publication *Prospects Legal*, available from your university.

▶ Vacation placement programmes. A number of firms run programmes for second-year undergraduates (or final-year if you are a non-lawyer), when they will size you up for a training contract. To get accepted for a placement programme is in itself an achievement, but it is certainly no guarantee of success.

Max Planck Institute for Intellectual Property, Competition and Tax Law: IMPRS for Competition and Innovation - Legal and Economic Determinants

Degree
Dr. jur. (for law students), Dr. rer. pol. (for economics students)

In Cooperation with
Max Planck Institute for Intellectual Property, Competition and Tax Law and the Faculty of Law, the Munich School of Management and the Department of Economics (Volkswirtschaftliche Fakultät) at the Ludwig Maximilians University Munich.

Course Language(s)
Mandatory courses are held in English; elective courses at the Ludwigs Maximilians University may also be taken in German.

Beginning of Programme
Winter semester - October each year

Programme Duration
3 years

Description of Content
The last decades have seen an exponential increase in the significance of intellectual property rights in the larger framework of innovation and competition which has stimulated the demand for experts in this field. There has also been an enormous increase in the significance of law and economics opening up new methods for the analysis of intellectual property and competition law. The IMPRS-CI doctoral programme was, thus, founded in 2008 to meet the demand for experts in these fields. It also closes a gap in European law education, which still lacks an interdisciplinary law and economics approach to intellectual property and competition law, by offering several doctoral fellowships to outstanding students interested in the integration of law, business administration and economics and the study of the nexuses between patent law and innovation, copyright law and creativity, and market transparency and competition.

Course Description
Educational Organisation: The duration of the programme is three years.
First year - students take a full schedule of introductory, advanced and elective courses and work on their doctoral research project.
Second year - students take a full schedule of advanced and elective courses and a research seminar and make substantial progress on their dissertation.
Third year - students take research seminars and devote full time to accomplishing their dissertation and defence of their thesis.
General Promotion/Funding of the Programme: International Max Planck Research School
ECTS Credits: 120
Diploma Supplement: No

Costs, Fees, and Funding
Funding Opportunities within the University: Fellowships and stipends of about EUR 1,100 monthly are granted to all accepted students for the duration of three years.

Required Entry Qualification Profile
Language Requirements: Applicants must provide proof of their English skills unless they have received a degree from an institution where English was the language of instruction. English: TOEFL (Test of English as a Foreign Language) of at least 620 (paper-based) or 260 (computer-based) or 105 (internet-based iBT). IELTS (British Council International Testing System) of at least 7.0. Test scores older than three years are not accepted.
Required English Language Test: Yes, IELTS or TOEFL
Academic Requirements: All applicants must satisfy the general postgraduate admissions requirements of the Faculty of Law, the Department of Economics or the Munich School of Management of the Ludwig Maximilians University Munich. Please refer to the individual faculty homepages for further details.

Contact
Max-Planck-Institut für Geistiges Eigentum, Wettbewerbs- und Steuerrecht
Prof. Dr. Reto M. Hilty
Marstallplatz 1, D-80539 München
Tel.: +49.89.24246.402
imprs@imprs-ci.ip.mpg.de
http://www.imprs-ci.ip.mpg.de/

▶ Law Society Bursary Scheme. Available for students taking CPE/GDL and LPC. They are very limited, competitive and include hardship criteria – but worth trying. The bursary is made up from a variety of funds and grant-making trusts which have been grouped together under an umbrella scheme. Applications for awards for 2009–10 were invited in March 2009. More information and application form for next year available from the Law Society's Information Services hotline – tel: 020 7316 5772 or email: bursaryapplications@lawsociety.org.uk. See also www.lawsociety.org.uk.

▶ Law Society Diversity Access Scheme. This aims to provide support to those with talent who will have to overcome particular obstacles to qualify as a solicitor. These could relate to social, educational, financial or family circumstances or to disability. For further details see www.lawsociety.org.uk or email: dascheme@btinternet.com.

▶ Local authority grants. Local authorities are not obliged to fund GDL or LPC students, and rarely do, but they do have discretionary funds available for a wide range of courses and, providing you meet their criteria for awards, you could strike lucky. There are no set rules, as every local authority has its own policy. Your local authority may well issue a leaflet giving information on study areas eligible for financial support. Enquire at your local education authority. Failing that, contact the Law Society (see website above).

▶ Loans. If all other lines of attack have failed there is always a loan (see pages 252–6).

Laura's story

Laura is studying at the College of Law (London).

'Most of the top law firms recruit for training contracts two years in advance, i.e. in the third year of uni or at the beginning of the GDL. This can lead to the bizarre situation I found myself in where you get a job in a law firm before you have even started studying law!

'Competition for places at the top firms is extremely stiff: applicants are all expected to have at least a 2:1 degree, As and Bs at A level and a lot more besides – they must have something extra to make them stand out.

'Despite maintenance grants and the funding of law college fees by law firms, it is quite usual for students to finish law college with up to £30,000 of debt. Many take professional studies loans of up to £20,000 because the maintenance grant usually only covers rent in London and little else!

'It can be quite stressful to be in so much debt, but I think most people view it as an investment – in themselves. The debt repayments can be quite crippling when you are a trainee, but are less significant on qualification as there is usually a big pay rise when you qualify. The debt is manageable, but it may not be great if you suddenly decide after law college or the training contract that law is not for you!

'For the top law firms, the recruitment process is long and laborious, involving long and testing application forms. If your application is successful, there are usually up to three interview stages, which include verbal reasoning tests, a team exercise, a written exercise and interviews with partners.

'The careers department in my college was fantastic and gave one-on-one advice and guidance about firms, how to tailor application forms to present yourself in the best way, and they also provided mock interviews and feedback from other students.'

Further information for law students

▶ For the most comprehensive information about firms offering sponsorship see www.prospects.ac.uk or ask your university for details.

▶ *Lawyer 2B* is a dedicated magazine for law students and those considering a career in or around the legal profession. A sister publication of *The Lawyer*, it provides news, comment, features and careers advice in an informal yet informative style. It is published five times a year and is available free from most UK law schools. In addition to the magazine, *Lawyer 2B* has launched a new website, www.lawyer2b.com, which gives breaking news along with features, comment and advice to reinforce the information in the magazine.

▶ For vacation placements and mini-pupillages look at the Prospects website: www.prospects.ac.uk.

▶ For general information see www.lawsociety.org.uk. Click on 'Student Guide'.

Facts and Figures

BPP Law School is among the top law schools

	Fees 2008 GDL*	Fees 2009–10 LPC**
Leeds	£6,500	£9,995
London	£8,100	£12,500
Manchester	£6,500	£9,995

*Graduate Diploma Law
** Legal Practice Course

Other professional qualifications?

Accountants, engineers, actuaries – all usually join firms that specialise in that kind of work. The firm will pay for your training and pay you while you are being trained.

I want to study in the United States

It's not cheap. Tuition for one nine-month academic year in state universities ranges from $4,000 to $13,000 and in private universities from $8,000 to $35,000. On top of that you will have living expenses, which vary tremendously: from $7,000 to $20,000. Last year over 2,500 UK students chose the US for postgraduate study. Don't automatically rule out the more costly courses, as the university may offer financial help through:

▶ scholarships or fellowships

▶ teaching/research assistantships

▶ a loan.

Funding for Postgraduate Study in the US

Thinking of postgraduate study? Worried about the costs?
Fortunately there are many funding options available, particularly if you're one
of the thousands of UK students considering postgraduate study in the US.

Types of Funding:

There are four main types of funding for study in the US: savings, loans and funding from a US university or an external funding body.

US universities spend $47 billion on research and development, which they pass along to students in the form of fellowships (grants) and assistantship packages. Assistantships will offer funding in exchange for ~20 hours of teaching or research in the department, allowing you to gain valuable work experience alongside your degree. Funding packages will vary, but many include tuition and fees, health insurance and a living stipend. Typically, the process of applying for university funding is integrated into the admissions application and may be as simple as submitting your admissions application by an earlier date.

Awards from professional, charitable or government organisations, such as the Fulbright Commission, are also available. They generally are awarded based on academic merit and specific personal qualities related to the mission of the organisation. For example, to apply for a UK Fulbright Award (worth approximately $40,000), one must be a UK citizen interested in US study or research, as this correlates to our aim of promoting US-UK study exchange. Although you will have to submit a separate application to each funding body, funding applications tend to follow the format of university applications.

Finally, as the cost of higher education rises, more students are taking out loans from a lender in the US or UK to cover all or part of their studies. For example, UK Career Development Loans can also be a great way to fund your studies, if you are working toward a professional degree or are in a field with practical applications and plan to return to the EU to work.

Steps for Success:

1. Start early: Applying for funding often happens simultaneous to, or in the case of the Fulbright Awards prior to, the admissions process.

2. Be committed: The more time you put in and the more opportunities you apply for, the better your chances of getting funding!

3. Chose universities carefully: Look for 'best buys' such as public (state-funded) universities or those at which you are well above the average admissions exam scores and marks of last year's admitted students, as most university funding is awarded on the basis of academic merit.

4. Network with faculty: You may wish to network with faculty doing research or teaching a class in your area of interest prior to submitting your admissions or funding application. You never

know whether this faculty member could be involved in admissions or funding decisions!

5. Keep in mind additional funding will be available, when you enrol: Rest assured there will be additional sources of funding available after beginning your studies, such as new assistantships or working on campus (international students can work up to 20 hours per week during term time).

Resources:

The US-UK Fulbright Commission is a not-for-profit organisation, funded by the US and UK governments to offer scholarships and advice to UK students interested in US study and vice versa. As part of the EducationUSA network, we are the official source of information on US study in the UK, and our website www.fulbright.co.uk serves as a clearinghouse for funding opportunities and information on postgraduate study in the US, with links to scholarship search engines and loan providers. You will also want to consult each university's departmental and/or graduate studies webpage for information on available funding and application procedures.

FULBRIGHT COMMISSION

www.fulbright.co.uk

Awards from bi-national exchange programmes, foundations or corporations, etc. may also be available. See the appendix in the Fulbright Commission *Guide to Postgraduate Study in the US*, available from the Fulbright Commission (details on page 121), or log on to www.fulbright.co.uk. and find out about USA grad school days, postgraduate study seminars and Fulbright awards for postgraduate study.

See page 258 for studying abroad – what to read, who to contact.

advice note

Seeking a career in the legal profession? Check out *Graduate Prospects Law Directory* for training contracts and law course vacancies published annually in September. See www.prospects.ac.uk.

Extra funding

Are there any other funds I can apply for?

There may be. But not all councils and funding bodies give them, and these are under review.

Child Tax Credit

Available to students with dependant children and paid by the Inland Revenue. The amount you get will depend on circumstances. Call 0845 300 3900 8a.m. to 8p.m. for more details, or visit www.taxcredits.inlandrevenue.gov.uk and check out how much you could get.

Access to Learning Fund

Usually given as a grant to students with higher-than-expected costs and according to need; part-time students can apply if studying at least 50% of full-time course. Contact your university.

Help for people with disabilities

The Disabled Students' Allowance for postgraduate study offers up to £10,260 p.a. for full- or part-time students on a course that requires first-degree entry. See *Bridging the Gap*, free from the DIUS Publications Department.

Are funding arrangements the same for all parts of the UK?

No. For residents of Scotland, Wales, Northern Ireland, the Channel Islands and the Isle of Man, funding arrangements are slightly different.

Loans

OK, so nobody is going to fund me: can I get a loan?

Yes, but not the student loan. There are four excellent alternative schemes.

1. Career development loan

Available only to those taking vocational training of up to two years. You can borrow up to £8,000 and not less than £300. The loan is designed to cover course fees (only 80% given if you are in full employment) plus books, materials and living expenses where applicable. The loan is provided by three banks only: Barclays, the Co-operative and the Royal Bank of Scotland.

Loans can be for a full-time, part-time or distance learning course. Interest on the loan is paid by the government while you are studying and for one month after your course has finished (or up to six months if you are unemployed when repayment should start). Phone 0800 585505 for a free booklet on career development loans (line open seven days a week 8a.m.–10p.m.) or contact the banks direct. It is worth talking to all three banks as pay-back arrangements may differ.

See page 254 for other loans from banks.

2. Business School Loan Scheme

If you want to take an MBA, the Association of MBAs (AMBA) should be able to help. It runs a special scheme to assist graduates and other suitable applicants to study for a Master's degree in business administration. The scheme is run in conjunction with NatWest Bank. To take advantage of the scheme you need to have a Bachelor's degree or other suitable professional qualification, a minimum of two years' relevant work experience or five years' experience in industry or commerce, and to have secured yourself a place on an MBA course at a business school that is on the association's approved list. Maximum loan for full-time students is two-thirds of present or last gross salary, plus tuition fees for each year of study. Preferential interest rates are given during the course. Repayment starts three months after completion of your course and you have up to seven years to pay it off. See www.mbaworld.com.

Facts and Figures !

What do Master's graduates do?

▶ 22% worked in management positions six months after completing their course

▶ 12.5% went to work as education professionals

▶ 9% were employed as business and finance professionals

▶ 7.1% became health professionals

▶ 5.8% worked as social and welfare professionals

▶ 11.9% were in general professional and technical occupations.

Unemployment among Master's graduates was 4.2%; far lower than the 6% of first-degree graduates who were unemployed.

(HECSU, *What do Master's Graduates do?* report, 2007)

The rise and fall of our business schools

International business school ranking: where the top UK schools are ranked in the world's top 100	2009	2008
London Business School	1 (Joint)	2
University of Cambridge: Judge Business School	11	10
University of Oxford: Said Business School	20	19
Lancaster University Management School	27	22
Manchester Business School	32	22
Cranfield School of Management	35	30
Warwick Business School	37	29
Imperial College London Business School	39	35
University of Strathclyde Business School	41	30
City University: Cass	41	41
Leeds University Business School	57	48
Aston Business School	77	–
Durham Business School	80	–
University of Bath School of Management	83	69
Birmingham Business School	83	–
Bradford School of Management	87	53
Edinburgh University Management School	92	44
Nottingham University Business School	100	76

Source: *FT (Financial Times) Business School Ranking*

3. Law school loans

Assisted by the Law Society, a number of major banks run a special scheme to help students fund law school courses. The loan, which currently stands at up to £25,000, is given at very favourable rates. For more details and an application form contact the banks directly.

4. Postgraduate loan

What loans do banks offer to postgraduates?

Bank	Course area	Amount offered
Barclays	Career Development Loan (for vocational training lasting at least one week)	£300–£8,000
Co-operative	Career Development Loan	£300–£8,000
HSBC	Graduate Loan Only available to existing customers	Up to £25,000 (minimum loan £1,000). Available up to 5 years after graduation
Lloyds TSB	Further Education Loan, only available to existing current account customers studying full-time for a professional qualification: architect, barrister, chartered engineer, dentist, doctor, optometrist/optician, pharmacist, solicitor, surveyor or veterinary surgeon	Up to £10,000 at a preferential rate (min. £1,000). Can delay repayments for 48 months and can take up to 5 years to repay. Must be permanent UK resident studying at a recognised UK institution
	Graduate Loan	Up to £10,000 (min. £1,000)
NatWest	Professional Trainee Loan: for barrister, solicitor, doctor, dentist, pharmacist, vet, chiropractor, optometrist, osteopath, physiotherapist	Up to £20,000 for full-time students (full-time trainee solicitors and barristers can borrow up to £25,000)
	MBA Loan	Full-time students can borrow up to two-thirds gross pre-course salary plus course fees up to 80% (less any grants). Repayment holiday for 3 months after completion of course. Tranche draw-down option available
	Graduate Loan	£1,000 to £15,000 if graduated in last 3 years and have full-time job or job offer
	Interest-free Graduate Overdraft Repayment Plan	Interest-free loan to repay your student overdraft – up to £2,000 in the first year, £1,000 in the second year, £500 in the third year after graduation. Whole sum must be repaid within 3 years from graduation

(Continued)

Bank	Course area	Amount offered
Royal Bank of Scotland	Law Student Loan (GDL/LPC full-time or part-time)	Up to £15,000 repayable over 7 years (conversion courses limited to £5,000)
	Healthcare, chiropractic, dentistry, veterinary, osteopathy	Up to £15,000 repayable over 7 years
	Career Development Loan	£300–£8,000
	Graduate Loan	£1,000 to £15,000 for those who have graduated in last 3 years and who have full-time job or job offer
	Interest-free Graduate Repayment Loan	Up to £2,000 in the first year after graduation, £1,500 in the second year and £1,000 in the third year. Whole sum must be repaid 3 years from graduation

For more details on career development loans, see page 252.

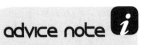

advice note

Want to know more about the cost and routes to funding for postgraduates? Log on to www.prospects.ac.uk and access 'Funding for further study'. The guide is designed to cater to the needs of the myriad of people who might consider participating in further study. Information on how to secure employer sponsorship makes it as relevant to those returning to study as to those going straight from university; and it also offers specific advice for both international students and those with disabilities.

Overseas students

What help is there for students coming to the UK from abroad?

There are scholarships specifically for overseas students, but there aren't very many, so apply early.

The best source for finance is your own home government. Failing that, try the British government through the British Council, the Foreign and Commonwealth Office or the Overseas Development Agency schemes.

International Students House provides accommodation bursaries for postgraduates from developing countries who are studying in London. Students should already have won a scholarship to cover fees. Last year some 40 bursaries were given. It also administers the Mary Trevelyan Fund, a hardship fund that will give up to £1,000 to London-based final-year postgraduates and undergraduates from developing countries who are facing financial difficulties. Last year this scheme was under-subscribed. Contact:

ORSAS

The Overseas Research Students Award Scheme (ORSAS) was set up to attract high-quality international postgraduate students to the UK to undertake research. The scheme is administered by individual universities on behalf of the Department for Innovation, Universities and Skills. Awards provide funding to pay the difference between the fees charged by academic institutions to international students for tuition and those charged to home/EU students. Awards do not cover maintenance or travel expenses.

Further information on eligibility and a list of higher education institutions taking part in the scheme can be found at www.orsas.ac.uk.

Sadly, for institutions in England, ORSAS funding will be phased out gradually over 2009–2010 and 2010–2011 and so far nothing is expected to take its place. For further information on available funding and deadlines for application, you should contact your intended institution or, if you cannot find the information you need, email orsas@hefce.ac.uk. In Wales, funding for new ORSAS awards is no longer being provided.

International Students House, 229 Great Portland Street, London W1W 5PN. Tel: 020 7631 8300. Accommodation: 020 7631 8310. See also www.ish.org. uk, which includes details of accommodation. (Also see *Sources of Funding for International Students* in the book list on page 258.)

There are also the Commonwealth Scholarship Plan, the UN and other international organisations. Some universities give awards and scholarships especially to students from abroad – but each university needs to be contacted individually. Some charitable trusts also cater for foreign students. EGAS (the Education Grants Advisory Service, see details on page 208) might be able to help you winkle them out, or check for yourself in appropriate directories (see further information in this chapter). EU students can compete for UK postgraduate awards already listed in this chapter, but on a fees basis only.

As a student from abroad, what is it really going to cost?

Fees

There is no set rate of fees for postgraduate courses. In the past a minimum has been recommended, but each institution can charge what it wants. Fees for overseas students are generally substantially more than those for home students. EU nationals are generally eligible for UK home student rates. Science courses are usually more expensive than arts courses. For average overseas postgraduate fees in 2008–2009 see page 220.

Living expenses

International Students House recommend that you will need at least £10,000 (excluding fees) to live in London. Our research in Chapter 1 will give you some idea of what living in Britain is likely to cost.

Further information for foreign students studying in the UK

▶ *Sources of Funding for International Students*, free from the British Council Information Centre, Bridgewater House, 58 Whitworth Street, Manchester M1 6BB. Tel: 0161 957 7755. Email: generalenquiries@britishcouncil.org.

▶ *The International Student's A–Z: A guide to studying and living in England, Wales or Scotland* (three editions). Published annually by International Students House, 229 Great Portland Street, London W1W 5PN. Tel: 020 7631 8369.

▶ Association of Commonwealth Universities scholarships: www.acu.ac.uk.

Who to contact/what to read

▶ *Postgraduate Directory*. Free from your careers service.

▶ *Prospects* postgraduate magazine: options for further study and research. Free from your careers service.

▶ Prospects website – it's massive: www.prospects.ac.uk.

Top 10 book-buying/course equipment universities

	Weekly spend
Glasgow	£14.83
Exeter	£11.98
Leicester	£11.94
Liverpool	£11.70
Edinburgh	£10.70
Nottingham	£10.53
Bristol	£10.51
Birmingham	£10.48
London	£10.32
Belfast	£10.05

Source: *NatWest Student Living Index 2008*

Studying abroad: what to read, who to contact

► Directory of Study Abroad Programme. Website: www.studyabroaddirectory.com.

► *Scholarships and Funding for Study and Research in Germany*, German Academic Exchange Service, 17 Bloomsbury Square, London WC1A 2LP. Tel: 020 7235 1736. See also www.daad.de/deutschland/foerderung/stipendiendatenbank.

► *Beginners' Guide to Postgraduate Study in the USA*. Information on applying, tuition fees, etc. Educational Advisory Service, Fulbright Commission, Fulbright House, 62 Doughty Street, London WC1N 2JZ. Tel: 020 7404 6994. Include an A4 SAE with 48p stamp. Email: education@fulbright.co.uk. Website: www.fulbright.co.uk.

► Try the UK Embassy or High Commission of the country where you are interested in studying: they may well have guides on awards and assistance offered.

► See also www.intstudy.com and www.studyoverseas.com.

CHAPTER 10

Making the money go round

In this final chapter, we look at banking and budgeting, and try to give you some advice on how to manage your money, with the help of students, a bank student adviser who has first-hand knowledge of some of the financial difficulties students get themselves into, and how best to help them.

The main topics covered in this chapter are:

Problems and predicaments

'My rent is over £70 a week. There's gas and electricity and telephone on top of that; I'm not making ends meet.'

'I've got an overdraft of £3,500, the bank is charging interest; if I've got an overdraft how can I pay the interest charges?'

'I thought: "£1,500, wow!" at the beginning of the term and blew the lot in the first few weeks. I haven't even the money for my train fare home.'

'I'm a geography student and have to go on a compulsory trip. Where on earth am I going to
find £120?'

'I know now that I shouldn't have bought the car and spent all that money on booze, but . . .'

Budgeting: what it is and how you do it

The principles are incredibly simple. Putting them into practice is, for many people, incredibly hard. It is a matter of working out what your income and expenses are and making sure the latter don't exceed the former. It may sound rather boring, but it's a lot better than being in debt. The students quoted earlier obviously didn't budget.

A bank student adviser's view
'A student loan of over £4,900! It certainly sounds a lot, but is it really? If all you are receiving is the standard funding for students then you haven't got wealth beyond your dreams, just the absolute minimum for survival. Bear that in mind right from the start and every time temptation looms, then you shouldn't go far wrong. There will always be those who like to live on the edge – spend now and cope with debt and disaster later. Most students who get into debt are genuinely surprised at how easily the money "just slipped through" their bank account. Debt has a way of just creeping up on you if you let it. So be warned.'

Where to keep your money: bank, building society, under the mattress?

Before you can start budgeting you need to choose somewhere to keep your money. In fact the Student Loan Company won't pay out your loan unless you have an account. We would recommend either a bank or a building society. They are generally quite keen to attract students' accounts because they see students as potential high-earners, as you'll see on page 267, where we look at the enticing freebies they offer. These are worth looking at, but they shouldn't be the deciding factor. More important is to choose a bank or building society that is located close to your home or place of study. While these days you can use the cash-dispensing machines in most branches of most banks and building societies, they haven't yet invented a machine that can give advice.

Beware the private enterprise cash machines; cash crisis they generally charge for withdrawals, sometimes as much as £2. Not a good deal if you are only drawing out £10. Most banks' cash machines are free to users whether you are a customer of that bank or not. The machine will always tell you if it is making a charge, so always check.

What type of account?

There are a number of different types of account. At the bank you'll need to open what's called a current account so you can draw money out at any time. Many banks offer accounts specially designed for students, so it's worth checking with them what they have. Some current accounts give interest – not as much as a savings account, but every little helps. Check your bank for interest rates. A building society current account is very similar to a bank account. They, too, give instant access to your money, and also pay interest on any money in your account. How much depends on the going rate and your building society. Look for 'free banking' – this means that you don't pay charges when in credit or within your interest-free overdraft.

advice note *i*

Caution

► Don't keep your cheque guarantee card and cheque book together. If they're stolen, somebody could clean out your account.

► Keep your personal identification number (PIN) secret. Never write it down or tell it to anyone else.

► Cheques take three days to clear from an account. So don't go on a mad spending spree if you find you have more money in your account than you thought. The read-out on the cash machine may not be up to date.

Shariah-compliant accounts

There are a number of banks that offer Shariah-compliant accounts, including HSBC, Lloyds TSB, and the Islamic Bank of Britain, However, you would not be entitled to the special student incentives mentioned later in this chapter – at the moment. But things could change!

Shop around

If you are looking for a bank account, shop around and compare the banks and what they can offer you in terms of overdrafts, etc. If you want an overdraft, the simplest way to compare charges is to ask for the EAR – Effective Annual Rate. This is a standardised way of expressing the total cost of borrowing if you were continually overdrawn for a year. It is, banks advise, also worthwhile asking the following questions.

► How much interest will I earn if I am in credit?

► Do I get a free overdraft facility? If so, how much?

► If I want to arrange a larger overdraft, will I be charged an arrangement fee?

► What will the interest rate be on my overdraft?

► If I am overdrawn without consent, how much will I be charged for:

  ▷ the unauthorised balance

  ▷ the bounced cheques?

► How easy is it to get an overdraft?

- ▶ What are the rates of interest charged if overdraft goes beyond limit, and how easy is it to extend it?
- ▶ What are the interest rates on graduate loans? (Some are much better than others.)
- ▶ What happens to your overdraft once you graduate?
- ▶ How close is the local branch to your university/lodgings?
- ▶ Are there reciprocal cash point facilities close to your institution? (Otherwise you could be charged for making withdrawals.)

What will you get when you open an account?

When you open an account you may receive some or all of these services and facilities.

- ▶ Cheque book, which you can use to pay big bills and for large purchases.
- ▶ Cheque guarantee card, which could be for up to £100. Some banks limit it to £50 for students. This states that the bank will guarantee your cheque up to the amount shown on the card, so the shop where you are making your purchase will let you take the goods away there and then. This is often incorporated into your cash card.
- ▶ Cash card, which enables you to withdraw cash from a cash machine, and may offer additional payment functions.
- ▶ Debit card (SOLO, Switch, Maestro or Delta) which will automatically debit your account for goods bought when passed through a terminal at the point of sale.
- ▶ The three-in-one card. Most banks and building societies combine the facilities listed above into multifunctional cards, which act as cheque guarantee cards, give access to cash machines and can be used as debit cards so you can purchase goods and services without writing a cheque.
- ▶ Account number, which you will need for any correspondence with your bank.
- ▶ PIN – this is your personal identification number, which you will need to remember and use when getting money from the cash dispenser.
- ▶ Paying-in book containing paying-in slips, probably with your branch name printed on them, which you can use when paying in cheques and cash. Just fill in the slip and pass it to your bank. Most banks provide pre-printed envelopes, which you can pick up in your branch and then post through a letter box in the banking hall. You can also pay in cheques through some cash machines.
- ▶ Statements sent to you at regular intervals (we would advise you to ask for them monthly). The statement will give details of the money going in and out of your account – an essential factor in budgeting properly.
- ▶ Internet banking.

- ▶ 24-hour telephone banking, which allows you to keep in touch with your student account and credit card account day and night.
- ▶ Student contents insurance.
- ▶ You may also be able to apply for a credit card, but think about it seriously before doing so – it could mean more debt.
- ▶ Freebies (see below).

Overdrafts, loans, freebies

Which bank should I choose? What's the carrot? What will they do for me?

So what's on offer?

Overdraft

The most useful offer made by banks to students is the interest-free overdraft. Our research with students showed that around 50% of students took advantage of this. As you will see from our chart on page 268, it could add between £1,000–£3,000 to your spending power. But it eventually has to be paid back. And don't assume it is yours as a right: you must ask first. Most banks also offer special arrangements for paying the overdraft off once you graduate. Again, check what these are before you step on the slippery slope to debt. How long will they give you to pay it off? What will the charges be then? How long does the interest-free loan last? These are the questions to ask.

Banks are the Student's Friend

Despite all the talk of students and their financial difficulties (our research shows that most students are likely to be in debt to anything up to £20,000 or even £40,000 by the time they qualify) banks are still falling over themselves in an effort to gain your custom. Nearly all offer students some kind of carrot to get them to open an account, and promise some kind of interest-free loan which, for most students, is an essential part of their funding package. How generous, you might think. But banks aren't charities. Their reasoning isn't difficult to fathom: they are in the business of long-term investments. Students are the country's potential high earners. Statistics show that people are more likely to change their marriage partner than their bank. The strategy is: get 'em young and you've got 'em for life.

Freebies

Most banks keep their new student offer under wraps right until the very last minute – largely so that their competitors can't top it with a better inducement.

This means the new offer is on the table from around June/July. Some banks have a closing date for their main offers, which could be as early as November, when the first loan cheques have been happily banked. The offer is generally open only to first-year students. Before giving you the benefit of their freebies, the bank of your choice will ask for some proof of your student status, such as your loan award letter or your first term's loan cheque.

To give you some idea of what you can expect, and to check the next round of offers, we looked at how students fared in 2008–2009 (see the table on pages 268–71). When comparing the facilities offered, if an interest-free overdraft facility of £3,000 sounds an attractive inducement, and well it might, remember it could also be temptation and will add to your overall debt.

What's the best banking buy?

Compare the current facilities offered by some of the major banks. Remember, student packages are usually revised each summer, so check with the banks for the latest information.

Graduates

There are other benefits to be considered once you graduate, such as covering your student bank overdraft and terms for paying it back, and finding the money to tide you over while you get started in work. If you are thinking of undertaking further study, the banks may be able to help.

But should one be bribed into choosing a bank? Forward-thinking students may well decide that interest-free overdraft facilities carry more weight in making the choice than a paltry once-off cash offer. You would do well to look carefully at the small print before making a decision. Some banks offer more in the second and third years. But do you want that kind of temptation?

'I went for the freebies – rather than the most sympathetic bank manager – bad move when debt loomed.'

3rd year student, Glasgow

Current facilities offered by some of the major UK banks

	Abbey	Bank of Scotland	Barclays	Halifax	HSBC	Lloyds TSB	NatWest	Royal Bank of Scotland
Free banking	Yes	Yes	Yes	Yes	Yes	Yes	Yes	Yes
Interest on current account	Yes, paid monthly – 3%	Yes, paid monthly	Yes, paid quarterly	Yes, paid monthly	Yes, paid monthly	Yes	Yes, paid monthly	Yes
Free overdraft	1st year £1,000; 2nd year £1,250; 3rd year £1,500 4th year £1,800; 5th year £2,000	1st–5th year and 1 year postgraduate: £3,000	£200 on opening account. Up to: 1st year £1,000; 2nd year £1,250; 3rd year £1,500; 4th year £1,750; 5th year £2,000	Up to £3,000, 1st–5th year and one year postgraduate	Up to: 1st year £1,000; 2nd year £1,250; 3rd year £1,500; 4th year £1,750; 5th year £2,000	1st–3rd year: £1,500 (tiered in 1st year); 4th–6th year: to £2,000	Up to: 1st year £1,250; 2nd year £1,400; 3rd year £1,600; 4th year £1,800; 5th year £2,000	Up to £2,500, 1st–5th year
Student adviser	Yes – in all university campus branches	All branch advisers can help	Yes, major campus branches/ university towns	All branch advisers can help	Yes	Call centre advisers available 24 hours + branch advisers	Yes – on/near campus branches	Yes – on/near campus branches

Student insurance	No special package	See freebies	Student possessions insurance	See freebies	Four levels of possessions cover from £2,000 to £5,000	Student possessions insurance	Student Essentials Insurance	Yes – Student Essentials Insurance
Freebies	Free Visa debit or Electron card	Commission-free travellers' cheques and foreign currency. 25% off AA membership for one year. 20% discount on card care insurance	£200 interest-free loan on opening account. Online shopping discounts at Barclays and Me website	Commission-free travellers' cheques and foreign currency. 25% off AA membership for one year. 20% discount on card care insurance.	2 years free worldwide travel insurance. Overdraft limit alerts at cash machine. Fee-free credit card with £500 limit. Banking 24/7 via internet banking. Graduate service.	£20 cash when opening account (check details). Free NUS Extra card giving discounts. Free YHA membership. 35 free music downloads	Free 5-year 16–25 Railcard worth £120. Student discounts at range of retailers including Cineworld, Domino's Pizza, Specsavers. £100 off selected ASUS laptops. £50 off mobile broadband. Free Microsoft webcam and microphone for online applicants. Free mobile phone/online banking	Scotland: £100 cash or travel package worth £149. England: travel package worth up to £165. Free 2 for 1 value cinema card. Commission-free travellers' cheques. Discounts on books, CDs, videos, computer games, concert tickets, travel and more. £50 off mobile broadband. £100 off selected ASUS laptops

(Continued)

	Abbey	Bank of Scotland	Barclays	Halifax	HSBC	Lloyds TSB	NatWest	Royal Bank of Scotland
Paying off undergraduate overdraft	Interest-free advance overdraft of up to £2,000 decreasing to £500 p.a. over 3 years.	Can keep student account for a year after graduating	Interest-free overdraft: 1st year £1,500; 2nd year £1,000. Double if you pay £5 monthly charge	Can keep student account for a year after graduating	Interest-free overdraft: 1st year £1,500; 2nd year £1,000	Interest-free overdraft: 1st year £2,000; 2nd year £1,500; 3rd year £1,000	Interest-free overdraft: 1st year £2,000; 2nd year £1,000; 3rd year £500	Interest-free overdraft: 1st year £2,000; 2nd year £1,500; 3rd year £1,000
Low-cost graduate loan	Up to £10,000 (minus any interest free overdraft)	No		Up to £10,000	Up to £25,000 at preferential rate. Range of repayment periods	Up to £10,000 with up to 5 years to repay	Up to £15,000 at preferential rate over 7 years (5 years for loans of £10,000 or more)	£1,000–£15,000 at preferential rate over base rate with 7 years to pay if amount £10,000 or over

Professional study loan, e.g. for medicine, dentistry, optometry, veterinary science or law	No	Career development loan £8,000 max.	Considered on individual basis	Further Education Loan up to £10,000 to existing Lloyds TSB current account holders	Up to £20,000 (barristers/ solicitors up to £25,000) MBA loan available	Up to £15,000
Career development loan		Yes – up to £8,000	No			Yes – up to £8,000

Can I open two student bank accounts?

The banks don't like it, but the fact is you can and there isn't much they can do about it. However, two overdrafts to pay off are not to be recommended, especially if you are also paying off student and fee loans.

What is a bank student adviser?

A student adviser is somebody in the campus branch of the bank, or the branch closest to your college, who has been earmarked to deal with student problems. They are usually fairly young, and they are always well versed in the financial problems students face. Certainly you will find them sympathetic and full of good advice on how to solve your particular problems. But you won't find them a soft touch, as one student adviser pointed out: 'It's no good us handing out money like confetti – it just builds up greater problems for the student later on.'

Never run up an overdraft without asking the bank first. They are much more sympathetic if you put them fully in the picture. And unless they know you are a student, you could find you miss out on the interest-free loan. Talk to your bank's student adviser – ideally before you hit a problem.

What is a low-cost graduate personal loan?

This can be a life-saver for the newly qualified graduate. It is a special personal loan scheme offered by some banks to graduates to help tide them over the first few months while they get settled into a job. Most banks offer anything up to £10,000, some up to £25,000 and more, and some up to 20% of your starting salary. A graduate loan can be individually negotiated. The loan could be used to pay for suitable clothes for work, a car, advance rent – whatever you need. But remember: nothing is for free. You will have to pay interest, and if you already have a student loan and a substantial overdraft, this might be just too much debt. The graduate loan should not be confused with the many other types of loan banks offer to postgraduates to assist with study. (See Chapter 9.)

Banks' websites

Check out the banks' websites for the latest information and offers.

- ▶ Abbey – www.abbey.com
- ▶ Bank of Scotland – www.bankofscotland.co.uk

- Barclays – www.barclays.co.uk
- HSBC – www.hsbc.co.uk
- Lloyds TSB – www.lloydstsb.co.uk
- NatWest – www.natwest.com
- Royal Bank of Scotland – www.rbs. co.uk.

'I ended my first term at uni £300 overdrawn. What a shock! How did it happen? It's only too easy if you don't keep a close watch on your account. I now bank online so can check-up all the time. Okay, so I do have an overdraft, but at least I know.'

2nd year Languages student, Durham

'Create a spreadsheet with all your outgoings and income – unless you see it written down it's very hard to see how much you're spending.'

4th year Medicine student, St George's

'Have a budget. Only way to really keep track of things. Helps you realise how much you do spend. Good way to do this is to take out cash at the beginning of the week and never use cards.'

4th year Classics student, St Andrews

Your income: how much?

It's all very well to have an official piggy bank in which to keep your money, but where is the money going to come from and how much is it likely to be? If you have read the rest of this book, you should by now have some idea how much you are likely to have as a student. We have listed some of the likely sources in our budgeting plan. With a little ingenuity you may have discovered others.

A step-by-step budgeting plan

1 Take a piece of paper and divide it into three columns (see page 274). On the left-hand side write down your likely income sources and how much they will provide, for example:

- maintenance grant
- student loan
- fee loan
- parental contribution

- bursary
- money from Access to Learning Fund
- money earned from holiday job
- money earned from term-time job
- sponsorship
- interest-free overdraft

2   The trouble with budgeting, especially for students, is that money generally comes in at one time, often in large chunks at the beginning of a term, and your outgoings are needed at other times. When you work you will probably find it easiest to budget on a monthly basis, but as a student you may have to do it either termly or yearly, depending on how the money comes in.

3   In the middle column write down your fixed expenses – things that you have to pay out – like rent, gas, electricity, telephone, food, etc. Don't forget to include fares. Now total them up.

Income		Outgoings	Predicted	Actual
Grant	£	Fees	£	£
Bursary	£	Rent/college board	£	£
Parental contribution	£	Gas	£	£
Fee loan	£	Electricity	£	£
Student loan	£	Telephone	£	£
Sponsorship	£	Launderette/cleaning	£	£
Job	£	Food	£	£
Access to Learning Fund	£	Fares – term time	£	£
		Fares – to college/home	£	£
		Car expenses	£	£
		Books/equipment	£	£
		TV licence	£	£
		Student rail/bus card	£	£
		Broadband	£	£
Total:	£	Total:	£	£
		Socialising	£	£
		Hobbies	£	£
		Entertainment	£	£
		Clothes	£	£
		Presents	£	£
		Holidays	£	£

4   Subtract your fixed expenses from your income and you will see just how much you have, or haven't, got left over to spend. Draw a line under the list in your right-hand column and now list your incidental expenses – things like socialising, clothes, the cinema, hobbies, birthdays, etc. This is your 'do without' column: the area where you can juggle your expenses to make ends meet.

5   Apportion what's left over to the things listed in this final column, making sure you've got at least something left over for emergencies. Do the figures add up?

6   Seems simple enough and logical on paper. But of course it doesn't work quite as easily as that. There's always the unexpected. You can't get a job. Your car needs a new battery. People use more gas than expected. Did you really talk for that long on the phone?

7   Having worked out your budget, use the final column on your budget sheet to fill in exactly how much your bills do come to. In this way you can keep a check on your outgoings and how accurate your predictions were, and do something before the money runs out.

If you are having difficulty putting together a budget, look at the student examples at the end of Chapter 1, page 32.

Hot tip from a burnt student

'There are so many hidden costs at uni – expenses pop up all the time. It's impossible to budget at the beginning of term, which makes financial management a nightmare – sports levies, balls, tours, travel, books – and that's just for starters.'
2nd year Music student, Durham

What is a standing order?

Regular payments such as rent can be paid automatically from your bank account through a standing order. You just tell the bank how much to pay out and to whom, and they will do the rest. The system is ideal for people who are bad at getting round to paying their bills. Oops – forget to pay the electricity and you'll soon know.

Standing orders are not so easy to organise when you are in shared accommodation with everyone chipping in to pay the bill. However, we did discover one student household in Durham which had a special bank account, just for bills, which they all paid into.

What is direct debit?

With a direct debit set up on your account, the bill is again paid automatically, but it works in a different way. The bank of the organisation you are paying the money to will collect the money direct from your account. This is an ideal way of paying when the amount being paid out is likely to change.

Cards and the catches

Credit cards

These are an easy way to pay for things but they can also be an easy way to get into debt. When you have a card such as Mastercard or Visa you are given a credit limit. This means you can make purchases up to that sum. Each month you receive a statement of how much you owe. If you pay back the whole lot immediately there are no interest charges. If you don't, you will pay interest on the balance. There can be an annual charge for credit cards. You can use your card in the UK and abroad at most shops and many restaurants. They are a way of getting short-term credit but are an expensive way of borrowing long term. On the plus side they are a way to spread payments or ease temporary cash flow problems. If you live, as most students do, at two addresses (college and home), make sure you don't miss a monthly bill that needs to be paid.

Store cards

Many stores offer credit cards that operate in much the same way as described above, but can only be used in that particular store or chain of stores. Although most stores will check your credit rating before issuing you with a card, they are still too easy to come by – get a stack of them and you could find you're seriously in debt. A store card is quite different from a store loyalty card – the type issued by Boots, Tesco and many other organisations. These give you points for everything you buy in that store, which you can save up and use to purchase products. A good thing to have if you are a regular customer.

cash crisis

While most big stores and pubs will not charge for giving cash-back, some of the smaller stores may. Always check.

Debit cards

You've probably seen the Switch/Maestro card in action, as most stores and garages have the system installed. By simply passing your debit card through a Switch/Maestro terminal, the price of the purchase you are making is automatically deducted from your account. What could be easier? Details of the transaction will show up on your next statement. Some stores will offer you 'cash-back' on a debit card, which could save you a trip to the bank.

Safety check

Most banks and building societies will not send plastic cards or personal identification numbers to customers living in halls of residence or multi-occupancy lodgings, because they could go astray or sit unclaimed in the hallway for days. All too easy to steal. You may have to collect them from a branch nearby.

What if the money runs out?

Help, I'm in debt!

Don't panic, but don't sweep the matter under the carpet and try to ignore it, because it won't go away. In fact it will just get worse. Get in touch with the student welfare officer at your university, the student adviser at your local university branch or your bank manager. Or all three. They will have plenty of experience of helping students in debt and will be able to give the best advice and help. Impoverished and imprudent students are not a new phenomenon.

'I needed £200 to put down as my deposit for renting a house next year, but I hadn't got it, so I went round to my bank and they extended my overdraft.'

Getting an overdraft

If you are struggling, don't turn your back on the interest-free overdraft facilities that most banks offer students and are considered by many students to be an essential part of their income – helping to fill that financial black hole between loan payments. As you can see from our chart on page 268, free overdraft facilities vary enormously, as do the amounts you can borrow – up to £3,000 in your first year.

If you go over your overdraft limit, get on the phone or call in immediately to your bank. Many of the clearing banks have campus branches or at least a branch in the town geared to dealing with students. They'll probably be sympathetic and come up with a helpful solution.

> *'Don't borrow from a lot of places. If you've got an overdraft and a student loan, that's probably enough.'*
>
> 1st year Urban Planning Studies student, Sheffield

A planned overdraft

'I'm going for an interview and need something to wear.'

This is not an unusual request from students in their final year – jeans and a scruffy T-shirt rarely make a good impression. Banks are very good at coming up with a plan to help you out with an obvious or specific need. After all, an interview success could mean you'll clear your overdraft that much more quickly.

An overdraft is often the cheapest way of borrowing, even if it is not part of the special student package. There are charges and interest rates, which need to be checked out. The advantage of an overdraft is that you don't have to pay it back in fixed amounts, though the bank has the right to ask for its money back at any time.

Borrowing on credit

'Haven't got the money at the moment so I'll buy it on Mastercard.'

Easily done, but be warned – though Mastercard/Visa is excellent as a payment card, credit can cause problems. If you don't pay off your bill by the date given on your statement, you will have to pay interest and, compared with other sources of borrowing, this is very high. Unlike your friendly bank, credit card companies are not the sort of people you can negotiate with, and are very likely to sue. Don't see them as another source of income.

Personal loan

This is quite different from an overdraft. It is usually used when you want to borrow a much larger sum, over a longer period – say several years. It differs from an overdraft in that you borrow an agreed amount over a set period of time and the repayments are a fixed amount, generally monthly. You might take out a loan to pay for your course fees, but not for short-term credit to tide you over until your next grant cheque arrives.

Thrift Tips

Leeds University Union Welfare Service suggests these ways of managing your money.

▶ *Get value for money – use markets or large supermarkets for fresh fruit and vegetables. Your local corner shop may be convenient, but is often more expensive.*

▶ *Make the most of student discounts for coach and rail travel, clubs, restaurants and hairdressers.*

▶ *Use the library rather than buying books – has your uni got a second-hand bookshop?*

▶ *Withdraw only the amount of cash you actually need on a weekly basis from the bank – otherwise it will disappear.*

A bank manager's view

'The problems students have are very real. As a bank manager, all too often we find we are just picking up the pieces when things have gone too far. Debt brings stress, and that will affect your ability to study. Come sooner rather than later.'

Don'ts

(Which unfortunately some students do!)

▶ Don't fall into the hands of a loan shark. Any loan offered to students, except from a recognised student-friendly source, e.g. banks, building societies, parents or the Student Loans Scheme, should be treated with the utmost caution and suspicion. It's bound to cost you an arm and a leg, and lead to trouble.

▶ Don't run up an overdraft with your bank without asking first – even the much-vaunted interest-free overdraft offered by most banks to students should be checked out first, otherwise you might find you are being charged. They need to know you are a student.

▶ Don't forget to pay your gas and electricity bills. Make them top priority. A week or two on bread and (cheap) jam is better than having to pay court costs.

▶ Don't pawn your guitar, only to find you can't afford to get it out to play at the next gig.

- ▶ Don't try 'kiting'. The banks have got wind of what's been going on, and you're bound to be found out and get into real trouble. For the uninitiated (like this author), kiting is the dishonest practice of making the most of the time lapse between people reporting that their credit card is missing and it being recorded as stolen. Be warned: it is a criminal offence, and could end up increasing your debts – or even worse.
- ▶ Don't get blacklisted with the bank. 'Kiting' is a sure way of getting a bad record. Running up an overdraft is another.
- ▶ Don't see credit cards as another source of income.

A final word of advice from a student

'Before starting a degree, students don't realise just how tough it's going to be. You think, how on earth can anybody be so irresponsible as to get into £22,000 worth of debt? But once you are into university life, you know only too well. Despite the hardship, don't be put off; university is excellent – an incredible experience not to be missed!'

Savings?

Most books on budgeting give lengthy advice on saving. We think it unlikely that students will do more than just make ends meet, and even that will be a struggle. However, if you do find that you have some surplus cash, or are in the lucky position of being able to do without the student loan and decide to take it out as an investment, you could put it in an ISA, or open a savings account at a bank, a building society or the Post Office. Check out the interest rates and the terms and conditions. Many high-interest accounts give limited access to your money – so watch out.

Barclays' Money Managing Tips

Most banks close to universities have student advisers. Barclays has a national network of over 200, whose full-time job is to advise students on how best to manage their money while at university. This is their list of top tips on managing your money. Some have already been suggested by students elsewhere in this book, but repetition can't hurt if it keeps you out of debt.

► Don't wait until you get to college to open an account. Open one at your local branch. You will need it in order to apply for a student loan.

► Once you know how much you will have to live on per term, ask your bank for advice on budgeting. Don't be worried about going back for further guidance if you're finding it hard to cope.

► Limit your borrowing to a few sources. Spreading debts around too much makes it difficult to keep track of them and can only create problems later.

► Be cautious about how much money you borrow on your overdraft, even if it is interest free.

► Arrange to have your monthly statements sent to your term-time address to help you monitor your budget.

► Try to limit your trips to the cash machine to once a week, otherwise you could easily lose track of how much you are spending.

► Insurance is vitally important, but ask your parents first if you can be included on their house insurance.

► Wait until you arrive at university before buying expensive books and equipment; then you will know what you really need. Ask around for places offering the best deals, such as your university bookshop, or buy second-hand textbooks from students in the years above you.

► As your loan comes termly, it is often a good idea to get your loan money paid into your savings account and then transfer money over perhaps every week or every month. This will help you budget and spend within your means.

► Familiarise yourself with the student services available to you at your university. Student support centres are in place to help you with all aspects of student life, including your finances.

► Keep checking your account to ensure all payments are made.

► Always deal with bills and statements as they arrive – try to avoid putting them to one side or forgetting to pay bills. We recommend paying by direct debit if possible.

► If you've got problems, remember that your bank's student adviser is there to offer advice and support. Don't ignore a problem, hoping it will go away by itself – because it won't.

University is a great experience. Enjoy every moment of it. Be concerned about money, but don't get stressed out. Most students do find a way of making the financial sums add up and have a good time.

Index